BERLIN
JOURNAL

1989-1990

Robert Darnton

W.W. NORTON & COMPANY
NEW YORK · LONDON

FOR MARGARET

The text of this book is composed in Plantin, with the display set in
Kabel Bold Condensed. Composition and manufacturing by the
Haddon Craftsmen, Inc. Book design by Charlotte Staub.
First published as a Norton paperback 1993.
The author gratefully acknowledges the assistance of Isaak Behar for
material used in Chapter Two. Any dramatic or other rendition of the
material in this chapter requires the permission of Isaak Behar.
Library of Congress Cataloging-in-Publication Data
Darnton, Robert.
Berlin journal: 1989–1990 / Robert Darnton.
p. cm.
Includes index.
1. Germany (East)—Politics and government—1989–   2. Berlin
(Germany)—History—Allied occupation, 1945–   3. Anti–communist
movements—(East)—I. Title.
DD289.D27 1991
943.1087′8–dc20   90–19745
ISBN 0-393-31018-3
W.W. Norton & Company, Inc.
500 Fifth Avenue, New York, N.Y. 10110
W.W. Norton & Company Ltd
10 Coptic Street, London WC1A 1PU
2 3 4 5 6 7 8 9 0

BERLIN JOURNAL

CONTENTS

CONTENTS

INTRODUCTION

This book offers an account of a revolution in a strange land: Germany, or, more precisely, East Germany, the German Democratic Republic. The East Germans themselves sometimes use a humbler term to describe what happened in their country in 1989–1990: *Wende*, meaning turn, or turnabout. But they generally prefer *revolution*, perhaps because it fits in better with their Marxist tradition. The events of 1989–1990 hardly conformed to the Marxist theory of class struggle, however; and insofar as they did, they were directed against the class of apparatchiks, who dominated the country from the upper ranks of the Communist Party (SED).

Also, the events lacked blood. No guillotines, no barricades, no storming of a Bastille. Do they deserve to be called revolutionary at all?

I would gladly leave the definitional problem to the experts. But then I am supposed to be an expert myself, a historian of Europe during the era of the French Revolution. Having spent most of the year celebrating the bicentennial of the Revolution, I arrived in Berlin on September 1, 1989, with the intention of writing yet another monograph about the eighteenth century. But then something that looked suspiciously like a revolution exploded under my nose, and it helped set off a chain reaction of other revolutionary explosions throughout Eastern Europe. I decided to put my monograph aside, and to follow the events as closely as I could.

The result is this book, or rather journal. Instead of writing an academic analysis in which I might arrive at some theoretical notion of what a revolution really is, I tried to produce a journalistic account of the events as they occurred. Now, "event history" has come in for a lot of scorn from historians who pretend to penetrate below the surface of the past in order to understand its deep structures. I must admit that I once belonged to the scorners. But when swept up in a flood of revolutionary events, I found myself questioning my earlier assumptions. "Event history" is not as straightforward or as superficial as it may sometimes seem. Two considerations especially stood out.

The first concerns the importance of accident, error, improvisation, misunderstanding, and unintended consequences. Looking back a year later, I think that the two most important events of the East German revolution were the two that took me most by surprise and that still are the most difficult to understand. On October 9, someone somewhere in the GDR power structure called back the troops deployed to repress a demonstration in Leipzig. Everyone present at that demonstration was convinced that the government had prepared to commit something comparable to China's Tiananmen Square massacre. At the last minute, however, the troops withdrew. How? Why? We still do not know. The responsibility probably lies somewhere along a line of command that stretches from Mikhail Gorbachev in the Kremlin to the second secretary of the Communist Party in Leipzig. But where? At a specific point or among many points still diffused through certain segments in the machinery of power? Could the non-massacre have resulted from poor communication—a short-circuit in the system for transmitting orders, or a switch thrown by an anonymous apparatchik who wanted to prevent a bloodbath? Whatever the cause, the effect was momentous: from that moment on, it was clear that the government would no longer repress the demonstrations, and the demonstrations continued until they overwhelmed the government.

The second event now looks as decisive and as mysterious as the first. It already stands out as a major historical date: November 9, the "fall" of the Berlin Wall. On the ninth itself, however, the East German government did not decide to dismantle the Wall. Indeed, there was no East German government. The entire ministry had just resigned, and the caretaker administration under Willi Stoph was feuding with the caretakers of the Communist Party, who had just engineered the collective resignation of the Politburo. Meanwhile, refugees continued to stream out of the country via Czechoslovakia, and the East German parliament, which had always approved everything passed on to it by the Party, demanded a liberal new travel law.

In the midst of this crisis, the Party's spokesman, Günter Schabowski, announced that, pending the new law, East Germans could travel to the West without the usual elaborate restrictions on visas. He made the announcement in an off-the-cuff manner at the end of his evening press conference. No one present thought he was proclaiming the end of the Wall. But East Berliners began arriving in such numbers at the border that the guards finally let them through. According to one version recounted to me by a friend from East Berlin, the crowd at the border insisted that the government had decreed the opening of the Wall. "How do you know?" asked a guard. "We saw it on television," came the reply—an allusion to Schabowski's statement at the press conference. "In that case," said the guard, "you can cross over." Far from being planned, November 9 might have been a colossal misunderstanding—and, quite literally, a media event.

The problematic character of October 9 and November 9 bears on a second consideration about "event history." Events do not simply happen. They come charged with meaning, and people make their meanings at the same time as they improvise actions. Before we knew it, Schabowski's statement about visa requirements had become the fall of the Wall and the end of the Cold War. By pouring into West Berlin, the East Germans had transformed the mental geography that millions of people had used to impose some order on the world for nearly half a century.

"Mental geography" takes us far away from a conventional "event history." So in observing the events, I did not feel compelled to revert to an older tradition of straight political narrative. Instead, I tried to combine a record of what happened with reports on how people understood the happenings—that is, to marry two genres known to the professionals as "event history" and "the history of mentalities," or, in ordinary language, to read the significance of the events as it was being generated by the actors themselves and to keep an eye on the symbolic dimension of their actions. This kind of reportage is less esoteric than it sounds, because symbolic statements were spread so thickly across the East German political landscape—sprayed on walls, carried on banners, and shouted in demonstrations—that everyone had access to them. Of course, I may have read them wrongly, and their ultimate significance may not be clear until we can contemplate them from a distance of many years. But seen up close, they seemed to express two basic themes: a concern for legitimacy and a need to confront the past.

No one in the GDR believed that the revolution could have succeeded if the Soviet Union had tried to stamp it out in the same way that it crushed the uprising of June 17, 1953. Without Gorbachev, the old regime might have continued for another generation. But the collapse of the regime cannot be reduced to the force of personalities—a progressive Gorbachev, on the one hand, and a moribund Erich Honecker, on the other. More fundamental, in my view, was the delegitimation of the Communist Party, a process that went back many years and that could be followed in the growing protest against the privileges of the apparatchiks in 1989. It came to a climax with the revelations about the Volvos and saunas and hunting lodges appropriated by Honecker and the other Party leaders. To Westerners, these luxuries looked harmless; to East Germans, they represented the ultimate betrayal of socialism by an elite that had demanded sacrifices so that socialism could prevail. A political folklore about Wandlitz, the luxury ghetto of the Party bosses in East Berlin, undermined the support of the Communist Party just as the mythology about the decadence of the court in Versailles had eroded the authority of the monarchy in eighteenth-century France. In the end, the East Germans came around to the view that the Party ruled in its own interest and by sheer force. This lesson was not lost on the leaders of the new

regime. As soon as they assumed power, they took elaborate measures to assert their legitimacy—through inaugu-
ration rituals, constitutional debates, and demonstrative
voting procedures.

Contrary to what one might have expected, the new
regime did not begin with a declaration of independence,
but rather with a confession of guilt. It assumed responsibility for the entire burden of German history, including
the horrors of Nazism. The Communists had refused to do
so because they considered themselves victims and enemies of Nazism. In casting off Communism, the new leaders of East Germany confronted the past that they shared
with Germans in the West. By act of parliament, they
apologized to the Jewish people and promised to pay reparations to Israel.

At the same time, the East Germans began to uncover
disturbing information about what they referred to as the
"blank spots" in their own history. They learned that victims of Stalinism lay hidden in mass graves near the victims of Hitlerism at Buchenwald and the sites of other
concentration camps. When they followed the tortuous
history of repression and the secret police, they discovered
that it led from the Gestapo of the 1930s to the Stasi (secret police) of the 1980s—in fact, right into the parliament
itself, where the deputies set up a special commission to
determine how many of their own number had worked as
Stasi agents. The East Germans found it painful to peel off
so many layers from a living past, but they considered it
necessary for the fulfillment of their revolution.

Soon they will encounter a man who embodies the past
they have repressed: Isaak Behar, a Jew who survived the
Holocaust by hiding underground in the midst of wartime
Berlin. For years Herr Behar has gone from school to
school, telling his tale to the children of West Berlin; and
now that the city is united, he will bring it to the East.

Paired with his story in Part I are some stories of my own, which are meant to show how the past weighed on an outsider who attempted to make sense of the events that transformed Germany in the years 1989–1990.

My accounts of these events appear in Parts II and IV, which cover the two main phases of the revolution: the overthrow of the old regime (Part II: September 1989 to January 1990) and the establishment of the new (Part IV: January 1990 to July 1990). I have published them in their original form, as essays written in the heat of the events and completed on the dates that appear after the chapter titles.* They are meant to convey something of the flavor of the revolution as I observed it, even though I sometimes got things wrong. In retrospect, my two biggest mistakes were a failure to recognize the importance of the push for unification with West Germany in the late autumn, and an underestimation of the strength of the Christian Democrats during the election campaign. Like many observers, I thought (and even hoped) that the GDR might find a "third way" between socialism and capitalism, one that would permit it to preserve its own identity, and I wrongly predicted that the Social Democrats would win the election. Where I differed from the other commentators was on the question of an *Ausverkauf* or sell-out to the consumer society of the West. I did not see why East Germans should be condemned for desiring washing machines and bananas, or why that desire should be considered incompatible with the demand for free elections and civil rights. After breathing in a few lungfuls of the air in Bitterfeld and Halle, I could understand why so many people emigrated to the West. And after spending a few evenings in

*The first chapter in Part II is an exception. It was written in July 1990, in order to provide a context for the crisis that led to the fall of the Wall. Several of the chapters in Parts II and IV were published in abridged form as articles in *The New Republic*.

the tenements of Leipzig and East Berlin, I learned to respect those who remained behind in order to do battle on the home front.

Part III is intended to flesh out the account of events in Parts II and IV, by exploring the peculiarities of life in the GDR. It consists of interviews and essays based on chance encounters from the time I first arrived in East Germany. Although I came to West Berlin to spend a year at the Institute for Advanced Study, my first stop was Halle, *terra incognita* deep in East Germany, where I attended a colloquium on the Enlightenment. The colloquium did not seem to be very different from academic meetings in the West, until a French friend, who had just spent a year in Halle, took me aside and said, "Something strange is going on. One of the East German professors just cited Nietzsche, in public!" As I had not known that Nietzsche was taboo in the GDR, I suddenly realized that I was in a very foreign country.

That realization grew with every day that I spent in the GDR, and I spent a great many, because my East German colleagues generously invited me to give lectures all over the country; and once it became possible to travel freely, I set off on my own, to attend demonstrations and have a look at anything that seemed interesting. But everything seemed interesting, even the simplest remarks by the most ordinary people, because, as I soon discovered, East Germans did not think like Westerners. They began from different assumptions, and lived in a different world.

Perhaps I should have been prepared to find everything so strange, but I had assumed that East Germans were essentially the same as West Germans, except for varying degrees of political persuasion. They spoke the same language and shared the same culture. But they had lived apart for forty years. I had not realized how effectively they had been divided and how deeply the division had cut into the two societies. It extended to the everyday lives of ordinary people, their ways of handling social contacts, time and money, friendship and family, and even words, despite their common language.

Not only was East Germany another world; it was suddenly accessible. Before November 9, travel into the GDR involved elaborate preparations, expense, visas, nasty inspections at the border, further check-ins with the police at every stop, and fruitless efforts to make contact with a population too terrified to talk. After November 9, everything opened up. The border crossings became increasingly easy and the guards positively cordial. Whenever I wanted to see something, I simply got in a train or car and went there. And when I arrived, I found myself in an East that was also Western.

Cities like Leipzig, Halle, and Weimar lie along the main route of Western European history. They look and feel Western. Their inhabitants speak a Western language, although I must admit that I felt speechless when trying to communicate with peasants in Saxony and workers in Schwerin. Educated East Germans share the same high culture as their counterparts in West Germany. In June 1990, I spent an evening in Magdeburg with a doctor whose great passion was the art of Paul Klee. To his delight, he had just seen a Klee exhibition in Hannover. Before November, Klee had been taboo—and Hannover also. The city was just ninety miles to the west, but he had never been able to visit it, although all the East was open to him and he had traveled to the farthest reaches of Siberia.

Not only were the East Germans now willing to talk; they had a great deal to say. The collapse of the Wall released a great flood of words, from a people who had been suffering in silence for forty years. They wanted to explain what they had experienced; so I spent most of 1989–1990 trying to listen.

They surprised me by their openness. They talked frankly about the rigging of elections, the censoring of books, the polluting of the environment, and the pervasive influence of the secret police. Of course, they did so in a way that made their own roles look innocent. Everyone I met was a victim of the system; no one was ready to assume responsibility for it. I have tried to allow for this tendency toward self-exoneration in the essays that follow, but I have not felt any urge to pass judgment on the East Germans. On the contrary, I wanted to write in a way that would capture their points of view and permit their voices to be heard.

My greatest handicap was my ignorance. I have never spent much time studying German politics or culture. But at least I knew that I knew nothing, which is an advantage in a way. In fact, I was surprised to discover how little East and West Germans knew about each other, and how rarely they recognized the limits of their knowledge. Many West Berliners, to my astonishment, had never set foot in East Berlin. "Why should we?" they would say. "We don't know anyone there; there is nothing to do; the border guards are nasty; we have to change money into a worthless currency; and when we go into a shop there is nothing to buy." Those who wandered east across the Wall generally stayed in the old center of the city, the artificial world between the Brandenburg Gate and Alexanderplatz. But East Berlin, even the livelier East Berlin of the Prenzlauer Berg, is not East Germany. The far north and the deep south remained off limits to most *Wessis* and *Bundis,* as West Germans are known in the GDR. People from the Rhineland and Bavaria seemed to have little interest in what went on in Thuringia and Saxony, so thoroughly had the Wall done its work.

Of course the lack of contact was more severe for East Germans who wanted to go West. *Reisekader* (usually privileged members of the Communist Party) got to travel, and ordinary citizens often received permission to visit relatives, especially if they had passed retirement age and left their wife or husband at home. But most *Ossis* (as East Germans are known in the Wests) had never set foot in West Germany. They lived in another world, close but cut off from everything taken for granted in the West. That is the fascination of the GDR at the moment of its opening: alien but accessible, strange but familiar, so near and yet so far, it works on the visitor's imagination like a gigantic ghost town that is not yet dead. Now Ossis and Wessis can easily move across the porous borders of East and West, exchanging goods, money, ideas, and ways of life. The pieces in Part V touch on these movements between worlds.

Taken together, the essays in this book should provide a journalistic account of an extraordinary year, but nothing that can claim to be a definitive history. Although I am a card-carrying historian, I do not feel apologetic about writing in a journalistic mode. Indeed, I admire the masters of the craft, from Louis-Sébastien Mercier to Meyer Berger, more than I admire many professors in the American Historical Association. My only regret is that I cannot live up to the standards set by those masters of journalism.

But there is a kind of journalism that I do not admire. It thrusts the reporter onto center stage by abusing the first person singular. At every point it dangles his or her "I" before the reader, as if to say, "I was there" and "Look how clever I am." Yet there is an equal danger implicit in the opposite style, the kind that hides the reporter's voice behind an inexorable third person singular. It creates an illusion of omniscience, laying everything out as if everything had been taken in and as if the writing were reality. I have tried to find a middle way, experimenting with different voices in Parts I, III, and V and keeping the first person to a minimum in Parts II and IV.

Finally, I would like to thank the Wissenschaftskolleg zu Berlin, which invited me to spend the academic year 1989–1990 in West Berlin and which did not object when I spent so much of it in nonacademic fashion in the East.

R.D.
Paris
August 1990

CHRONOLOGY

1989

May 2 Hungary begins to dismantle its border with Austria.

August East German refugees flock to Hungary and seek asylum in the West German embassies in Prague and Warsaw.

Sept. 11 Hungary opens its border with Austria; approximately 55,000 East Germans escape to the West.

Oct. 1 6,000 refugees travel from Prague to West Germany via the GDR in special trains.

Oct. 3 The GDR closes its border with Czechoslovakia as refugees continue to flood into the Prague embassy.

Oct. 5 A second set of special trains brings 11,000 refugees from Prague to West Germany via the GDR; riots in Dresden.

Oct. 6 Gorbachev arrives for the fortieth anniversary celebrations of the GDR in East Berlin.

Oct. 7 Counter-demonstrations during the celebrations are repressed, resulting in injuries and arrests.

Oct. 9 A mass demonstration takes place without violence in Leipzig. The security forces withdraw, averting a civil war.

Oct. 18 Egon Krenz replaces Erich Honecker as general secretary of the Communist Party (SED). Under increasing pressure from demonstrations and the emigration of refugees, Krenz begins to reorganize the Party and the government.

Nov. 3 East Germans are now allowed to enter Czechoslovakia without a special visa; a new wave of refugees sweeps across the Czech–West German border.

Nov. 4 Nearly a million people demonstrate in East Berlin for free elections, the freedom of the press, and the freedom to travel.

Nov. 7 The government led by Willi Stoph resigns. A committee of the parliament declares a draft of a new travel law to be inadequate.

Nov. 8 The Politburo resigns. In replacing it, the Central Committee of the Communist Party confirms Krenz's position as general secretary and recommends that Hans Modrow be selected by the parliament to form a new government.

Nov. 9 Günter Schabowski, the spokesman of the Central Committee, announces that East Germans can travel to West Germany without getting special clearance. Hundreds of thousands of East Berliners flood into West Berlin, where the entire city celebrates the opening of the Wall.

Nov. 13   The parliament chooses Modrow as prime minister and demands free elections.

Nov. 17   After taking the oath of office, Modrow announces the formation of a new government and promises far-reaching reforms.

Nov. 28   In Bonn, Helmut Kohl announces a ten-point program for the unification of the two Germanys.

Dec. 1   The parliament votes to eliminate the reference to the leading role of the Communist Party from the constitution. Leading members of the Party are accused of corruption and abuse of office in a report of an investigating commission.

Dec. 2   In a demonstration before Central Committee headquarters in Berlin, Party members jeer Krenz, demand the resignation of the Politburo and the Central Committee, and call for a complete reorganization of the Party.

Dec. 3   Krenz, the Politburo, and the Central Committee resign. A temporary committee takes charge of the Party pending the choice of a new leadership at a special convention. Honecker and his collaborators from the previous regime are expelled from the Party; some of them are arrested.

Dec. 4   As the mass demonstrations in Leipzig and other cities continue, the call for unification with West Germany becomes increasingly strong.

Dec. 5   Honecker and some of his collaborators are placed under house arrest, as the investigation into corruption and abuse of power continues.

Dec. 7   The Round Table, which includes representatives of the main citizens' movements and political parties, holds its first meeting. It urges the government to call for free and secret elections on May 6 and to dissolve the secret police (Stasi).

Dec. 8–9   At a special convention, the Communist Party

chooses Gregor Gysi as its leader and reorganizes itself, renouncing all forms of Stalinism.

Dec. 16 Continuing its restructuring, the Communist Party (formally the Socialist Unity Party of Germany, or SED) adopts a new name: the Party of Democratic Socialism (SED–PDS—the SED component of the new name will be dropped on February 4). Meanwhile, the Christian Democratic Union (CDU) reorganizes itself under the presidency of Lothar de Maizière, and other parties begin to prepare for the election campaign.

Dec. 22 The Brandenburg Gate is opened.

1990

Jan. 1 A half million East and West Germans celebrate New Year's on and around the Wall.

Jan. 15 Under growing pressure from demonstrations demanding the immediate dissolution of the Stasi, the government issues a report on the former secret police, and Modrow assures the Round Table that it can supervise the Stasi's dismantling. Later that afternoon, a crowd storms Stasi headquarters in East Berlin.

Jan. 28 Modrow agrees to move the date for the parliamentary elections up to March 18 and to create a new coalition government. This "government of national responsibility" will include representatives from the major citizens' movements and parties and will work closely with the Round Table in order to hold the country together until the election.

Feb. 5 With the blessing of Kohl, the CDU joins the DSU (Democratic Social Union) and the DA (Democratic Beginning) in an election coalition named Alliance for Germany.

Feb. 7   The citizens' movements, New Forum, Democracy Now, and Initiative for Peace and Human Rights, form an election coalition named Alliance '90.

Feb. 10   After meeting with Gorbachev, Kohl announces that the Soviet Union respects the right of the German people to unite in one state.

Feb. 11   The Liberal Democratic Party (LDP), the Free Democratic Party (FDP), and the German Forum Party (DFP) form an election coalition named the Alliance of Free Democrats. By now most of the parties have regrouped, and the election campaign is under way.

Feb. 25   The Social Democrats (SPD), led by Ibrahim Böhme, announce their election program at their convention in Leipzig; the PDS does the same at its convention in East Berlin. By now, all the major parties have come out in favor of union with West Germany, the CDU and DSU most emphatically, the PDS with the most reservations.

Mar. 18   The Alliance for Germany wins a surprisingly strong victory in the election: 48 percent of the vote and 193 of the 400 seats in the new parliament, the first freely elected parliament in the history of the GDR.

Mar. 31   The Central Bank of West Germany recommends that East German marks be converted to West German marks (DM) at a rate of two to one when the future currency union takes place. The East Germans protest, demanding a one-to-one rate.

Apr. 2   Böhme withdraws as leader of the SPD after being accused of having collaborated with the Stasi. He is replaced by Markus Meckel, while the SPD and the Free Democrats negotiate with the Alliance for Germany over the formation of a broad coalition government.

Apr. 5   The new parliament holds its first meeting and elects a president.

Apr. 9 De Maizière completes the negotiations for a coalition government under him as prime minister. The twenty-four ministries will be distributed among the Alliance for Germany, the SPD, and the Free Democrats, giving the government the two-thirds majority necessary for modifying the constitution and settling terms for unification with West Germany.

Apr. 12 The coalition agreement is signed, and the new government is sworn in before the parliament.

Apr. 19 De Maizière outlines the policies of his government to the parliament. The subsequent debate on his speech marks the beginning of parliamentary politics.

May 2 The two German governments agree on terms for the currency, economic, and social union, which will take place on July 1. East German wages and pensions will be paid in deutsche marks at a rate of one to one, savings for most adults at one to one up to 4,000 DM and at two to one thereafter.

May 6 In elections for local and regional governments, the CDU remains the strongest party in East Germany. It takes 34 percent of the vote, although it loses 6 percent compared with its showing in the national election on March 18.

May 18 The treaty for the currency, economic, and social union is signed in Bonn.

July 1 The treaty goes into effect, uniting the economies of the two Germanys. All border controls in and around Berlin are dismantled, uniting the city.

Oct. 3 The two Germanys are united in a single polity, the former GDR incorporated as five new states in the Federal Republic.

Dec. 2 In the first all-German parliamentary election, the voters confirm their support for the CDU (44 percent of the vote) and its ally, the FDP (11 percent).

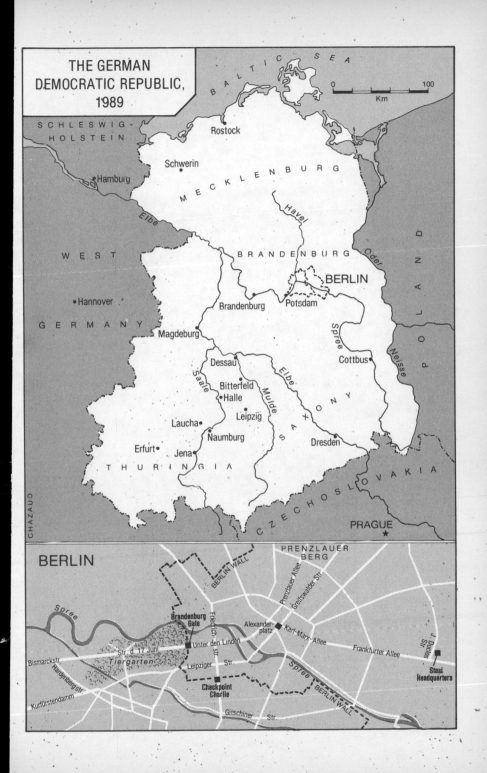

THE GERMAN DEMOCRATIC REPUBLIC, 1989

0   100
Km

BALTIC SEA

SCHLESWIG-
HOLSTEIN

Hamburg

Rostock

Schwerin

MECKLENBURG

Havel

WEST

Hannover

GERMANY

BRANDENBURG

BERLIN

Brandenburg

Potsdam

Magdeburg

Spree

Dessau

Cottbus

Saale

Bitterfeld

Halle

Mulde

Elbe

SAXONY

Laucha

Leipzig

Naumburg

Erfurt

Jena

Dresden

THURINGIA

Oder

Neisse

POLAND

CZECHOSLOVAKIA

PRAGUE
★

CHAZAUD

BERLIN

PRENZLAUER
BERG

BERLIN WALL

Spree

Prenzlauer Allee

Greifswalde Str.

Brandenburg
Gate

Unter den Linden

Alexander-
platz

Karl-Marx-Allee

Friedrich Str.

Str. d. 17 Juni

Tiergarten

Leipziger   Str.

Frankfurter Allee

J. Duclos
Str.

Bismarckstr.

Hardenbergstr.

Spree

BERLIN WALL

Stasi
Headquarters

Kurfürstendamm

Checkpoint
Charlie

Gitschiner   Str.

BERLIN JOURNAL

PART I

CONFRONTATIONS WITH THE PAST

CONFESSIONS
OF A GERMANOPHOBE

I always wished that the soldier who killed my father had been a German, but he wasn't. He was an American. It didn't even happen in Germany. It happened, in the language of wartime Washington, "somewhere in the Pacific," actually at the Battle of Buna in Northern New Guinea on October 18, 1942. An American gunner strafed the wrong side by mistake. But I put it right in my mind, simply by making it happen in Germany. I was three at the time and didn't know much about geography. Living on the East Coast, I heard about nothing but "bad people" who were all German. They had pencil-mustaches, wore their hair smeared diagonally across their foreheads, and walked like geese. In my mind, I arranged it that Hitler himself had killed my father, and in my dreams I saw him coming to get me. He usually came in the window, with a knife between his teeth. I still have Nazi nightmares made up mostly of jack boots and torture chambers. Or do I? Are they really Nazis or some other species of "bad people" picked out of the trash stored in my head—death squads in Argentina, perhaps, or even "New York's finest"? How can we know what seeps into the mind and settles into memories? How can we assess what we remember?

I had a chance to play with those questions just before I left for Berlin, when I ran across an article I had supposedly written, or rather dictated, at the age of four for the Sunday *New York Times Magazine:* "ROBERT, AGE 4, IN WONDERLAND. What he saw in a tour of Washington is set down here in his own language." My father had been a war correspondent for *The Times.* One of his friends, Meyer Berger, took me around the city and recorded my quasi-baby talk in order to draw a picture of wartime Washington as it appeared to a little boy. It was to be a modern version of the story about "The Emperor's New Clothes," and it made a good Sunday feature because I came up with supposedly cute comments, such as "Penny-gone" for Pentagon.

The cuteness has worn off by now, but I find the article disturbing, because as a four year old I apparently spoke the words that appear in it. Meyer Berger, who took them down in shorthand, was famous for the accuracy and integrity of his reporting. In reading those words printed under the by-line, "by Robert Darnton as recorded by Meyer Berger," I can know what I said forty-six years ago, a year after my father's death. I can step into a stream of consciousness that had disappeared into the lower strata

of my mind, and dive into a world that had been completely inaccessible—unless I could have reached it by a
long and painful detour from a psychoanalyst's couch. Of
course, Meyer Berger may have made mistakes, and he
may have edited out the most important passages. But how
accurate is the note-taking of the psychoanalyst? How un-
mediated is his contact with experiences stored in other
people's minds for half a century?

A few passages from "Robert in Wonderland":

In the car we passed horses that don't go, and men that
don't go (Statues in Washington's streets). We saw the
house (German Embassy, in Massachusetts Avenue)
where the Bad Men lived. The taxicab man said the Bad
Men wasn't there. I said: why? and he said they are in the
war shooting down houses. A truck tried to pass our car,
but it didn't go as fast as each other. I said why didn't they
shoot down the Bad Men when they lived here so they
wouldn't shoot down the Good Men's Houses?

In the newspaper office I saw a thing (news ticker). It
tells how much dead men are killed and how did they get
killed and it tells it very quickly and it jumps up and down.
It makes a funny noise, Bup-bup-bup-bup, and it goes
back so quickly. When it is stopped writing it purrs like a
kitten. We got a kitten that purrs. My kitty's name is
Patches. It's a she. It just really is. . . .

(Pentagon) The Penny-gone is a big building for cars
and for people. Everybody has badges. If they wouldn't
have badges Bad People would come. Real soldiers don't
live here. They live in War. . . .

(Walter Reed Hospital) Soldiers have to walk with
sticks. I saw a soldier in pajamas and the Bad Men cut off
his leg and his pajamas too. The Bad Men made these
soldiers sick. Maybe his wifes will put his foot on again.

(Arlington Cemetery) It is so quiet here because the
good soldiers are asleep. He has to sleep here all the time in

the world. If a big tank would come and it could run over that Big Thing (Tomb of the Unknown Soldier) it would wake him.

All these soldiers are covered with little houses but without windows and no doors so they can't come out. So they won't shiver and chilly. This is where the Good Soldiers are.

Now, this is a book about Germany, not about Robert Darnton. I want to get on with it and to avoid detours into soulful introspection. At the same time, my readers should know that what follows does not come from a neutral observer. It is a book about Germany by someone who had looked upon Germans with fear and hatred since before he can remember. For me and millions of others in my generation, Germans were the "Bad People." Many of us tried to shake off this prejudice, but it remained hidden below the threshold of our consciousness—until the fall of 1989. The Peaceful Revolution of 1989 did not just free the Germans from the last vestiges of more than a half-century's dictatorial rule. It freed us from what we thought of them.

My first thoughts, as I flew toward Berlin on August 28, 1989, were recollections of three incidents. The first went back to my first trip to Germany, in the summer of 1958. I was visiting an American friend at the University of Tübingen. One night the whole town, or so it seemed, gathered under an enormous tent to sing songs and drink themselves into a stupor. I had never seen grown-ups behave like that as a collectivity. They linked elbows and rocked to the rhythm of the beer-hall songs. The girls danced on the tables, while the men grabbed at their dresses. And at midnight, punctually, the place closed down. Drunken revelers staggered about outside in the dark still clutching their mugs. When they met, they clinked mugs, slapped backs, and bellowed out *"Prost!"*

I set out for the student residence, cold sober and feeling as if I had been trapped inside a hellish scene by Brueghel or Bosch. *"Prost!"* called out a figure that loomed up out of the dark. My feeble German made it obvious that I came from the United States. *"Amerikaner!"* said the figure, and he began to tell his story.

He had known many Americans during the war. He had guarded them, in a camp. One day an officer picked one of them out. "Make that man kaput!" he ordered. "What could I do?" The man shrugged his shoulders. Then, weaving on his feet, he put his beer mug down and reached into his pocket. Out came a pack of matches. He lit a match and held it up to the back of his hand. There, flickering in the light, I saw an SS tatoo. *"Amerikaner! Brüder!"* he called out, as if all were now forgiven. He extended his tatooed hand and took mine in it. Not knowing what to do, I let him shake my hand and walked off into the night feeling dirtied and sick.

The second episode did not happen to me but to a friend of mine, Suzanne. Like many French Jews, she was sent to a family in the south during the war, and she attended school in her adopted town under a false name, as if she were an ordinary Catholic. When the Germans moved into the unoccupied zone, a detachment of troops took over the town. They paraded past the school every day. To the tiny children, they looked funny in their strange uniforms with their odd way of walking. One day as they marched past, a boy in Suzanne's class pointed his finger at them and laughed. The commanding officer stopped the parade, stood the boy up against the school wall, and had him shot by a firing squadron.

For the rest of the war, whenever she saw a group of

German soldiers, Suzanne felt an irresistible impulse to laugh. If she spotted them marching through the street, she would run inside her house to a hiding place behind a curtain. Then she would peer through the window; and as they stomped by, she would bury her face in the material and laugh and laugh and laugh.

The third episode involved my friend Horst. He recounted it to me over coffee in his room under the roof of an ancient building in Wolfenbüttel, the Lower Saxony town where we were both spending the summer as research fellows in the Herzog August Bibliothek. "It's not easy to be called Horst," he began. It took me a minute, but I soon realized he was alluding to Horst Wessel, the Nazi "martyr," who was killed in a brawl in 1930. Everywhere for the next fifteen years sons of Nazis had Horst foisted on them as a name.

By way of explanation, my friend told me that his father was, as he put it, "a shit"—a petty-minded *petit bourgeois,* who joined the Nazi party at the first opportunity and threw his weight around as a minor official. On July 20, 1944, Horst, then four or five years old, was traveling with his father and mother in a train. The only other person in their compartment was a man reading a newspaper. After the train pulled into a station, they heard the public address system announce that there had been an attempt on the Führer's life but fortunately he had escaped unharmed. "Too bad they didn't get the bastard," said the man behind the paper.

Horst's father leaped to his feet. He grabbed the man by the lapels, screaming that he would denounce him to the Gestapo. He could do so easily before the train pulled out, because a Gestapo office stood just across the platform. But then Horst's mother stood up. She put her hand on Horst's head and shouted at his father: "I swear on the head of this boy that if you do that I will leave you this minute and never come back!" Horst sat there staring at his parents. The man did, too. They were frozen in a silence that seemed to last forever while the father made up his mind. At last he sank back into his seat, the train pulled out, and they all resumed their journey.

Everyone who traveled in Germany during the 1950s and 1960s has a collection of such stories. The war touched so many lives that it left its mark everywhere, and anyone who strayed among the ruins would hear horrific tales from survivors with too much on their minds or too much beer in their bellies. But the caricature of the bloated, beery German would not wash by 1989, when I flew off for a full year at the Wissenschaftskolleg in Berlin. By then, I had discovered that I had a great deal in common with the Horsts of my generation—and that other generations had come of age, innocent of any responsibility for Nazism, since they were born after it had ended.

What set my generation off from theirs? I asked myself. It was not so much the war as it was a conviction, the only unshakable, almost metaphysical conviction that could be shared by people of my age and cast of mind. Germany represented the Absolute—not the Absolute of Hegelian philosophy, but the only Absolute we could imagine in a world without a God or any clear, transcendent truth: Absolute Evil, the evil of Nazism. Whatever our opinions about politics or ethics or all the other issues we discussed in college bull sessions, we knew that one thing was true: Nazism stood out as a basic point of reference in a landscape composed of endless shades of gray; it was black, pure black, so black that it defined the color of everything around it.

An odd thought to entertain before arriving in Berlin. Was I about to land in the capital of the "evil empire," or was that idea as empty as Ronald Reagan's rhetoric about the Soviet Union? I looked down trying to locate the spot where Hitler's bunker had existed, and tightened my safety belt.

A WANDERING JEW

Isaak Behar has never taught school, but he has a passion for pedagogy. You should not offer children abstractions, he explains. You show them your yellow star, the real thing. You let them touch it, hold it to their chest. You pass around your identity card with "Jew" stamped on it. You tell them about things that happened at places they walk by every day—the yellow bench for Jews in the Tiergarten, the Gestapo in the Jewish school at the Roseneck, the burning of the synagogue on Fasanenstrasse.

"It is okay if they cry," Herr Behar says. "Sometimes I cry with them. How can you talk about such things, things that you have been carrying in your memory for fifty years, without being moved? But children often cry at the sight of a dead cat, at suffering of any kind. They empathize for a moment, and then they forget. I want them to understand."

So Isaak Behar fills his talk with concrete details. The words spill out of him in a great flow—anecdotes, jokes, homely observations about daily life in a world the students can barely imagine, and a precise account of how the Nazis annihilated his family and friends and came within an inch, time after time, of destroying him.

Isaak Behar is a man with a mission. One of the few Jews who survived the Holocaust by hiding in the heart of Berlin itself, he goes from school to school telling his story to the next generation of Berliners. He prefers small classes, where he can look the students in the eye, and high schools, where they are old enough to ask searching questions. "Grandfather, what did you do during the war?" The question hangs over many German families, and it often goes unanswered. Herr Behar brings the students face to face with their families' past, because he embodies it.

Is he then a man possessed? A modern version of the Wandering Jew? Or another Ancient Mariner, who has traveled to the bottom of hell and returned with a tale that he is determined to inflict upon an uncomprehending public? Herr Behar does not look the part. He is short and roly-poly. He talks with gusto, chopping the air with his hands, jumping up to write names on the blackboard, plunging down narrative by-ways that seem to lead nowhere but suddenly intersect the main story at an unexpected point, making it denser and often funnier—for he splices his talk with jokes and even a little ribaldry. He laughs at himself, and the students laugh with him, when they are not crying. They hang on every word. They are in

the presence of a great storyteller, and they know it, even
if they do not suspect the pedagogy that lies behind it.

Isaak Behar slaps his bald pate in astonishment at what
he has just said: he had an Aryan girl friend! A real Berliner sweetie! He is standing before Herr Ladewig's eleventh-graders at the Walther Rathenau Gymnasium and
trying to explain the Nuremberg laws. On their side, they
are trying to imagine him, at age nineteen in 1942, squiring
around one of the blondes like the Sabines and Brigittes in
their own class. How can they understand that a Brigitte
and a Jew would be executed for sleeping together in 1942?

Herr Behar confesses that he was not much of a student.
He copied his friends' homework while riding to school in
the tram on the Kurfürstendamm. The only two subjects
in which he held his own were drawing and gym. (The
students laugh.) But girls! (The students laugh again.) He
lets them understand that he was something of a ladies'
man, and indeed the face that looks out from his earliest
identification card shows a handsome young man with a
glint in his eye.

Young Isaak used to rendezvous with Inge Meyer on
Sunday mornings. She knew she was risking her life, but
who has ever been deterred by risk when they were young
and in love? Besides, Isaak knew how to minimize the
danger. He took different, round-about routes when he
slipped out of his family's apartment at 154a Kant Strasse;
and he never wore his yellow star, although that, too, was a
potentially fatal offense. As he was leaving the apartment
house on Sunday, December 13, 1942, two men in leather
coats stopped him.

"Do you live here?"

"No, certainly not. I just came for a visit."

For some reason they let him pass without even asking
him to show an identification card. He hurried off to seek
help from some friends, a family of Bulgarian immigrants

who lived nearby. The father went out to reconnoiter; but he got too close and the two men seized him, thinking he was Isaak. By then a detachment of Gestapo had ordered Isaak's family to pack up some belongings and had discovered that Isaak was missing.

"Now we've got you," said one of the men.

"But I am not Isaak Behar," said the Bulgarian in broken German and produced his Bulgarian passport to prove it.

"What are you doing here?

"I just stopped by to say hello."

"You can say good-bye now," the man replied, and led him up to the Behar apartment on the third floor. When the door opened, Frau Behar screamed. She thought it must be Isaak. But as soon as she saw the Bulgarian, she knew her son was safe. After another round of passport checking, the Gestapo released the Bulgarian and drove the Behars into the street. They were carted off to an internment center for the night, then marched to the Grunewald freight station and loaded into a box car bound for Auschwitz. Shipment number 25; 811 "pieces" of Jews (811 *Stück Juden*). Isaak never saw his family again.

The room is silent. The students stare at the floor. Herr Behar stands up and draws an *x* through the first four names that he had written on the board at the beginning of his talk:

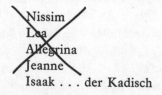

Nissim
Lea
Allegrina
Jeanne
Isaak . . . der Kadisch

"Some say there were six million. Some say seven or five. The number is too big to comprehend. For me it was four, everything I had in the world." Herr Behar pauses, letting the words sink in. Then, from somewhere deep inside him, a question sails across the room and hits the students like a slap in the face: *"Why?"* Another silence. Herr Behar answers softly, "Because they happened to be born Jews."

"Do you remember what you said to your parents when you left the house this morning?" he asks. "Probably not. Perhaps you said nothing. I said next to nothing when I left my house on December 13, 1942. It was early, and I was in a rush to see Inge. But I should have said a prayer, because I was the Kadisch."

The students look bewildered. Herr Behar explains that he was the third child and the first boy. According to Jewish tradition, fathers wanted to have sons, because sons were ideally suited to say the prayer for the dying known as the Kadisch. A first-born son was often called "the Kadisch," and a father counted himself happy if he had a Kadisch in the house to pray over him. At the time of Isaak's birth, his father could not believe his good fortune. "Mir ist der Kadisch geboren! Mir ist der Kadisch geboren!" ("The Kadisch has been born to me"), he kept repeating, beside himself with joy. But Isaak never got to say Kadisch. He never even said good-bye.

The Behars were not especially pious, but they kept up the traditions and observed the rituals. They lived on the corner of Kant Strasse and Fasanen Strasse, just a few yards down from one of the biggest synagogues in the city. Herr Behar pulls two enlarged photographs from a plastic carrying case and props them up against the blackboard. One shows the synagogue, an imposing structure covered by three huge domes, as it appeared in the 1930s. The other is a current view of the street corner. He points to the windows of his apartment, which somehow survived the war, and to the site of the synagogue, an empty space across the street behind an Esso station.

The apartment was cramped and the family poor, because Isaak's father had to feed five people from his meager income as a repairer of Turkish carpets. But as Herr Behar sees it in retrospect, he had a blissfully happy childhood. His sisters doted on him; his father spoiled him as the Kadisch; and to his mother he was a *Macher,* a feisty little guy who could fight or talk his way through anything. He felt proud and protective when he took her on his arm during their walks through the Tiergarten. She could not make it all the way across, because she had been nearly crippled in a traffic accident opposite the Gedächtniskirche. They always stopped to rest on a bench in the middle of the park, but after Hitler seized power Jews could sit only on certain benches painted yellow. Why yellow? The students cannot come up with an answer; so Herr Behar explains. If an epidemic breaks out on a ship, the captain runs up a yellow flag. If a package is filled with dangerous material, it often has a yellow label. Yellow means poison or the plague. So he did not feel like much of a *Macher* when he sat by his mother on the yellow bench, exuding as much protection as he could from beneath his yellow star.

Anti-Semitism did not begin suddenly when Hitler seized power in 1933, Herr Behar warns the students. There were always fights and insults—"Jew-swine," "Jew-whore," and, worst of all, "matzoh-baker." Does anyone know what matzohs are? Most of the students look puzzled, but one girl says they are a kind of flat bread, like the Turkish Fladenbrot everyone eats in Berlin. "Right!" says Herr Behar, looking pleased. "I'm a Turk, too." He explains that his ancestors settled in Turkey in the fifteenth century, when the Jews were driven out of Spain. That was how his father got to know about carpets. After World War I, when Turkey and Germany had been allies, his father traveled to Berlin. When he returned, he said to

Frau Behar, "Lea, I have seen a country where they do not just clean the houses; they scrub the doorsteps and the sidewalks in front of the houses!" So the Behars moved to Berlin. And after World War II, when he no longer knew where he belonged, Isaak Behar requested and received a Turkish passport. He reaches into his bag of tricks and pulls the passport out. The students looked impressed. They see Turkish immigrants (Gastarbeiter) every day, but not Turkish Jews. Herr Behar adds that he later received a German passport. In fact he has a whole collection of passports, some with false names, some with "no country" (staatenlos) stamped on them.

Herr Behar reaches into the bag again and pulls out . . . a matzoh. "This is a matzoh," he proclaims, holding it up high. He breaks the matzoh into pieces on a paper plate and passes it around. While the students taste it, he gives a brief account of Passover and notes that it has some similarity to the Communion rituals in Christian churches. But when he was a boy, many Germans held the Jewish people responsible for the death of Christ. Many believed that Jews used to eat Christian babies and that the brown spots baked on the matzohs came from the blood of Christians.

So he and the other Jews in his class were called "matzoh bakers." Actually, they got along quite well with the non-Jewish children at first. Young Isaak was surprised when his friend Hans Müller arrived in school one day wearing a new black tie. "Yes," Herr Behar says to the students. "I know it seems unbelievable, but we wore ties to school then." He wanted one like it, but Hans said that was impossible, because you had to be a member of "our organization" and Isaak was a Jew. More black ties appeared. One day the black ties ran their flag up the school flag pole, and everyone sang the hymn of the Nazi youth organization. It was a good tune, Herr Behar says, and he hums a few bars. As a school boy he had wanted to sing along, too.

But then things got nastier. "No Jews" appeared in shop windows. Isaak could not go to certain cafés, sports grounds, and swimming places. He had to attend a separate school for Jews. And then came November 9, 1938, Crystal Night. On the morning after the smashing and looting, Isaak stood before his reflection in the window of his room, putting on his new school tie. Suddenly he looked out the window and saw the synagogue burning across the Fasanenstrasse, not a hundred meters away. A large contingent of firemen had stationed themselves around it, with their backs to the flames, and were spraying water on the surrounding buildings so they would not catch on fire. The Behars gathered in front of the window, staring dumbfounded. As the synagogue's roof collapsed, Isaak sensed a change in his mother. Tears ran down her cheeks, but she did not sob: instead, something seemed to snap inside her. His father put his arm around her shoulder.

"They are only burning stones, Lea."

"Once these stones burn," she replied. "They will burn people."

"How right she was," says Herr Behar. Soon afterward his school was closed. Then came the war. Then forced labor for his sisters in a factory making uniforms, for his father and himself in a munitions factory. Then the fatal night of December 13, 1942, and Auschwitz. How can he explain it? How can he make a class of secular seventeen year olds understand the importance of synagogues and matzohs and the Kadisch? Most of them have never known a Jew. Only a few thousand of the 170,000 Jews in prewar Berlin survived the Holocaust. The city itself was almost totally destroyed. The Berlin familiar to the students in the Walter Rathenau Gymnasium is another city, one that has been divided by the Cold War and filled up, in some of its Western neighborhoods, by Turks. The students seem to imagine young Isaak as a Turkish *Gastarbeiter*, but one with perfect German and without a mustache.

Above all, how can Herr Bchar convey the reality of the Holocaust? It began here, just down the road, he says. Grunewald, your local stop on the elevated railway, used to be the main point of departure for the deportations. The Jews were marched through the streets and loaded onto special trains, forty to a boxcar, in the Grunewald freight yard. It all happened in broad daylight, and with Prussian precision, down to the booking of the victims and the synchronization of their departure with the preparation of the gas in Auschwitz. When your grandparents claim they never knew about it, don't believe them. Say to them, "Grandfather, grandmother, I can understand that you would rather not talk about it. You don't have to lie."

Herr Behar explains that he, too, was forced to ride that train. But the Gestapo did not catch him for more than a year. After his family disappeared, he went underground, living by his wits and the few rules for survival that he picked up among the other hunted Jews: 1. Do not form a group; the more isolated you are, the better. 2. Do not talk with strangers, and have a false story ready in case you are required to talk. 3. Once you have found a hiding place, venture out as little as possible, and always return by a different, roundabout route.

At first, Isaak thought he could hide in public bomb-shelters. But the special military police known as *Kettenhunde* (guard dogs) checked identity cards there. So when an air raid occurred, he did the opposite: he climbed onto a roof. However, he soon learned that wardens always inspected the roofs for firebombs after a raid; and he narrowly saved himself during one inspection by hiding behind a water tank. He knew better than to try to sleep in movie theaters because they, too, were inspected by *Kettenhunde*. So he usually spent the nights in cellars and the days in subways or the streets, walking about and trying to look inconspicuous.

At least money was no problem. When the Jews were forced to turn in all their jewelry and other valuables, many of them slipped some of their possessions to Gentile friends with the understanding that the friends would use them to provide help in time of need. Isaak's father had turned over his savings to such a friend, who gave them back to Isaak after the family was deported. Of course, Isaak did not have a ration card, but he could buy cheap food without rations just before meal times in certain restaurants. He avoided old friends, because he knew that he was on every Nazi wanted list and that anyone who helped a Jew would be killed as an enemy collaborator. He even stayed out of barber shops, where he felt exposed to spies. And he did not dare use public baths, because the *Kettenhunde* often swept through them.

By April 1943, Isaak was so hairy and unkempt that he feared his looks alone might provoke a policeman to demand his identity card. In desperation, he called his former boss in the munitions factory, a man named Behrens, who had shown some sympathy for the Jews condemned to forced labor under him. Of course, Behrens might also turn him in to the Gestapo. But sometimes, Herr Behar assures the students, you have to gamble on the existence of some good will in the world. When he phoned, Isaak said only "Behar" in a muffled voice. Behrens replied, "6:00 today, the usual clock."

What clock was that? Herr Behar asks the students. None of them knows. So Herr Behar produces another photograph from the 1930s: the clock by the kiosk in front of the Bahnhof Zoo at Hardenbergstrasse—the best-known meeting place in old Berlin. Isaak got there early and stationed himself across the street, in order to see whether Behrens might be followed by any suspicious-looking characters. When Behrens arrived, he seemed to be alone; so Isaak swallowed hard and walked past him, saying "Behar." He was so transformed in his appearance that Behrens had not recognized him. They walked off to a café, where Isaak explained that he could not go on like this. He needed to get himself cleaned up and to find a hiding place. Behrens took a deep breath. It won't be easy, he said. But he would see what he could do, and they would meet again in a day or two.

At their next meeting, Behrens gave Isaak a slip of paper with a typewritten name and address. He had a cousin, who had a colleague, who had a friend, who knew a porter in the Hotel Adlon named Koslovsky. Koslovsky was willing to tidy Isaak up and to hide him in his apartment in Wedding near the Wittler bread factory. Everything worked perfectly. Koslovsky insisted only that Isaak leave the room not more than once a day and that they meet every evening at 8:00, when the porters changed service, in order to be sure that neither had been arrested.

After several weeks, Isaak regained his normal appearance and began to feel human again, although he had to lie low and to avoid using any light at night. One night while going to the toilet in the dark, he slipped on the stairs and woke up someone with the noise. A door opened, throwing a shaft of light in the stairway. Isaak dashed inside the toilet and bolted the door. No one came, but he decided that he would have to protect himself against a similar accident by buying a flashlight. The next day, as he bent over the flashlights in a shop on the Kottbuserdamm, his eyes met those of the saleswoman. She appeared to be much older than he, in her mid-thirties, he reckoned, but pretty; and she looked at him hard.

Now, the last thing he had thought of was women, Herr Behar assures the students, whose attention suddenly grows more intense than ever. But before he knew it, he had blurted out, "Do you want a cup of coffee?" "Why, yes!" she said with a smile. "Pick me up here at 6:00." Once outside the store, Isaak began to reflect. He would have to make up a story, but he wasn't very good at lying; and he needed an excuse to free himself in time to meet Koslovsky in the apartment at 8:00. He decided he would be Hans Müller, a translator working the night shift in a government office. Like many of the Jewish families expelled from Spain, the Behars spoke Ladino, a Spanish dialect. Isaak could fall back on that, as well as on bits of French retained from school, and trust to his luck.

The saleswoman turned out to be Betty Krug, thirty-three and divorced. Her former husband had given her the shop in place of alimony, and she seemed to want a man. There were not many suitable men in Berlin in 1943, Herr Behar explains to the students. But customs were different then. You did not use the intimate *Du* until after the first kiss, and the first kiss did not occur until after many dates. On the third date, he had barely touched Betty's hand, and the situation seemed impossible. "Something is wrong," she said to him. Once again, he was seized by an impulse, and he told her his whole story.

When he had finished, she said, "My God, a Jew! And illegal!" Then, after a long pause: "Couldn't you arrange to stay out later some night?" Back at the apartment, Koslovsky reacted with predictable horror: "As if things aren't already difficult enough! Now, a woman!" But as an exception, for one evening only, he extended the deadline until 11:00. Isaak and Betty had dinner at Habels Weinstube by the Roseneck on Hohenzollerndamm—just a few blocks from your school, Herr Behar tells the students. "You go by it every day." He would never forget that

evening. After dinner, Betty said that she had baked a cake
at home. Did he want to come to her place for some more
dessert?

The next morning, Isaak got back to the apartment in
time to meet Koslovsky when the porters began their
morning shift at 6:00. There was no time for a good-bye
and no need for an explanation. Isaak moved in with
Betty. She had wanted to install him in a summer house
that her sister owned in Grünau on the outskirts of the
city. But the sister did not want to get mixed up with a
"foreigner." (Betty did not dare to say that "Hans" was a
Jew.) So Isaak found himself in a three-room apartment—
the greatest comfort he had ever known—fussed over, fed,
and loved by another Berliner sweetie. He could hardly
believe it. Only a few weeks before he was living in coal
bins and alleys, like an animal. Now he really felt human.

Isaak was loved, but he was not really free. He could not
wander about Berlin at will; and whenever he ventured
out, he took a different route back, crossing the street if he
smelled a *Kettenhund;* for one I.D. check would be enough
to do him in. Little by little, however, he became more
relaxed, extending his forays into cafés, where other suspicious characters met and exchanged bits of information.
By the summer of 1944, it was clear that the Germans were
losing the war; but Berlin became more dangerous. The
deportation trains from the Grunewald station continued
unabated, and the Gestapo were finding it increasingly
difficult to fill them with the quota of Jews.

Isaak sometimes picked up reports about the situation
from other Jews, who surfaced from the underground in
the Café Dobrin. "You probably have had coffee there
yourselves," says Herr Behar to the students. "Today it is
called the Café Bristol. On the Ku'damm near Knesebeck-
strasse." They would sit at separate tables and talk
obliquely while keeping their eyes on the door. One day a

well-dressed man about forty-five years old sat down at Isaak's table. He offered Isaak a cup of the ersatz coffee served in the place and began a casual conversation. Isaak fell back on his Hans Müller–translator story, which seemed to go over well. The man, a Herr Wegener, who said he also worked in a government office, responded sympathetically without pressing Isaak for details. They met again a few days later. This time Wegener said he had two daughters, ages eighteen and nineteen, and invited Isaak to join them for a family meal.

At the reference to the daughters, Isaak's ears pricked up. Not that he was tired of Betty, but he would not say no to a chance to meet someone closer to him in age. Herr Behar pauses, giving the students time to exchange some looks. The daughters turned out to be uninteresting, but Wegener became increasingly sympathetic; and after the third dinner, he said, "We have taken you into our hearts. If you ever have any problems, we are friends. We can help." Isaak said thank you, but he had no problems. "Not even small problems? Not even middle sized?" Isaak hesitated for a moment, but then again, as with Betty, he blurted everything out, everything except his liaison with Betty.

"I can help you," said Wegener. He could arrange for Isaak to escape to Czechoslovakia. False passport, train ticket, money, everything. He would drive Isaak to the station himself, and his friend Prokop would pick him up in Prague.

Isaak thought it over on the way home. To get out of Berlin! And with the protective cover of a passport! But how could he leave Betty? How could he even tell her? He decided to keep it to himself and to let his new friend make the preparations.

A few days later, Isaak packed his belongings. He had

not told Betty and she was not in the apartment, so he wrote a note:

I am in safety. Thanks.

That was all. She had fed him, loved him, risked her life. He walked out, leaving the key behind. "I was a shit," says Herr Behar to the students. "A shit."

As promised, Wegener had everything ready. He dropped Isaak off at the Anhalter train station, saying, "Have a good trip. Greet Prokop for me." Isaak stood before the departure board, a bag in each hand, looking for the track number of the train to Prague. Two hands grabbed his arms from behind. His bags dropped. He spun around. And he found himself in handcuffs. "You can't do this to me!" he protested. "I am Hans Müller." "Müller, Behar, it is all the same to us," said one of the plain-clothesmen. They led Isaak off to a black Opel limousine, and soon afterward he was sitting in cell PI under the police headquarters in Alexanderplatz.

Herr Behar leans a photograph of the police headquarters against the board. It is a gigantic building, but the students do not recognize it because it was obliterated during the war. Besides, at that time (September 1989) very few of them had ever set foot in Alexanderplatz. It lay on the other side of the Wall, and they knew only West Berlin, a very different city from the Berlin of young Isaak Behar.

Cell PI was like an Oriental bazaar, Herr Behar explains. It was as big as their classroom, and it contained thirty prisoners—Jews, gypsies, homosexuals, and petty criminals of all varieties. They did a lively trade in cigarettes and newspapers while waiting for the police to dispose of their cases. Like everything else in Prussia, the jail was run with bureaucratic precision. If a guard took a prisoner out of a cell, he had to fill out a receipt, which in turn was entered in a register kept by a superintendent. Isaak got to know the system, because the police used him as a translator whenever they needed to interrogate prisoners who spoke Spanish or French.

One day, while waiting to translate for an interrogation, Isaak fell into conversation with a new guard who looked sympathetic. The guard asked him how he had been caught. And after hearing Isaak's story, he said, "Do you know anyone outside who can help you?" Once again, Isaak hesitated. He had concealed Betty's existence from the undercover agent who had befriended him in the café, and he knew that "nice" cops sometimes gathered intelligence in jails. But he decided to take a chance, and he gave Betty's name and address.

A few days later, the guard took him aside. "Betty greets you," he said and handed Isaak a tiny piece of cake. They devised a plan for Isaak's escape. The guard would summon Isaak for an interrogation, take him to a hallway leading to an exit, and turn in the receipt as if he had been locked back in the cell. On the agreed date, Betty was waiting outside to whisk Isaak off to her apartment.

But on that day, a few hours before the guard was to fetch him, Isaak was led off to the deportation center at the former Jewish old age home at the Grosse Hamburger Strasse. The Gestapo had been holding him until they had rounded up thirty-nine other Jews, the required number for a boxcar. By then they had difficulty in reaching their quota, because 98 percent of Berlin's Jews had already been killed. Isaak was to be in the final stage of the "final solution."

Enough information had reached Isaak through the underground grapevine for him to know what to expect. He knew that they would be trucked to the Grunewald station and herded like animals into a boxcar. A Jew named Star-

garter, who dressed in a pseudoNazi uniform, complete
with jackboots, would take charge of the operation, kicking and cursing them unmercifully in an effort to save his
own skin by ingratiating himself with the SS. The train
would slow down for a sharp curve near the Erkner Station, the last S-Bahn station within the city limits. That
was their only chance to escape. With three others, Isaak
planned to pry open two air slats, which would be boarded
over high up on the side of the boxcar, and to leap out at
the Erkner curve.

At first, everything happened according to their plan.
They had found an old lead tube and a curtain rod support, which could serve as tools and which they hid under
their clothes. Stargarter turned out to be even nastier than
expected, but they withstood his insults as they climbed
into the boxcar, the only carload of Jews on the train. It
was September 6, 1944, the fifty-seventh shipment to
Auschwitz.

A Gestapo officer with four ordinary soldiers guarded
them from the next car. In order to prevent escape at-
tempts, the officer had put Isaak in charge of the Jews and
had told him that if anyone tried to get away he and nine
others would be shot. Nonetheless, as soon as the train
pulled out of the station, Isaak climbed on the back of
another man and started to pry off the boards covering the
air slat. But shortly before they reached the Erkner station, there was a loud noise and the train ground to a halt.
"I'm done for," thought Isaak. "They saw us, and now
they are going to shoot me."

After a long wait, they heard the rest of the train drive
off. Their car had been uncoupled and left on a side track,
they didn't know why—perhaps so that the execution
could take place without disturbing the passengers. The
soldiers herded them out of the boxcar and held them at
gunpoint while the Gestapo officer took Isaak aside. In-

stead of drawing his gun, he produced an explanation. The car had broken an axle. They would have to spend the night at the siding and board another boxcar, which would be sent on the next day in time to make the late evening train to Auschwitz. Meanwhile, Isaak should choose two or three others to help him carry some pots of broth for the evening meal, which would be delivered to the nearest street by a truck from the deportation center.

Immediately Isaak began to formulate a new plan. He chose his three friends. While studying the terrain, they hauled the broth to the Jews huddled outside the boxcar, and they arranged to do the same thing the next evening at about 9:30, when their final meal would arrive. At a signal from Isaak, they would drop the pots, kick the soldier accompanying them in the testicles, and run off into the woods across the street.

After a sleepless night and a miserable day, the four set off with a soldier to fetch the broth. But before Isaak gave the signal, the other three panicked and ran for it. The soldier fired after them in the dark, while Isaak stood there helplessly cursing his fate. In order to prevent any more mishaps, the soldiers ordered all of the Jews back into the boxcar. Isaak said that he needed to relieve himself and asked for permission to do it behind a nearby bush so that he would not foul the car. As he had proven his trustworthiness, a soldier let him go off on his own. Isaak squatted down for a second, then dashed behind the boxcar, and sprinted for the woods.

Never did he, or perhaps any other human being, run so fast. He heard shots and shouts, but he kept running deep into the forest on the outskirts of Berlin. He knew, however, that it would be far safer to hide in a huge city than in a suburban forest. So after the shooting died down, Isaak found his way back to the Erkner station, took the next S-Bahn train to the Bahnhof Zoo in central Berlin, and soon was walking down Joachimstaler Strasse looking for a whore.

Why a whore? The students are astonished. Herr Behar explains that everyone in the underground believed that the best place to go if you got in a tight spot was a whorehouse. He found a woman—pretty or ugly, it didn't matter and he couldn't remember—and soon was inside a cheap hotel. She took offense when he told her he only wanted to sleep. He explained that he had just arrived from Cologne, where he had been bombed out of his apartment. But ten marks quieted her, and another three marks pacified the madame who ran the establishment. Fortunately for him, the police had paid Isaak for his interpreting in the prison—another example of Prussian exactness.

He could not yet feel safe, however, because the madame had warned him that the police sometimes made identity-card checks in the middle of the night. Sure enough, through a half sleep, Isaak heard knocking. At first he thought he was dreaming, but it came closer and closer; and soon it was only a few doors away, accompanied by a loud voice: "Open up! Police! Identity card!" For a second, Isaak gave in to hopelessness. But then his will to survive surged back. He had fallen on the bed without taking off his clothes. So he leaped up, threw open the window, and jumped into the dark.

He landed on a vegetable garden in a courtyard about fifteen feet below. Back into the street, to the Bahnhof Zoo, into the first S-Bahn train, and out again a few stations later. Only then did Isaak notice that he had ripped his trousers and that his left leg was throbbing with pain. He had torn his Achilles tendon. Also, he had reached the point of exhaustion. After staggering into a park outside the station, he collapsed on a bench and fell into a deep sleep.

When he woke up the next morning, Isaak discovered

that he was in the Lietzensee Park and that he could barely walk. His ankle was swollen to three times its normal size. Using a fallen branch as a cane, he managed somehow to hobble back to the subway and to make a train to the Kottbuser Tor. After an agonizing struggle up the Kottbuserdamm, he stood in front of Betty's shop window, waving to her as she served a client. She nearly fainted. But she excused herself without arousing the customer's suspicion and slipped him the key to her apartment: Planufer 4, another desperate walk.

At last, however, Isaak made it back to Betty's bed. This time, she persuaded her sister to let her hide him in the summer house in Grünau. Isaak had given out the address of Betty's apartment too often for it to be safe, and he needed several weeks of healing before he could walk again. So he remained in Grünau, on the eastern fringe of the city, while Betty took care of him, more a nurse than a lover. He stayed there through the winter and into the spring of 1945. Betty returned to her apartment. And the Allies advanced on Berlin.

One morning in May, Isaak looked out the window. Soldiers were posted outside, soldiers in strange uniforms. Russians! He ran out the door, shouting, "I'm free! I'm free!" The soldiers looked at him incredulously, then raised their rifles. "I'm a Jew! I'm a Jew!" Isaak screamed. But they did not understand German. All around them German soldiers had been stripping off their uniforms in order to pass as civilians. Isaak might well be a Nazi.

They marched him off at gunpoint to a neighboring villa, which was serving as headquarters for a Soviet general while the Red army overran Berlin. For three days, they kept him under guard, and he kept protesting, "I'm a Jew! I'm a Jew!" At last an intelligence officer arrived, looked him over skeptically, and spoke to him in broken German. Isaak insisted he was Jewish and offered to pull down his pants to prove it. But the officer was unimpressed. Many non-Jews were circumcised, he said; and many Nazis were masquerading as victims of Nazism.

The Russian left and returned with a copy of a Hebrew prayer book. "Read!" he said, putting the book in Isaak's hands. Isaak, the Kadisch, knew how to open a holy book. He had been Bar Mitzvahed; so he could read in Hebrew. He read and read, as if his life depended on it—and, indeed, it did. *"Landsmann!"* cried the officer. He took Isaak in his arms in a great Russian-Jewish bear hug; and from that day to this Isaak Behar has been a free man.

Freedom? Russians? Sephardim? Jews who are Turks and Spaniards and officers in the Red Army? The categories bounced off the walls, confounding the realities in the well-ordered classroom of Herr Ladewig's eleventh-graders. Could such things have happened in this very city? To this very man? It was a lesson they would never forget.

PART II

"WE ARE THE PEOPLE"

THE EMBASSY IN PRAGUE

November 3, 1989

O ctober 30, 1989, the train to Prague. After two
months in Berlin, I was indulging in some tourism. Like any student of the eighteenth century, I
had always wanted to see the most beautiful of
baroque cities. But how could I take time off to visit the
eighteenth century in Czechoslovakia when the twentieth
century seemed about to explode in East Germany?

I found it easy. I sat back in my seat, the Baedecker in
my lap, and dreamed of domes and arches—the Loreto-
kirche designed by Christoph Dientzenhofer, the Wald-
stcinpalast built for Albrecht von Wallenstein, Mozart's
residence in the Villa Bertramka, Kafka's in the shadow of

the Hradschin Castle, and the Magic Lantern Theatre, where Václav Havel had thumbed his nose at the regime.

The thought of Havel brought me back to the present, or rather to an incident that had occurred two weeks earlier. Sitting in the kitchen on a sunny, Sunday morning, I happened to turn on the radio and caught the broadcast of Havel's talk when he was awarded the Peace Prize of the German Booksellers' Association. The Czech authorities would not let him out of the country, so a German actor read the speech for him to the audience assembled at the Frankfurt Book Fair on October 15.

When the words reached me, I found them strangely moving. They were words about words, the power of the Word, composed by a Czech, uttered by a German, and picked up by chance in the ear of an American. Without dwelling on his own case, Havel listed all his friends who had been thrown in prison for daring to speak out against the Czech regime. He did not celebrate them as martyrs but rather as persons who had borne witness to a force that could shake an empire even though it did not come out the barrel of a gun. Then, instead of congratulating his audience on the power of the press in a free country, he reversed directions and showed how the power of words could undermine freedom. He discussed the misuse of words under the Nazis, not merely by Hitler but by Martin Heidegger, the greatest philosopher of the era. And before his non-German listeners could begin to feel comfortable, he cited a half dozen other cases in which the abuse of words had degraded and enslaved mankind, beginning with the perversion of the Gospel. Even "perestroika" could be made into an instrument of totalitarianism if it were used to beat its opponents into submission.

Havel did not leave us with a comfortable conclusion. He merely advocated vigilance. Only by making our words do what we intend and by questioning our intentions could we turn speech into a force for liberty rather than oppression. A Sunday sermon? A creed fit for a playwright but not for ordinary mortals confronted with power in the form of billy clubs? True, Havel was preaching, but he had earned the right to do so by many years in prison, and he did not simply speak as an intellectual. He spoke for humanity. Never had I felt so struck by the unmistakable accent of authenticity, certainly never on a Sunday. Something prophetic was stirring in the strange, baroque world I thought of as the "East."

The train itself belonged to the commotion. At that time every train out of East Berlin contained East Germans attempting to escape from the GDR. The Iron Curtain had begun to crack in May, when Hungary dismantled the electrified, barbed-wire border separating it from Austria. Throughout the summer, East Germans had poured into Czechoslovakia and Hungary, ostensibly to take vacations in sister socialist countries where they could travel without a visa, but in fact to find a route to the West. They could get a passport in any West German embassy, because West Germany did not recognize the existence of two German states and therefore considered them as citizens of the Germany ruled from Bonn. But Czechoslovakia and Hungary would not let them cross into the West, arguing that the new passports were invalid because they did not contain visas stamped at the point of entry. On September 11, however, Hungary decided to let the East Germans exit without producing visas, and 10,000 of them who had been camping at the border flooded into Austria in one day.

Of course, the Czechs could plug that hole by closing their border with Hungary. But throughout the rest of the month, the refugees poured into the West German embassy in Prague. They simply knocked on its front door and demanded asylum. Because Bonn had defined them to be fellow citizens, they could not be refused; and because the embassy was West German territory by diplomatic convention, they entered the Federal Republic of Germany as soon as they crossed its threshold.

The problem was how to get them out. The embassy staff could not force them out any more than it could refuse to let them in. Otherwise it would violate the policy set in Bonn and stir up a political reaction that might bring down the government. By the end of September the embassy contained so many refugees—3,500 of them camping in hallways, the back garden, anywhere they could find a few spare feet—that it was nearly paralyzed.

Meanwhile, a different kind of pressure was mounting in the headquarters of the Communist Party in East Berlin. Mikhail Gorbachev was due to arrive on October 6 in order to stand by Erich Honecker's side at the ceremonies celebrating the fortieth anniversary of socialism in the GDR. Honecker had no love for Gorbachev and perestroika, but he also seemed to be incapable of continuing his own variety of Stalinism. He had been so enfeebled by a mortal case of cancer that no one seemed to be in charge of the country. Moreover, Gorbachev's visits had a way of touching off revolutions. His visit to Beijing had nearly brought down the Chinese government in June, and his support of reformers in Poland and Hungary looked seditious to the Stalinist old guard of Czechoslovakia and East Germany.

Of course, Germans were not supposed to revolt. On the rare occasions when they had tried to do so, they had always failed. "Quiet is the citizen's first duty," was the unofficial motto of the GDR. But the East Germans had become increasingly noisy throughout the summer, and an outburst of angry noise, to say nothing of violence, could spoil the triumphal tone of the festivities in October. The clamor coming out of the Bonn embassy in Prague might be contagious. At the very least, it suggested that the East Germans felt something less than satisfaction with their forty years of socialism.

Therefore, as an extraordinary measure, the GDR permitted six trains packed with refugees to travel from Prague back through the GDR—where officials tried to save face by pretending to expel them—and into West Germany on October 1. This incident produced some spectacular scenes on West German television: sealed trains arriving in the dark, rapturous greetings from the platform, passengers leaning out the windows and answering questions about how it felt to breathe the air of freedom. No one can know just how those scenes affected the East German population, most of whom watched West German television. But within two days, the Bonn embassy in Prague was overrun once more.

At this point, the Czech police joined the miniature Cold War drama being played out around the embassy. First, they tried to block access to its front door, but retreated when the West Germans protested. Then they set upon a crowd of refugees attempting to climb over the embassy's rear fence, but the West Germans seized hold of the climbers and freed them with the magic touch of diplomatic immunity. Finally, the police withdrew. Unable to win in the local game of tug-of-war, East Germany closed its border with Czechoslovakia on October 3, creating an iron curtain behind the Iron Curtain. By then, however, at least 7,600 refugees had crammed themselves into the embassy, and it was more urgent than ever to get them out before the world turned its attention to the celebration in East Berlin.

On October 4–5, the East German government permitted a second wave of refugees, 11,000 of them in eight special trains, to travel from Prague to West Germany by means of the same detour through the GDR. The secret police, known as the Stasi (Staatssicherheitsdienst), beat back East Germans attempting to leap on the trains all along the route. Riots broke out in and around the Dresden station, and it began to look as though the GDR was drifting toward civil war. Somehow the country made it through the great socialist birthday party on October 6 and 7. Honecker got his parade, along with some triumphant oratory, while the Stasi put down demonstrations in Berlin, Dresden, Leipzig, and other cities with a great deal of brutality. Gorbachev came and went without provoking a Tiananmen Square massacre—perhaps because he warned Honecker that the Soviet Union would not support repression of the sort that was used to stamp out the uprising of June 17, 1953. In fact, a massacre nearly occurred after the Monday night prayer meeting in Leipzig on October 9. The Stasi and other armed forces were prepared to mow the Leipzigers down as they left the Nikolaikirche; but at the last minute—no one knows precisely why or how—they withdrew, leaving the streets to the people.

From that time on, the Leipzigers' cry, "We are the people," swept through the country, touching off peaceful demonstrations everywhere. On October 18, Egon Krenz replaced Honecker as general secretary of the Communist Party. He began to drive the old Stalinists from the top positions in the Party and the government, and to announce reforms in a desperate effort to prevent the protest movement from turning irrevocably against the regime—that is, in fact, to stave off a revolution. But the protests kept growing, especially in Leipzig. Every Monday night hundreds of thousands of people marched through the streets demanding free speech, free elections, and freedom to travel.

Nonetheless, the Czech border remained closed and the Iron Curtain intact. That did not prevent more East Ger-

mans from seeping into Prague and taking refuge in the
Bonn embassy. By the time I took my seat in the Berlin–
Prague express, the embassy had filled up again with
about 4,000 refugees. It was to become even fuller in the
next few days, because on November 1 the government no
longer required a special visa for travel to Czechoslovakia,
and the embassy became once more the main target of all
the hopes of East Germans who wanted to escape to the
West.

Had I walked through the train peering into compart-
ments, I probably would have spotted a great deal of
drama as the East Germans prepared themselves for the
confrontation with the Czech border police. But I only
had eyes for my guidebooks and the beautiful scenery
along the upper Elbe. I was traveling with my wife and our
two daughters, who were enjoying the first holiday allotted
to them by their German *Gymnasium*. We wanted to put
Germany out of our minds for a few days and to see some
new sights.

Nothing is more boring for teen-age girls than a professorial father armed with a guidebook. Sated with baroque
churches, they let me go my way. I had moved on to palaces, the magnificent structures spread out beneath the
castle on the left bank of the Moldau. Bumbling up Vlas-
ská Ulice, my nose in the book or my eyes fixed on cor-
nices, I did not notice the abandoned Trabis. But when I
spotted a particularly splendid façade half way up the
street at number 19 and let my gaze wander down to the
front door, I finally realized that I had strayed into
the front line of the current combat zone in the Cold War:
the West German embassy.

A couple of Czech police stood across from the building
at a discreet distance, watching but not interfering. Every
few minutes some East Germans, easily recognizable from
their haircuts and their clothes, would walk up to the door,

ring the bell, and disappear inside. Many had crammed their favorite possessions into a few suitcases and had driven to Prague in the most valuable possession of all, their Trabi, the product of years of saving and waiting. They usually left it on a side street, unlocked and with the key in the ignition, and walked the last few hundred yards. Those must have been the longest yards they had ever walked, for they left almost everything behind—not just the Trabi, but family, friends, a whole way of life. You could see the sense of loss mixed with hope in their faces as they arrived. Some smiled, some wept, some clenched their jaws and looked ahead. None of them stepped lightly over the threshold.

It was a threshold that separated two worlds. Once across it, they were in the West, a piece of that fabled other Germany they had seen so often on television and talked about so frequently with friends. In taking that step, they left everything they had ever known behind them. They took a leap of faith. And there was no stepping back, because however they reached mainland West Germany, they had to abandon their claim to citizenship in the GDR. The Stasi would see to it that their property would be confiscated, their apartment let, and their file closed with a final report: "enemy of the people."

Never had I seen such a momentous threshold in such a concrete form, nor had I observed such a succession of decisive instants, when everything hung in the balance, as one refugee after another passed through the doorway and into another life. Perhaps the scene was less metaphysical than I imagined. But the refugees seemed to be struggling with something much stronger than the anxieties that had come within the range of my experience in the United States—the ordinary, American varieties of stage fright and vertigo or the knotting of the viscera that precedes an examination and a side-arm fastball. Those East Ger-

mans—most of them young and certainly not destitute—
were going through a gamut of emotions undreamt of in
my philosophy. And whatever they felt, it was impossible
not to feel for them.

I was especially struck by a young couple who arrived
with a baby in a taxi. The mother stepped out. She lifted a
pram from the taxi's trunk, unfolded it, and placed the
baby inside. Then she pushed the pram ahead of her,
while her husband carried two large suitcases, looking
grimly at the embassy door. When they stopped in front of
it, she suddenly burst into tears. I nearly did, too. But
why? Were they victims of the Cold War, or deserters who
would rather abandon socialism than fight to improve it?

What would Václav Havel say? He had made his own
commitment clear, but would he condemn those who
chose differently? I did not know; but I suspected that
wherever he was and whatever words he was putting together in the baroque labyrinth of Prague, he would respect thresholds and the moment of decision—to cross or
not to cross.

THE MEANINGS
OF THE WALL

November 16, 1989

On the morning after, November 10, when both Berlins woke up wondering whether the first flood through the Wall had been a dream, the West Berlin tabloid *Volksblatt* ran two headlines, shoulder to shoulder, on its front page: "The Wall Is Gone" and "Bonn Demands the Destruction of the Wall." Both were right. The Wall is there and it is not there. On November 9, it cut through the heart of Berlin, a jagged wound in the middle of a great city, the Great Divide of the Cold War. On November 10, it had become a dance floor, a picture gallery, a bulletin board, a movie screen, a videocassette, a museum, and, as the woman who cleaned

my office put it, "nothing but a heap of stone." The taking
of the Wall, like the taking of the Bastille, transformed the
world. No wonder that a day later, in Alexanderplatz, East
Berlin, one conqueror of the Wall marched in a demonstration with a sign saying simply, "1789–1989." He had
helped dismantle the central symbol around which the
postwar world had taken shape in the minds of millions.

To witness symbolic transformation on such a scale is a
rare opportunity, and it raises many questions. To begin
with the most concrete: What happened between November 9 and 12, and what does it mean?

The destruction of the Wall began in the early evening
of Thursday, November 9, soon after the first wave of East
Berliners, or *Ossis,* as they are called by the West Berliners
here, burst upon the West. One Ossi, a young man with a
knapsack on his back, somehow hoisted himself up on the
Wall directly across from the Brandenburg Gate. He saun-
tered along the top of it, swinging his arms casually at his
sides, a perfect target for the bullets that had felled many
other wall jumpers, like Peter Fechter, an eighteen-year-
old construction worker, who was shot and left to bleed to
death a few feet in front of Checkpoint Charlie on August
17, 1962. Now, twenty-seven years later, a new generation
of border guards took aim at a new kind of target and
fired—but only with power hoses and without much conviction. The conqueror of the Wall continued his prome-
nade, soaked to the skin, until at last the guards gave up.
Then he opened his knapsack and poured the water toward the East, in a gesture that seemed to say, "Good-bye
to all that."

A few minutes later, hundreds of people, Ossis and
Wessis alike, were on the Wall, embracing, dancing, exchanging flowers, drinking wine, helping up new "conquerors"—and chipping away at the Wall itself. By
midnight, under a full moon and the glare of spotlights

from the watchtowers in no man's land, a thousand figures swarmed over the Wall, hammering, chiseling, wearing its surface away like a colony of army ants. At the bottom, "conquerors" threw stones at its base or went at it with pickaxes. Long slits appeared, and the light showed through from the East, as if through the eyes of a jack-o'-lantern. On the top, at the center of the tumult, with the Brandenburg Gate looming in the background, one Ossi conducted the destruction with a sickle in one hand and a hammer in the other.

By Saturday, November 11, chunks of the wall were circulating through both Berlins. People exchanged them as souvenirs of what had already taken shape in the collective consciousness as a historical event: the end of the Cold War. A sidewalk entrepreneur sold bits of wall from a table on the Ku'damm*: 20 DM for a piece of the past. At one point, an East Berliner walked by and objected, with a smile on his face: "You can't sell that. It's our Wall. It belongs to us."

Like any powerful symbol, the Wall has acquired many meanings, and they differ significantly from West to East. The Wall even looks different if you study it from one side and then the other. Seen from the West, it is a prison wall that encloses the East Berliners in totalitarianism. Tourists climb on observation towers and shudder deliciously at the spectacle: the monstrous, graffiti-covered concrete structure, the no man's land beyond it—which, until 1985, was mined and rigged with rifles that fired automatically at anyone who dashed across—the barbed wire, the dog patrols, the turrets with armed guards staring back through binoculars, and the second wall or windowless buildings on the far side of the deadly, desolate, space.

East Berliners see a different Wall. Theirs is painted in

---

*The Kurfürstendamm, West Berlin's elegant shopping avenue.

patterns of light and dark blue, clean, bright, and free of
all graffiti. It shuts off the view of the repressive apparatus
beyond it. If you lose your way or stray into outlying areas
in East Berlin, you can drive along the wall for miles without noticing that it is something more than an ordinary
part of the urban landscape.

Just after the metaphorical fall of this wall, I visited an
East Berlin friend on his side of the city. A non-Party
intellectual who has supported the demonstrations and
opposed the regime throughout the current crisis, he had
one word of advice: "Don't tear down the Wall. We need it
as a protective barrier. It should be permeable but it
should stay up. One of the great mistakes in Berlin history
was to tear down the customs wall in which the Brandenburg Gate was embedded in 1867. After that the tragedies
of the modern age began."

A young professor from Leipzig had made a similar remark two months earlier. She described the Wall as a dike
against dangerous influences from the capitalist world. I
had thought she was repeating a Party line, but the same
idea can be heard on East German television, in pubs, and
in the streets now that the East Germans are debating
their future openly and the Wall has changed its nature.

Not that they feel any nostalgia for the old police state.
On the contrary, they still pour into the streets, night after
night, demanding the dismantling of the Party dictatorship. But the very success of the demonstrations has created a new political consciousness, and the conquering of
the Wall has raised a new question: how is the rebirth of
popular sovereignty, the "We the People" of a truly democratic German Democratic Republic, to constitute itself as
a viable political unit? That is the question that determines
the meaning of the Wall for East Berliners.

Westerners commonly imagine that East Germans are
hungering and thirsting for the chance to earn large sala-

ries and to spend them on the consumer goods that are available in the West. This theme prevailed above all others in the media blitz surrounding the emigration of East Germans to the West, and it drowned out a more significant refrain that was chanted by the hundreds of thousands who remained home, demonstrating in the streets of Leipzig, Dresden, and a dozen other cities for weeks before the storming of the Wall: "We are the people! We're staying here!" Between 500,000 and a million people chanted that theme in the supreme demonstration of November 4 in East Berlin; not a nose was bloodied, not a window broken.

The demonstrations have operated as an Estates General in the streets, sapping legitimacy from the Communist Party and transferring it to the people. In conquering the Wall, the people brought that process to a climax. But then they faced a problem: what are they to do if nothing stands between them and the West?

To be viable, a state must define its boundaries and assert its identity in contrast to neighboring states. In the eyes of East German intellectuals, that means maintaining the Wall, but with unrestricted access to exits through it. They seem less comfortable with the idea of traffic in the other direction, however, because they know that their economy is floundering and their currency cannot stand up against the West German mark, which is officially exchanged in the GDR at a rate of one to one and is negotiated on the black market at one to ten. West German industrialists and financiers have declared themselves ready to pour billions of deutsche marks into the GDR, but that is not the Ossis' idea of liberation.

Ask anyone in East Berlin what he thinks of the country's economic prospects, and you will get a prophecy of doom, followed by defiance: "We do not want to be sold."

In the last few days about 6 million East Germans, a third
of the country's population, crossed the previously in-
penetrable border to the West and returned. Most of them
grew up under a system that called itself socialist. They
believe in socialism. They want to give it a try—by getting
rid of the monopoly of the so-called Socialist Unity (i.e.
Communist) Party and, if necessary, by maintaining some
kind of protective wall against economic domination from
the West.

Of course, it is very difficult for a visitor from the West
to know what people are really thinking in the East. But at
a time of popular uprising, voices are raised and they can
be heard. Few East Germans have clamored for reunification with the Federal Republic, despite the blandish-
ments of Chancellor Kohl. The East Germans probably
want what they say they want in the banners they carry in
their demonstrations. Although the banners lend themselves to slogans, they provide a running commentary on
the events as they have been seen since the "fall" of the
Wall from the East:

> "Let the wall be painted on both sides."
> "We are the people, and we are millions."
> "No more wall in the head."
> "Travel, yes. Beg, no."
> "Change the border to a nature preserve:
> 1 national park and 2 states."

Since the name of the new general secretary of the Communist Party, Egon Krenz, lends itself to punning with the
word for border (Grenze), the signs show how the East
Germans are playing with the notions of politics and
boundaries:

"Reforms, but without limits [*Krenz*]" *(Reformen—aber unbekrenzt).*

"At last we see through" (an allusion to the cracks in the wall and also to Krenz, whose eyes appear above the lettering).

On the Western side, the wall carries its own commentary, because it has been covered with layers of graffiti for years. The bottom layers of the palimpsest contain some witticisms, but they lack the bite of the word play in the East:

> "Tear along dotted line."
> "Make love not wall."

The Western Wall has been taken over by tourists, who often treat it as a neutral surface for spray paint:

> "Lisa ti amo"

Or whose high-mindedness says little about the divisions of Berlin:

> "Essex University condemns all forms of political oppression."

In places the palimpsest reads like a dialogue, in which the present answers the past with a comforting reflection: the Wall has fallen, even though it is standing before your eyes as a surface on which the writer sprays his assertion of its nonexistence:

> "A pity that concrete doesn't burn."
> "It falls, though."

> "This wall will fall."
> "We saw it fall, Nov. '89."

The graffiti sound triumphant, even when they joke, as in this message sprayed near Checkpoint Charlie:

"Charlie's retired. 10 Nov. 1989."

But the messages are essentially the same: they distinguish between totalitarianism on one side and liberty on the other. The theme is reinforced by the Checkpoint Charlie Museum, which displays devices used to escape under, over, or through the wall, and by crosses set up opposite places where persons were gunned down while attempting to escape.

The sense of heroism and suffering is undercut, however, by souvenir shops, which sell Wall postcards and Wall trinkets in a kind of fairground that has grown up between the old Reichstag, which is now a museum, and the breach in the wall opened opposite the Potsdamer Platz, which was once the busiest traffic center in Europe and is now an enormous field covered with mud and weeds. The postcards were snapped up by the Ossis who swarmed through the area after November 9 and who were fascinated by views of the Wall that they had never seen. But they did not know how to consume in the Western way. The vendors had displayed the postcards on stands outside their shops, and the East Berliners, who had never seen goods exposed so openly, assumed they were handouts and walked off with them without paying.

Was the breakthrough to the West an orgy of consumerism? One of the many radical sects in West Berlin tried to march against the flood carrying a banner, which proclaimed, "Your liberty is that of the West German Banks." But they were lost in the waves of Ossis, who swept through the Wall echoing the chant of the first wave, which arrived on Thursday: "Zum Ku'damm, zum Ku'damm und dann wieder zurück" (To the Kurfürstendamm, and then back again.) The *zurück* was the crucial term in the refrain, because the East Berliners did not come simply to buy up or sell out but rather to see the forbidden city with their own eyes and to return home. There was plenty of consumption, but much of it was free. The Federal Republic offers 100 DM (about $50) in "greeting money" once a year to every visitor from East Germany, and many banks stayed open on Saturday and Sunday to provide cash for Ossis who surged through the wall and then found themselves stranded with unconvertible currency. Where the banks failed, individuals stepped in to help. One West Berliner stood outside a break in the wall and handed out fifty-mark notes, for as long as his supply held out, to every Easterner who came through. Another came across a teen-age girl crying in front of the McDonald's on the Ku'damm. She said that all her life she had wanted to eat a McDonald's hamburger, and now she had no money. He pressed a fifty-mark note into her hand and she disappeared, into paradise.

The incoming Ossis collided with waves of well-wishers from the West, who thrust drinks in their hands, loaded them down with pizzas and sausages, took them for rides through residential neighborhoods, and put them up overnight. Ossis were given free rides on all busses and subways, reduced prices in restaurants and movie theaters, free admission in discothèques. They pressed their noses against store windows displaying fine clothing and Mercedes. And when they got their hands on deutsche marks, they spent them—for the most part on tropical fruits, which are not available in East Berlin; on toys, which are relatively shabby on the other side of the Wall; on books, which are often forbidden; on Coca Cola, which is restricted to Western Europe (Pepsi has the East); and on a wide variety of cosmetics, trinkets, and flowers.

A consumer orgy? A few West Berliners spoke conde-

scendingly of "banana freedom," referring to the inex-
haustible appetite of East Germans for bananas, which
most of them had never tasted. But one bite of forbidden
fruit does not a capitalist make. In fact, the East Berliners
often contented themselves with walking through stores
and staring at shop windows. Instead of loading themselves with consumer goods, they went souvenir hunting
and returned with little pieces of the West, just as the
Westerners took chunks of the Wall.

Above all, the two populations of Berlin sought to make
contact with one another. In exchanging hugs, drinks, and
flowers, they performed a collective ritual of *Bruderschaft*.
As the *Volksblatt* put it, "In the night when the gates
opened, it seemed as though there were no more East Berliners and West Berliners. Everyone felt as though they
belonged to a huge family, and everyone celebrated the
festival accordingly."

To someone unfamiliar with Berlin, it may be hard to
imagine how successfully the Wall had divided the city.
Soon after 1961, when the Wall went up, the million or so
inhabitants on the Western side and the 2 million or so on
the Eastern began to lose contact. By 1989, a whole generation had come of age within the shadow of the Wall.
Most of them never crossed it, even from West to East
when that was allowed. They accepted the Wall as a fact
of life, as something inexorable, built into the landscape—
there when they were born and there when they died.
They left it to the tourists, took it for granted, forgot about
it, or simply stopped seeing it.

Before the fall, an old woman was interviewed on her
balcony, which overlooked the Wall from the West. She
spent hours every afternoon staring into no man's land.
Why did she look so hard at the Wall, day after day? the
reporter asked, hoping to find some expression of Berlin's

divided personality. "Oh, I'm not looking at the Wall at all," she replied. "I watch the rabbits playing in no man's land." Many West Berliners did not see the Wall until it ceased to exist.

For the Wall enclosed the West Berliners even more thoroughly than it shut off their counterparts in the East. In 1961 it was perceived as a noose that would soon choke the life out of the western half of the city. But by 1989, West Berliners had come to regard the Wall as a source of support. Thanks to its presence, the government in Bonn poured billions into Berlin, subsidizing everything from the philharmonic orchestra to teen-age jazz groups. A whole population of underemployed intellectuals grew up around the Free University, which now has about 60,000 students. As residents of Berlin, they are exempt from the draft; they also can drink beer and talk politics in pubs throughout the night, for Berlin is the only city in the Federal Republic where the pubs are permitted to stay open past midnight, the only place where you can order breakfast in the afternoon. Many of these free-floating intellectuals became freeloaders. They lived off the Wall; and if it really falls, they may face a greater economic disaster than the Berliners in the East.

To Berliners, therefore, the Wall means something very different from what it means outside the city. But most of them realize that their local barrier is bound up with larger divisions, the Oder–Neisse line in particular and the general dividing line between the Warsaw Pact and NATO. Having gone to bed one day in a world with clearly defined boundaries, they woke up the next in a world without firm national borders, without balanced power blocs, and even without obvious demarcations of time, because it suddenly seemed possible to produce a treaty ending World War II forty-four years after World War II had ended. They are living a truism of anthropology: the collapse of boundaries can be deeply disturbing, a source of renewal but also a threat to a whole worldview.

The mood remains euphoric, nonetheless. In East Berlin especially, the idea has spread that in conquering the Wall the people seized power. No one denies that power comes out of the barrel of a gun, but it has symbolic forms, too. The demonstrations in the streets sapped the legitimacy of the regime. Combined with the hemorrhaging of the population across the borders, they brought the government down, without a shot fired.

When well-informed East Berliners try to explain what happened, they sometimes produce Kremlinological accounts of splits within the Party. While Egon Krenz was occupied with purging the Politburo, his enemy, Willy Stoph, the former president of the Council of Ministers, allegedly gave word that the travel restrictions could be lifted. This tiny crack opened the way to rumors, and the first trickle of Ossis began to gather at the border crossings. Faced with questions from the border guards on one side and the press on the other, the new party spokesman, Günter Schabowski, remarked casually at the end of his daily press conference that the restrictions no longer applied. The press took it as a sign that the Party had renegotiated the terms of an agreement on liberalizing travel to the West, not as a declaration that the Wall had fallen.

But the East Berliners continued to flock to the Wall, demanding access to the West merely by showing their personal identification cards. The pressure grew in proportion to the confusion, and in the end the guards started letting a few people through. The crack became a slit, the slit a breach, and the Wall "fell"—without anyone decreeing it, least of all Egon Krenz.

We may never know the details of what happened inside the crumbling power structure of the GDR. But whatever produced the occasion, the force that broke through the

Wall was there for all to see on the night of November 9. It was the people of East Berlin. They took the Wall as they had taken to the streets for the previous two months, with nothing but their convictions, their discipline, and the power of their numbers.

When they came streaming into West Berlin, they spoke the language of liberty, but they expressed themselves by gesture, not by high-flown rhetoric. They took possession of the Wall physically, by pouring through it, climbing on it, and chipping it apart. They did the same thing in West Berlin itself. They occupied space, swarming through the Ku'damm, filling the busses and pubs, parking their tiny Trabis on the noblest sidewalks, and returning triumphantly to the East with a flower for a girl friend or a toy for an infant.

It was a magical moment, the possession of a city by its people. On Thursday, November 9, under a full moon, between the shadow of the Reichstag and the menacing bulk of the Brandenburg Gate, the people of Berlin danced on their Wall, transforming the cruelest urban landscape into a scene of hilarity and hope, and ending a century of war.

A THIRD WAY?

December 8, 1989

C an East Germany find a "third way" between capitalism and socialism? The question was laid squarely
on the table at the Institute for Advanced Study in
Berlin, and around it gathered a group of social
scientists, the first East–West meeting of its kind since the
opening of the Wall on November 9, and probably the first
since the Wall went up twenty-eight years ago.

The chairman introduced the East Berliners as members of "what I believe is still called the Marxist-Leninist
Institute for Sociology"—a joke, meant to break the ice,
which still exists at the level of social relations, even
though Mikhail Gorbachev declared an end to the Cold

War at the summit meeting with President Bush last weekend. "As a matter of fact, we changed the name a few
weeks ago," came the reply from the senior Eastern sociologist.

The ice was broken. Then, to churn up the waters, an
economics professor from West Berlin tossed out a provocative statement. There is no third way, he said. You
can have a planned economy or a market economy, but
mixtures will not work. They become mired in bureaucratic intervention and their inability to cope with the flow
of information in the computer age, to say nothing of the
problem of matching supply and demand.

Not so, said a young East Berliner. Socialism was like
Christianity; it had never really been tried. They did not
practice socialism in the GDR; they already had a mixed
economy—the Schalck System.

That brought a laugh, because the Easterner was alluding to the scandal that finally forced the Politburo of the
GDR into self-destruction on December 3: the revelation
that Alexander Schalck-Golodkowski, the secretary of
state for foreign trade, had been using public money to run
a private business in the arms trade. Schalck-Golodkowski
fled the country. Top members of the Communist Party
were put under house arrest. And East German television,
which used to be a joke and now is an addiction for millions of Germans on both sides of the border, flooded the
GDR with images of high living by the highest leaders of
the Party.

The public reacted with a new round of demonstrations, including an especially angry gathering of Party
rank and file in front of the Party's headquarters in East
Berlin on December 2. When Egon Krenz, the new general secretary of the Party, tried to calm the crowd, he was
hooted down. The comrades did not want to hear any
more speeches; they wanted heads to roll.

On Sunday, December 3, the decapitation actually occurred. The entire Politburo, Krenz included, resigned,
leaving a vast empty space at the top of the power structure. A special assembly was called to reconstitute the
Party and to select a new set of leaders on December 8, but
will anyone follow? The moral bonds that once attached
the Party to the people have snapped. There has been a
revolution.

Revolution was the term applied to the events of the last
few days by the East Berliners at the Institute for Advanced Study. They described the earlier explosion of
November 4–9 as a prerevolution, or *Vormärz,* in an allusion to the Central European eruptions of 1848, which is
the parallel most frequently cited in these parts. First the
bleeding of the population from emigration by means of
Prague and Warsaw, then the Leipzig demonstrations,
then Gorbachev's visit and the near-miss of a Tiananmen
Square massacre in Berlin, then the climactic rally of November 4, the fall of Honecker, and the "fall" on November 9 of the Wall—it was a spectacular sequence of events.
But the real shift of power took place during the weekend
of December 2 and 3, when the Party declared itself bankrupt and the first apparatchiks went to jail.

Such at least was the view of events that went round the
table at the conference, and it gave some urgency to the
next point on the agenda: if the communist Party has really lost its grip on power, what is the future of socialism in
the GDR?

Socialism has no future, said the economist from the
West. Why not? replied the sociologist from the East. We
can keep our medical service, our social security, our protection against unemployment; and at the same time we
can allow limited investment from the Bundesrepublik,
taxing profits to pay for the social services. There are
many possibilities advocated by many people at the bot-

tom of the Party: feminism, ecology, a break-up of the
state into self-governing communes.

The West Berlin professors looked a little startled at
this prospect, which summoned up the radicalism on their
own campuses rather than a notion of a viable economy.
Mixed systems don't work, insisted the economist. Socialism is retreating before Thatcherism everywhere, even in
France. "Planification" is an illusion, even in Sweden. We
have whole libraries of books on the subject and decades
of experience with experiments. In the end, if you open
the door to West German capitalists, you will go capitalist.

The problem is time, said a historian. East Germans—
the youngest and most skilled East Germans—are still
pouring out of the country at a rate of one or two thousand
a day. Instead of stopping the hemorrhage, the opening of
the Wall has compounded it by undermining the economy.
East Germans can now sell their cheap, subsidized goods
in West Germany for deutsche marks and then use the
strong currency to finance further rounds of speculation.
The GDR is being bled white, and no one is capable of
saving the situation, because no one is in charge.

An East Berliner agreed that things were moving so fast
that they could not be stopped. Only a little while ago a
friend of his had composed a militant statement for a protest meeting. It began: "We demand the resignation of the
Politburo." But when she stood up to read it at the meeting, she had to change it to: "We welcome the resignation
of the Politburo."

The GDR will be West Germany's *mezzogiorno,* said a
sociologist from West Berlin. Labor and wealth will mi-
grate to the Bundesrepublik, and the GDR will remain as a
tourist attraction or an economic colony, if it retains any
independence at all. The utopian moment has come and
gone. It lasted about a week, from November 4 to 12. It
was a carnival, a time of dancing on the Wall, pouring

champagne over border guards, and collective *Bruder-schaft*. Now the party's over.

"I love the GDR," came the reply from a sociologist from East Berlin. "I was born here in Berlin. My house was bombed by the Americans. I was raised in a good Communist family, and I believe in socialism. But I think the GDR is finished. It was a historical phase, an episode."

And so it went, academic talk but not academic questions. What the ordinary people in East Germany are thinking right now is difficult to say. A month ago they spoke out loud and strong in demonstration after demonstration, always with the same refrain: "We are the people! We are staying here!" Almost no one called for reunification, a subject that was left for right-wing politicians in the West. But since then, more than 10 million East Germans, 55 percent of the population, have visited West Germany, and reunification is being debated openly. Neues Forum, the main opposition group, has called for a referendum on the issue.

Something that sounds like nationalism seems to be swelling in the streets. A leader of the Lutheran opposition complained recently of having been awakened by a group of drunks singing the prewar national anthem under his window. They sang its first verse, the one that is forbidden in the Bundesrepublik today and that not only proclaims "Deutschland über alles," but also celebrates a Grossdeutschland, one that stretches far beyond the Oder–Neisse line, "von der Maas bis an die Memel/ von der Etsch bis an den Belt" ("from the Maas to the Memel, from the Adige to the Belt," i.e., a Germany that would extend into territory that now lies in Belgium, the Soviet Union, Italy, and Denmark).

What one sees on East German television and hears in East Berlin streets is, above all, anger. People are outraged

that the leaders of the Party, who have constantly called
for sacrifices in the name of the general welfare, should
have embezzled funds for ski lodges and vacation villas.
The fury may seem odd to Americans, who have been
jaded by scandal and accustomed to the spectacle of presidents flying off to pleasure palaces on the choicest spots of
the Pacific and Atlantic coasts. But the sight of a few Volvos parked in front of some rather dumpy hunting
lodges—all of them purchased with public money and exposed on television—brings an East German's blood to
boil. It takes years of waiting for most people in the GDR
to get a two-room apartment in a cement high-rise or a
two-cylinder, matchbox-type Trabi automobile. Now they
know that while they waited and sat through endless
speeches about the need to tighten belts, the men who
made the rhetoric were getting fat at their expense.

The scandals burst before the public during a spectacular session of the GDR parliament, which was televised
live on December 1. Word spread about the flight of
Schalck-Golodkowski, the arrest of the Party's best-
known leaders—Günter Mittag, Harry Tisch, Gerhard
Müller, Hans Albrecht—and fabulous sums, a hundred
billion marks according to a common account, stashed
away in Swiss banks. The television cameras picked up the
shock waves rippling through the house—the jaws drop-
ping, the heads shaking, the tears welling up in eyes.

At the height of the emotion, Egon Krenz stood up in
the speaker's box. He looked his hearers straight in the
eyes and seemed to speak from his heart. Yes, he had made
mistakes, he said. He had failed to seize the moment, at
the beginning of the Gorbachev years, when it had been
possible to restructure before the people took to the
streets. But he hoped he had learned from the mistakes—
that they all had learned, because everyone sitting there
had also failed to anticipate the public's anger.

He hoped, too, that they all knew how to distinguish between mistakes and crimes. Then, when he seemed to have the deputies in his grip, he shifted into a lower key, and lost them. "I myself do not possess a country estate, nor a hunting lodge, nor a summer house," he said with more than a hint of sanctimoniousness. "So I have the moral possibility of intervening to create a clean, new socialism." Suddenly, Krenz seemed to have his back to the wall. He was fighting for his political life, denouncing his former colleagues, and sounding as if staying out of jail mattered to him as much as staying in power. It was Krenz's last speech. Two days later he was shouted down by the demonstration in front of Party headquarters and forced to resign.

Since then, more extravagant rumors have spread—a symptom of a revolutionary situation spinning out of control. East Berliners passed the word that an airplane full of compromising documents was about to take off for Bucharest, the only fit place for the Party archives, and that workers in the airport saved the situation by refusing to fill the plane's fuel tank. The secret police, the Stasi, are said to be destroying files in order to save themselves and their former bosses from the newly appointed investigating commission. After spotting smoke coming out of Stasi headquarters in Leipzig, a crowd stormed the building and placed the files under the guard of a citizens' committee. Crowds have also marched on Stasi offices in Dresden, Cottbus, Rostock, and Suhl. Government officials constantly warn against disorder in the streets, while citizens' committees have sprung up in several cities to preserve the peace—and the documentation.

The count of Party members under investigation now comes to 109, of whom 9 are former members of the Politburo. The denunciations and arrests multiply day by day, and the Party seems to be falling apart as the apparatchiks turn on one another in a general *sauve-qui-peut*. Reeling under accusations that they failed to investigate government corruption, the entire top staff of the secret police resigned on December 5. The chief investigator in the inquiry about police brutality, Günter Wendland, also resigned because of charges that he was delaying the investigation.

On December 8, as the Party met to elect a new general secretary, its old leader, Erich Honecker, who had stood beside Gorbachev to celebrate forty years of socialist rule only a month before, was charged with having damaged the economy and enriched himself through criminal abuse of public office.

Poor Honecker. As soon as the merciless eye of the television camera spanned over the furniture in his not so impressive hunting lodge, his spotless record of opposition to Nazism disappeared from view. The folklore of corruption, the images of private wealth and public poverty, the stabs in the back and the antlers on the wall, are undoing the power structure of an old regime. The hunting lodges have doomed the Communists in the GDR just as Imelda Marcos's shoe collection delegitimized the dictatorship in the Philippines and Marie Antoinette's diamond necklace brought down the monarch in France. Now Honecker, the former monarch of a docile GDR, sits in house arrest, helpless and reviled, a captive to a revolution, like Louis XVI in the Tuileries.

LIBERTY IN LEIPZIG

December 21, 1989

Last week in Leipzig, they prayed for the secret police. Three months earlier, they prayed to be delivered from the police. And a week after that, on October 9, their prayers precipitated a revolution.

Whether or not prayers really move mountains, they certainly mobilized the population of Leipzig, a place that once was a bastion of the Reformation and now is the capital of a revolution. Every Monday evening at 5:00, the people of Leipzig crowd into four churches in the heart of the old city. Their pastors talk to them about Leipzig and the City of God. Laymen lead them in a round of prayers, taking their text from the Bible and the daily newspaper.

The congregation links hands and sings the old Lutheran hymns. Then they walk out into the dark, polluted streets, holding candles and banners. Their ranks swell as other citizens join them, and the crowd gathers to hear speeches from the steps of the opera house. Finally, they march through the boulevards that ring the center city, a river of humanity swirling around the core of the old medieval town.

It is a curious ritual, without leaders, organization, or a program. The citizens of Leipzig merely pray and repossess their city by walking for an hour through its streets, but in doing so they have shaken all of East Germany. For twelve weeks now the Monday "demos" have kept the pressure on the government, and the whole country has followed them, as if one could gauge the pressure by keeping count of the demonstrators and as if every body in the streets represented a vote against the Communist Party. On October 2, the crowd numbered 15,000; on October 9, 50,000; on October 16, 150,000; on October 23, 200,000; by November 6, it was 500,000 strong—nearly the entire population of the city.

The numbers have fallen off somewhat as the regime gave in to popular demands and the Leipzigers began to organize parties in preparation for the May 1990 elections. But the "demo" of December 18, the last of the year, included 150,000 persons. They formed a human chain all the way around the old city. The marchers walked along it, ordinary people from all classes, mothers pushing baby carriages, fathers with children on their shoulders, saying very little, simply carrying candles and bearing witness.

An hour earlier, in the Thomaskirche, the faithful prayed for peace, for their church, for their souls, and the souls of their enemies; they prayed for Gorbachev, and for Modrow and Kohl—the leaders of East and West Germany, who were to meet for the first time on the following day; and they prayed for the Stasi, the secret police, who had threatened to mow them down in the streets only a few weeks ago. Now the Stasi are being disbanded. Some have been sent to work in coal mines, but most cannot find jobs. Even the hospitals, which are desperately short of staff owing to the exodus to the West, refuse to hire Stasi. Stasi have become pariahs, and so the Leipzigers prayed for them.

They prayed standing in the aisles, crammed shoulder to shoulder. The church could hardly have been so full when Bach played fugues on its organ in the early eighteenth century or when Martin Luther preached against the Pope in 1519. To hear them sing "A Mighty Fortress Is Our God" is enough to make you believe it.

The Leipzigers needed such a faith when they took to the streets on October 9. Honecker was still in power and reportedly had issued orders for the demonstrators to be shot. The Stasi were deployed along the parade route, armed with water cannon, tear gas, and live ammunition. The regular police force—the Volkspolizei—had marched through town earlier in the afternoon and stationed themselves, with clubs, gas masks, helmets, and shields, at the main train station. The Betriebskampfgruppen, a kind of Party army notorious for dirty work, stood ready to intervene at the Hotel Stadt Leipzig. Rumors spread that tanks were poised at the outskirts of the city and that the army had been put on the alert in Cottbus, 150 miles away. Emergency rooms had been prepared in the main hospital along with extra supplies of blood.

That the Stasi were ready to spill blood had become clear two days earlier, when demonstrations erupted in a half dozen cities as a protest against the fortieth anniversary celebration of socialism in East Germany, which Honecker directed from East Berlin, with Gorbachev at his side. In Leipzig the Stasi broke some skulls and arrested at

least thirty demonstrators. The pastor of the Nikolaikirche received warnings that his church would be fire-
bombed and his congregation shot if they persisted in their
determination to demonstrate. By the time of evening
prayers on the ninth, the whole city expected a civil war to
break out. But when the people filed out of the churches,
there was not a Stasi in sight.

In retrospect, the decision to call off the police appears
as the most important turning point of the East German
revolution, the moment when the people stood up to the
authorities and forced them to back down. As in the case
of many historical moments, however, it is difficult to discover exactly what happened. Egon Krenz later let it be
known that he had intervened. But after he replaced Honecker as general secretary of the Communist Party on
October 18, he needed to live down his reputation as a
hardened apparatchik and as the man who had conveyed
the Party's congratulations to the Chinese for the massacre of Tiananmen Square. "I was in Leipzig and declared
there that we must find a purely political solution to political conflicts," he announced to the press on November 17,
only to be confounded by the East German News Agency
ADR, which reported that he did not set foot in Leipzig
until four days after the demonstration.

In a recent interview, Willy Brandt declared that Gorbachev himself had ordered the retreat, though it may be
that Moscow merely sent some general warning against
the use of force. Leipzigers tell stories, which cannot be
verified, about Soviet tanks barring the way to East German soldiers. Whoever made the crucial decision, one man
stands out as a key intermediary in the cause of peace:
Kurt Masur, the director of the great Gewandhaus orchestra in Leipzig.

On Monday afternoon, just before the demonstration,
Masur was to conduct a rehearsal of "Till Eulenspiegel."

He called it off and telephoned five figures with some authority in the city: a theologian, an author, and three members of the local Communist Party responsible for cultural affairs. The group met at Masur's house at 2:30 and drafted an appeal for a "peaceful dialogue" between the citizens and the authorities as a way to save the situation.

Apparently the appeal never reached the officials in East Berlin, including Krenz, who then was in command of all internal security forces. The first secretary of the Party in the Leipzig region was sick, so it seems that someone just below him in the secretariat, someone whose name is still unknown, accepted the Masur appeal just in time to call back the troops at 5:45.

Gorbachev? Krenz? Or a faceless second secretary of the Leipzig Communist Party? However disaster was averted, the effect electrified Leipzig and the entire country. "We are the people," the rallying cry of the Leipzigers, has become a manifesto of popular sovereignty. The "demos" demonstrated that the people could defy the state, that the Party had lost its legitimacy, and that democracy was thinkable in the so-called "democratic" republic of Germany.

As power seeped away from the Party in November and December, the demonstrations continued. Every Monday at four o'clock, shops closed, the police disappeared, and the people took over the streets. Instead of directing his orchestra, Masur conducted public discussions in the Gewandhaus, which turned into a kind of town hall. The Gewandhaus, the opera, and the university surrounding Karl Marx Platz, where the demonstrations begin, constitute a new public space in opposition to the actual town hall, farther down the ring of boulevards. Together with the churches, they represent the only institutions around which public life can form. In a system where the Party has monopolized power, politics has taken refuge in the sphere of culture, and legitimacy has shifted to the intellectuals—ministers, musicians, actors, writers, and professors, or at least a few dissident professors in the lower ranks of the faculty.

Curiously, some of the faculty dissidents come from the Section for Marxism-Leninism, which occupies two of the top floors of a twenty-seven–story high-rise, the tallest building in Leipzig. To make room for it and some other new buildings, the government destroyed all that remained of the ancient university, including a lovely Gothic chapel. Walter Ulbricht, a proud son of Leipzig, decided when he became the head of the Communist Party in 1946, to make his city a showcase of what the East Germans now call "cement socialism." Down came the medieval and baroque buildings that had survived the war. Up went a series of hideous concrete boxes.

To celebrate this architectural great leap forward and also its 550th anniversary, the university changed its name in 1950 to Karl-Marx Universität. It became the first in the GDR to adopt Marxism-Leninism as an academic subject and to require all students to take it, even if they were concentrating in fields like mathematics and medicine. But some of the 150 instructors of Marxism-Leninism began to lose faith in the system, especially last May, when the government banned the German-language issue of *Sputnik,* a Soviet periodical that included some distressingly frank talk about perestroika. On May 7, 1989, the professors and students staged the first "demo" on Karl Marx Platz, shouting "Wir wollen raus!" ("We want to get out of here").

By October, when East Germans began to leave the country in droves, the chant changed to "Wir bleiben hier. Wir sind das Volk" ("We are staying here. We are the people"). After October 9, the Section for Marxism-Leninism changed its name to "Institute for Social Theo-

ries"—theories in the plural. The students have a new
student council, and a new student newspaper called
"Without a Filter." It is limited to one sheet, owing to the
paper shortage in the GDR. But the students also air their
views by pasting manifestos and posters on every conceivable surface. They write on one another's graffiti, so you
can follow the dialogue and read your way through town.

Some examples from the walls of Leipzig on December
18:

> The time is right for dreams. . . . After forty years of for-
> eign domination we have the chance to make something
> different, something of our own out of this country. . . . No
> reunification!

Then below:

> It can't be done without reunification. That is our right.

And below that:

> Build a socialist alternative to the FRG.

And finally:

> Nonsense. The GDR is no country (then a hole in the
> paper and the word "Yalta").

Some of the remarks are witty—for example "Reini-
gung statt Einigung" (Roughly: "Purge, don't unify")—
but most are deadly earnest, unlike graffiti in the West,
and many are signed: "Cornelia Fromme," "Katrin Hat-
tenhauer," "Stefan Sauer." The students and young professors adopt the same tone in their talk. Most of them
have never been in a Western country, except for a hop
into West Germany after the border opened on November
9. In contrast to the students in West Berlin or Göttingen

or Cologne, they have a direct and unsophisticated manner, as if politics were a wonderful new discovery.

There is also some nastiness to be found amid the handwriting on the walls. "A new Reich," said a sign near the
train station, and after it came a trail of jagged lines, which
a Leipzig professor said were meant to be the top halves of
swastikas.

Nationalism and neo-Nazism surfaced in the demonstration of December 11. One banner read, "Germany with
the borders of 1254—Naples is ours." Many marchers
waved the West German flag and chanted, "Germany!
Germany! A united fatherland!" Some confronted left-
wing demonstrators with the salute of the neo-Nazi movement in West Germany: three spread fingers and an
outstretched arm. There was angry shouting, which nearly
led to fights.

In order to reaffirm its nonviolent character and to
avoid confrontations, the final demonstration of the year
took place in silence. The only banners raised were a few
appeals for reunification from members of the right, but
they were relatively mild and the demonstrators carrying
them seemed mainly to be moved by the desire to pose
before the television cameras, which have spread the
alarm about right-wing nationalism throughout the land.

Is it a real danger? In a pre-demo coffee gathering, a
graduate student said he had heard anti-Semitic remarks
directed against Gregor Gysi, the new leader of the Communist (or Socialist Unity) Party, who comes from a
prominent Jewish family. Unlike Krenz, Gysi has genuine
credentials as a reformer. As a defense lawyer, he argued
the cases for some prominent dissidents, including poets
and writers like Wolf Bierman and Rudolf Bahro, and he
helped New Forum, the main opposition group, gain legal
recognition.

Gysi doesn't look like an apparatchik. He wears a sober

suit but keeps his collar unbuttoned, cracks jokes, and slumps in his seat like a college professor. He sounded somewhat professorial when he addressed the special congress called to rescue and reform the Party on December 16. He outlined a program for academic freedom, a new legal status for universities, promotions for talent rather than ideological correctness, better living conditions for students, more support for artists and writers, protection of the environment, rescue of old buildings falling into ruin, and a gigantic festival of the arts to take place sometime in 1990: "It should be a lively, free-ranging celebration of the new culture, with writers, actors, songwriters, rock musicians, and artists, who will express the spirit of the democratic outburst in the German Democratic Republic."

Will this program find favor in Leipzig? The call for pollution control and urban renovation will probably win some votes next May. Like other university towns—Halle, Berlin, Jena—which were the glory of Germany in the nineteenth century, Leipzig is collapsing under urban decay. Its once proud buildings from the Wilhelmine and Weimar era seem to be suffering from leprosy: they have lost a cornice here, a balustrade there and chunks of plaster everywhere. What survived the war in the medieval heart of the city has been allowed to fall apart or has been replaced by concrete boxes. The renovated Rathaus and a few rebuilt townhouses only worsen the effect: almost nothing remains of what was a great center of civilization 500 years ago.

If you do not weep over it, your eyes will smart from the exhaust spewed out by the Trabi automobiles, from the brown coal burned in primitive furnaces in most apartments, and from the smoke given off by the chemical plants and metallurgical factories on the outskirts of the city. Leipzig's enormous working class has been active in politics since it was first organized by August Bebel and Wilhelm Liebknecht. How will the workers vote when they get their first chance in a half century to say what they want? Will Leipzig's skinheads and shopgirls respond to calls for academic freedom and freedom in the arts?

The professors and students are worried. One young historian said that neo-Nazism was a danger precisely because it has always been the biggest taboo in the GDR. In West Germany, he explained, former Nazis were reintegrated into business and government. They grew old, retired, and died off, while neo-Nazi fringe groups were confronted openly. In East Germany, Nazism was repressed—by its dialectical opposite, Stalinism, or "Stasinism" as it is called by campus wits. Now that the lid is off, the old, pathological nationalism may revive, and the common people may turn against the intellectuals, Gysi included.

The danger of a split between the intellectuals and the people was the main theme of a talk given at the university two weeks ago by Christa Wolf, the most influential writer in East Germany. Like Masur, she called for a continued dialogue and a constant avoidance of violence. That is why the Christmas demonstration of December 18 took place with such self restraint, and why the demos will resume in the new year.

The question remains, nonetheless: why do they go on, Monday after Monday, when they have achieved all of their objectives—freedom of speech, freedom of assembly, and free elections to be held next May? It may sound like mysticism, but when one sees the Leipzigers walk around what remains of their ancient city center, they seem to recreate the city in the ancient sense of the word—as a collectivity of souls rather than an agglomeration of buildings.

A more down-to-earth explanation was offered by a

graduate student marching in the Christmas demonstration. The revolution is not over, he said. A great deal could go wrong; the apparatchiks are still capable of perfidy if not violence; and besides, as a nearby placard put it, "A Citizen's First Duty Is Mistrust."

HISTORY IN BERLIN

December 23, 1989

The opening of the Brandenburg Gate was not like that of the Berlin Wall. It was a staged event, announced in advance and carefully planned by the authorities in both Germanys. Television crews had waited for six weeks in a small village of trailers and platforms erected just outside the Gate. When opening day finally arrived, on December 22, they took over, filming it from every conceivable angle, splicing in clips that went back to the Franco-Prussian War of 1870, and adding editorial comments that explained the significance of things as soon as they happened. It was prefabricated history—an event so carefully packaged that it seemed to have taken place before it occurred.

The opening of the Wall on November 9 was an event of a different order. It took everyone by surprise. Even now, no one knows exactly what happened. Egon Krenz, then general secretary of the Communist Party, probably did not give the order for the Wall to be breached. He was busy coping with a revolt inside the Party while attempting to push the older apparatchiks out of the Politburo. Had he meant to open the Wall—to play the trump card in his plan to pass himself off as a reformer—he would have done so with brio. He would have called a press conference, made a speech, cut a ribbon, or hammered out a chunk of wall himself in order to demonstrate his determination to dismantle Stalinism.

Instead, Krenz let himself be overtaken by the event, and the East Berliners ran away with it. In retrospect, it looks as though they created it themselves, even though the Party's spokesman, Günter Schabowski, made an ambiguous announcement at his evening press conference on November 9 that the usual formalities would be lifted for travel to West Berlin. Even before Schabowski spoke, East Berliners swarmed around the border stations, demanding access to the West. For days the guards had feared that a crowd would storm the Wall. They apparently received authorization from someone somewhere in the government to lower the pressure by letting a few people through. As soon as the crack appeared, however, the trickle turned into a flood; and suddenly a great event had happened: the supreme barrier between East and West had been swept away by a peaceful popular uprising.

The first chunk of the Wall to be removed by a crane at the Brandenburg Gate on the night of December 21–22 was spray-painted with an appropriate slogan: "Someday every wall must fall." But there was something staged about the shifting of the scenery. As the television cameras whirred, Chancellor Helmut Kohl stepped through the breach, exchanged a "historic handshake" with the head of the East German government, Hans Modrow, and the assembled politicians delivered speeches.

The Berlin branch of Kohl's party, the Christian Democratic Union, made sure that nothing went wrong. On November 9, when the Wall "fell," Kohl was on a state visit to Poland; and he hurried back, announcing, "My place is in Bonn." That did not go over well with the Berliners, who whistled and hooted him down on the following day as he attempted to make a speech about German unification at the Schöneberg Town Hall in Berlin. On December 22, the CDU faithful filled the rows in front of Kohl at the Brandenburg Gate. They applauded wildly and carried a banner saying, "Thanks, Helmut."

This time Kohl limited himself to some diplomatic remarks about the "historical moment" everyone was experiencing. Modrow also told the crowd that they were standing on "historical ground." And both men, along with the mayors of East and West Berlin, provided exegeses of Gate symbolism. The Gate stood for Berlin, for Germany, for world historical events, for war and peace, for division and unity, for despair and hope. There was enough hermeneutics to make your head spin, if you were listening.

Most people in the crowd were not. They had been satiated with Gate symbolism by hours of advance coverage on television. Before the speeches had ended, they broke through the police lines and made for the Gate. The wreckers had opened two passages through the Wall on either side of it, one marked "entrance," the other "exit"—"like a museum," as one Berliner put it. The

crowd paid no attention and swarmed through both openings, a great wave of humanity surging from west to east
and another from east to west.

Despite some bruising when the two populations
merged, the Berliners seemed to enjoy the sensation of
making history together. They clapped one another on the
back, exchanged glasses of champagne, swapped ad-
dresses, and took photographs (preferably with border
guards, who by now have become used to being treated as
props)—all in a driving rain.

By evening, the first graffiti had appeared on the Gate
itself. Some, like the West German flags carried from the
East, expressed a wish for reunification. Thus a heart with
"DDR" (East Germany) and "BRD" (West Germany)
scribbled inside it. But most seemed to register someone's
desire to establish their presence at a historical event: "I
was here. Christoph. 22/12/89."

The exhilaration at participating in instant history
turned sober, however, as the news of the street fighting in
Romania sank in. "Berlin celebrates, Romania bleeds,"
said a banner set up opposite the eastern face of the Gate.
Also, the East Berliners have begun to complain about
"revolution tourism." Planeloads of people have de-
scended on the city from Paris and London, seeking a
historical experience and a bit of the Wall to take home as
a souvenir of it. "I just wanted to come and kick the Wall
before it fell down," said one tourist from America.
Chunks of the Wall are being hawked by peddlers: 20 DM
for a small piece, 50 DM for one with some fragments of
graffiti.

East Berliners often react to this kind of capitalism with
a half-serious joke, "They can't do that. The Wall belongs
to us." They, too, are beginning to have graffiti on their
side of the Wall. One is a painting of a section of the Wall

itself, a wall within a wall, with a caption: "This piece of wall is not to be sold for foreign exchange." "Don't sell out to West Germany" is a common slogan.

Does it follow that the opening of the Gate was a moment of false consciousness or of specious history manufactured by the media? Not really. Ceremonies do not lack meaning simply because they are prepared. To argue otherwise is to miss the point of the coronations and peace treaties that have marked off the past and of the tears that really flowed in Berlin on December 22.

The magical sounds in the air that day could be heard far away from the center of the city, in the church bells that rang from all the parishes between three and four o'clock. Berlin is really a collection of villages, many of which still have greens and churches with great bell towers. The bells spread the news into quiet neighborhoods, where pensioners and widows told themselves that they never dreamed they would live to see such a day.

The day belonged to the people themselves, on both sides of the Wall. They made it theirs by the simple act of walking through the Gate—an unthinkable gesture only a few weeks ago. For the first time since World War II, they could travel along the east–west axis of their city without so much as showing a driver's license: down the long avenue of the Kaiserdamm, lined with lanterns built to the glory of the Third Reich by Albert Speer; down the Strasse des 17. Juni, named to commemorate the East Berlin uprising of 1953 (some of its street signs have now been papered over with placards saying "Strasse des 9. November); through the Brandenburg Gate and down the grandest stretch of all, Unter den Linden, to the heart of old Berlin.

Berliners spent the day and most of the night walking up and down this stretch of urban space, greeting one another and smiling happily under their umbrellas. They did not need any speeches to know what they were doing. They were pacing off their city and claiming it once again as their own: that was how Berlin made history on December 22.

THE LAST
DANCE ON THE WALL

January 2, 1990

The French have a term for it, *bain de foule* (crowd bath), and the Germans have made it into a national institution: every week for the past four months they have swarmed through the streets in East Germany, forcing the government to make concessions by the sheer pressure of their numbers. Having got what they wanted, they flocked to the Brandenburg Gate to celebrate their victory on December 31. It was a gigantic New Year's party. Everyone from the East and the West was invited—500,000 guests and no hosts, no program, no organization of any kind, simply half a million people in the streets enjoying a collective bath.

The French have also developed a literature about such phenomena. Emile Durkheim and Marcel Mauss showed that behavior in the aggregate bears little resemblence to that of individuals and that collective representations operate independently from individual psychologies. Gustave Le Bon went so far as to argue that crowds could be understood as persons, with psychologies of their own. And students of *mentalités collectives,* from Georges Lefebvre to Michel Vovelle, developed a history of crowds and crowd psychology as revealed in riots, carnivals, and revolutions.

You would think that someone familiar with the French literature would be prepared for a bath in a German crowd. But the theory proved to be of little help to this historian, who joined the crowd at its densest point on New Year's Eve—those who were dancing on the Wall. What follows, therefore, is merely an impressionistic report about a new phenomenon, which may arouse some old anxieties: the Germans in motion and en masse.

Berliners have danced on the Wall three times since the beginning of the East German revolution in September: on November 9–10, when the Wall was first breached; on December 22, when the Brandenburg Gate was opened; and on December 31, when all of Berlin feted the end of its old division. Before September, to climb on the Wall was to make oneself a target for the snipers in the gun turrets guarding no man's land. Afterward, except on those three dates, the East German border police have kept the Wall clear, especially near the Brandenburg Gate, the symbolic center of the divided city, where the Wall is nine feet thick and just right for dancing. They have mounted a guard on top of the Wall by the Gate, and they make their message clear: no climbing. You may chip some souvenirs off the bottom, but the top is taboo. It is a forbidden area, given over to the people only during extraordinary moments of collective jubilation.

What exactly is a Wall "dance," as the Berliners call it? It has no music and no steps, although it involves a good deal of wiggling and waving in the manner of crowds at rock concerts. Essentially, it is a crowd bath of a peculiarly intense kind, a way of submerging yourself in a mass of mobile humanity. It is friendly but frightening. Other dancers help you up; you help up your successors—no easy task since the Wall is twelve feet high, without footholds—and once up, you cling together, because there is nothing to hold on to except your neighbors, and you are packed so tight you cannot take a step. Instead of walking, you ooze through the crowd, centimeters at a time, like a morsel passing through a monstrous intestine. You move by parastalsis, wherever the collective muscle pushes. The crowd squeezes out your individuality and absorbs you into itself. It digests you.

It could also crush you, or expel you over the edge, for the dance is dangerous. No one has been killed by falling from the Wall, but many have been injured. The dance takes you right to the brink of disaster. Even at the center of the pack, you feel that the crowd could be seized by a collective convulsion and swept in waves onto the concrete below. You could not resist. You cannot regain your individuality until you find some way to be secreted from the crowd and lowered onto *terra firma*.

Even then you are not free, because you are surrounded by 500,000 people all converging on the same spot, the epicenter of the celebration at the Brandenburg Gate. True, you can elbow and shoulder your way through the mass. But as you walk, people throw firecrackers at your feet, a traditional New Year's joke, which is almost as funny to the Berliners as throwing firecrackers into the crowds climbing up the stairs in subway stations. The sub-

ways belch great sonic booms in the distance as they dis-
gorge more merrymakers headed for the Gate.

The crowd comes armed with skyrockets and Sekt
(cheap champagne). The corks seem more dangerous than
the fireworks. People shake the bottles to work up the fizz,
then set the corks off with tremendous force, and pour the
Sekt over one another. The empty bottles, held out at
arm's length, serve as launching pads for rockets. If the
bottles do not explode in the launchers' hands, the rockets
may crash into another segment of the crowd, for the most
effective rocketry is the kind that soars in the lowest possible trajectory over people's heads. You think you are in a
battle zone with bombs exploding above and grenades
below.

The biggest bangs come at midnight: rockets, firecrackers, corks, Sekt, hugs, kisses, shrieks, blood, and fire,
the night in flames above the Gate, a paroxysm of collective jubilation. Never did Berliners ring in the New Year
with such frenzy. But the crowd bath turned into a bloodbath. At 1:30 a sixty-foot television stand by the eastern
face of the Gate collapsed onto the crowd below with 80
people on it. One man was killed, 135 injured.

The crowd had swarmed over the stand in order to jump
onto the roof of a pavilion adjoining the main body of the
Gate. From there they climbed up lightning rods and gut-
ters to the statues at the summit of the Gate. They jumped
on the four horses pulling the chariot Quadriga as if they
were riding a merry-go-round. Then they hauled down
the East German flag above the statue, cut out the symbol
of the Communist Party in its middle, and ran it up the
flagpole again. Stripped of its central emblem, it looked
like the flag of West Germany—that is, it seemed to pro-
claim the unity of the two Germanys. The message
seemed more moderate a moment later, when someone ran
up the flag of the European Community, and then it sim-

ply looked funny, when a Canadian managed to hoist the
maple leaf flag over Berlin.

Good-humored, political cabaret performed before
thousands at the most inaccessible and symbolically
charged point in a landscape dripping with symbolism.
But soon afterward the whole show crashed. The base of
the Gate was covered with half-dead bodies. Yet the rev-
elry continued, because the uproar was so loud that people
only a few yards away did not realize anything had happened. They continued to sing drinking songs, arms linked
and bodies swaying in beer hall style, and they were
packed so thick that the ambulances could not get through
for half an hour. As they raced to the outskirts of the
crowd, the lights of the ambulances shone through the
trees of the Tier Garten like blue sparklers. It was beautiful and sickening.

What to make of it all? The spectacle of Germans waving flags and massing in gigantic crowds will not gladden
the heart of anyone who remembers the 1930s or who has
studied the rise of Hitler. But for all its latent and manifest
violence, the Berlin New Year's party had no resemblance
to a Nuremberg rally. Instead of being regimented, it was
chaotic. It had no direction, no staging, and no Führer. It
was good-natured, not angry, even when a few drunks got
out of hand. It looked less "fascistic," if the word can be
applied to such events, than a soccer crowd in England.

How many murderers, madmen, and deviants of all varieties are likely to be contained in a crowd of 500,000?
Whatever the percentages, it seems remarkable in retrospect that there was not more violence. And it seems
especially astonishing that the public authorities would
surrender the center of a city to a crowd of half a million.
True, someone had put up some outdoor toilets, and a few
policemen could be seen at the edges of the crowd, but

they did not make the slightest attempt to dam or to direct
the flow of humanity. Instead, they let it flood over the
Wall, the Gate, and anything that got in its way.

On ordinary days, Germans are notoriously orderly.
They will stand for minutes at a red light, even if there are
no cars within sight, and they still show a great deal of
deference to the police, or indeed to men in any kind of
uniform. Perhaps they break into anarchy on New Year's
Eve (and also during the carnival season in places like
Cologne and Mainz) precisely because they rein themselves in so severely for the rest of the year: the greater the
discipline in everyday life, the bigger the explosion on
extraordinary occasions.

The trouble with that line of thought is that it conjures
up stereotypes of national character, rather like the famous remark attributed (no doubt wrongly) to Karl Marx:
"There will never be a revolution in Germany, because
someone will have to step on the grass." Iron discipline,
latent violence, crowds gone beserk—we seem to be in the
1930s, not the 1990s, to be dealing with caricatures derived
from George Grosz or Bertolt Brecht rather than people
we could meet on the street, or even on the Wall.

The Wall dance did not look like a scene from *The Three
Penny Opera*. The dancers wore jeans and parkas. Many
of them were teen-agers; nearly all were under thirty—
that is, they were born after World War II, after the death
of Stalin, and for the most part after the Wall went up in
1961. They had never known Berlin without a Wall and
had probably assumed that the Wall would stand until the
end of the century, as Erich Honecker had proclaimed.
Their world came walled. So to dance on the Wall was to
turn the world upside down: *Wahnsinn* (crazy), as they
kept repeating.

Older Berliners have older reference points: the Potsdamer Platz (Berlin's Picadilly Circus before the war, now

a gigantic vacant lot next to the Wall), the Reichstag Building (home of the Weimar parliament, now a museum), Hitler's bunker (a barren area in no man's land behind the Wall), and the monuments along Unter den Linden (rebuilt but until recently inaccessible to Berliners from the West without a visa).

Those places all lie within a few hundred feet of the Brandenburg Gate, but they meant very little to the young people who formed the bulk of the crowd at the Gate on New Year's Eve. However much they misbehaved—and authorities in both Berlins have condemned the defacing of the Quadriga statue—their behavior bore no resemblance to the torchlight parades and triumphant marches directed to the Gate under Hitler. It suggested the very opposite: instead of regimentation, the anarchy, improvised theatrically, and sheer exhilaration at "being there" associated with the demonstrations and live-ins of the 1960s and 1970s.

The crowd expressed plenty of enthusiasm for the opening of the Wall and, in some cases, the reunification of the two Germanys, but it took its tone from the student movements and popular culture of the recent past, not from any deep-seated Teutonic nationalism. In fact, the key event that precipitated the demonstrations in East Berlin took place during a concert by Michael Jackson on June 19, 1988. While Jackson filled the air with noise near the Reichstag Building on the western side of the Wall, a group of young people gathered to hear him on the eastern side, where such music was forbidden. The police tried to disperse them, but the crowd fought back: they demanded the right to hear the kind of music that appealed to their generation and that they had learned to like from Western radio and television.

Rock on one side of the Wall, rioting on the other. The two came together in the great Wall dance of New Year's

Eve 1990. There may be nineteenth-century varieties of nationalism at work in the Soviet Union, Romania, and Poland. But the Germans are dealing with something more recent and more difficult to classify—neither Apollonian nor Dionysian but videogenic: crowd bathing in folk-rock.

STORMING THE STASI

January 19, 1990

Was it another storming of the Bastille? The images left over from the bicentennial celebrations of the French Revolution are still fresh enough for one to see it that way, but January 15 was no July 14 for the East Berliners. The crowd that stormed the headquarters of the secret police, the Stasi, in the Normannenstrasse did not bring down a regime or string up any victims. It went on a romp, kicking through doorways and trashing furniture. Worse has occurred in American college fraternity parties, not to mention English soccer games.

But the East German government was shaken to its

core. In a nationwide appeal, broadcast over television
and radio, it sounded as if it thought the country was on
the brink of civil war. "The democracy that is just beginning to develop is in great danger," it warned. "The government of the German Democratic Republic appeals to
all citizens in this critical hour to stay calm and collected."
As soon as they heard of the riot, the government and the
opposition parties broke off their negotiations at the
Round Table, which are setting the political agenda until
the May elections, and Prime Minister Hans Modrow
rushed off to the Normannenstrasse as if he were determined not to botch things in the style of Louis XVI. "Is
this a riot?" the king reportedly said on July 15, 1789. "No
Sire, a revolution," was the famous reply. Modrow seems
to have feared a revolution and to have found a riot.

Why did this little event produce such a big effect? Modrow was certainly not studying a script derived from the
French Revolution, but like everyone else in East Germany he saw that things were building up to a crisis. The
first round of price increases—children's clothing, up
50–150 percent—had just taken place, producing mob
scenes in department stores. The first important strike—a
twenty-four–hour stoppage by milk deliverers in Berlin—
had just been announced. Emigration to West Germany
continued unabated at a rate of more than 1,000 persons a
day. And above all, the political situation began to boil.

In the first two weeks of January, Modrow's government made it clear that it meant to govern. It announced
new measures without consulting the sixteen opposition
groups gathered at the Round Table. It refused the opposition parties' demands for equal access to offices, telephones, printing presses, automobiles, and television time,
which have all been monopolized by the Communist Party
(SED). It rejected demands for a law on joint ventures,
which would permit foreign firms to acquire controlling

interests in East German enterprises. And it refused to budge on the Stasi issue.

The Stasi occupy a key place in the new political consciousness of the East Germans. In a lecture tour of university towns in the GDR from January 11 to 17, I found the obsession with the Stasi to be as pervasive as the push for unification with West Germany. Every city has its Stasi citadel, a bastion surrounded by walls and covered with a forest of radio antennae. Every citizen has a collection of Stasi stories, which explain why he was not promoted or allowed to travel or admitted to an educational institution. A Stasi mythology about tapped telephones, steamed-open letters, and denunciations by domestic spies has spread everywhere throughout the country.

How much truth is there to it? No one could say before last November, when the Stasi stations were occupied by demonstrators and placed under the surveillance of Citizens' Committees. After a quick look through the secret files, mainly their own, the committee members decided to keep the files closed and sealed. To release the information, they announced, would be to set off endless feuds among people who had been denounced by their neighbors or betrayed by their spouses. As the government had promised the Stasi would be disbanded, it seemed that the myth could be allowed to dissipate in tavern talk.

In December, however, the government mounted a campaign for the suppression of neo-fascism, and the political spectrum began to change. Some Nazi-like graffiti had appeared on walls; some anti-Semitic remarks had been overheard in pubs, some Soviet memorials had been defaced, and a strong nationalistic current had surfaced in the opposition demonstrations, which have continued to take place in many cities, especially Leipzig.

How serious is this danger? The first alarm came from the opposition groups—a poorly organized and badly

splintered coalition of parties and civic organizations
which have only one thing in common: hostility to the
SED. Nationalists had shouted down some New Forum
speakers in the Leipzig demonstration of December 11,
and it looked as though a new right might attempt to seize
the antigovernment movement from the hands of the new
left, capitalizing on popular pressure for union with West
Germany.

By early January, however, most of the left opposition
groups, New Forum included, had endorsed unification in
some form or other, usually with guarantees of the current
borders and a proviso for the sanction of the major powers. Flag waving is no longer a monopoly of the right, and
the flag one sees everywhere—in demonstrations and even
draped from apartment windows—is the flag of the Federal Republic. As East German intellectuals now describe
it, neo-Nazism amounts to little more than spray-painting
by teen-agers, who get the greatest possible shock value in
their protests against the regime by playing with the most
powerful taboos in the regime's official culture: the symbols and slogans from the Hitler period. There is nothing
except frustration behind the occasional swastika on the
wall—no broad public support, no party, no Führer.

In fact, the lack of dominant personalities, in the government as well as the opposition, makes East German
politics look very different from those of Poland and
Czechoslovakia, where personality cults have formed
around Lech Walesa and Václav Havel. Gregor Gysi, the
new leader of the SED, looks and sounds like an intellectual. As a defense lawyer, he developed a strong record of
defending dissidents. And as Party secretary, he is known
for his wit. He may be the only politician in either Germany with a sense of humor. No one could be less like a
Hitler or a Stalin.

Yet the most common graffiti and demonstration banners now say things such as: "Gysi-Stasi-Nasi" and "Gy-STAsi." Instead of playing with neo-Nazism, the opposition is trying to brand the regime with the charge of "Stasinismus"—i.e., with attempting to reconstruct a police state. It began whipping up Stasi-consciousness, and in doing so it provided the spark that set off the riot of January 15.

The opposition groups adopted this strategy in response to a government line, which went roughly as follows: neo-fascism is a genuine threat; the public should rally to the government's struggle against it; to win the struggle, the government will have to take strong measures; and strong measures can only be effective by means of a security police, or *Verfassungsschutz* (constitution protection), in the language of the SED. To the opposition groups sitting at the Round Table, constitution-protecting sounded suspiciously like Stasi-reviving, all the more so as the promised liquidation of the Stasi seemed to have come to a halt. Was the danger of neo-fascism a bluff, used to cover up the creation of a new police state while the SED maintained its monopoly on the media and the means required to run a political campaign? As soon as the government sponsored the idea of the danger, the public began to disbelieve it: such is the state of confidence in public authority in the GDR.

On Monday, January 8, the opposition groups delivered an ultimatum to the government: either Modrow would inform them about the state of the Stasi—the number of agents, their activities, and the progress of their dissolution—or they would break off all negotiations, producing political chaos only four months before the general election. Modrow had tried to keep his distance from the Round Table, arguing that he had to concentrate on governing the country and that he reported to parliament—that is, the old Volkskammer, where there is no real opposition to the SED. But when faced with the ultimatum, he caved in.

On January 15, during the morning before the riot, he appeared before the Round Table and asked to make peace. He promised to abandon all plans for establishing a new security force before the elections, and he asked his main advisor, Manfred Sauer, to report on the Stasi. Sauer's report was astonishing, even to those with a highly developed Stasi-consciousness. The force consisted of 85,000 regular employees, of whom only 30,000 had been dismissed. It also included 109,000 secret informers: that is, almost 1 of every 80 persons in the country, whose population is about 16 million, worked for the Stasi. The surveillance involved 1,052 full-time specialists who tapped telephones, 2,100 who steamed open letters, and 5,000 who followed suspects. The force had doubled since 1980 and had set as its goal the perfection of an espionage network that would cover every citizen in the GDR.

The Stasi armory included 200,000 pistols, which were being turned over to the Ministry of the Interior; a huge fleet of cars, which would be sold to the public; and 3,000 telephone lines, which would be integrated in the public phone system (only a small minority of households now has a telephone). In short, the Sauer report confirmed the wildest fantasies of the Stasi alarmists. The hundreds of Stasi offices collectively constituted a forbidden city, with its own barbers and grocers and sports facilities as well as an information apparatus that could reach into everyone's life and that no one from the outside had ever penetrated—not until January 15, 1990.

At 5:00 that afternoon, a crowd of about 100,000 gathered at the central Stasi office in Berlin for a demonstration organized by New Forum under the slogan "Imagination against Stasi and Nasi [sic]." The Sauer report made it unnecessary for them to use their imagination. Shouting "We are the people," they climbed a wall, forced open a door, and went on a rampage. They smashed furniture, urinated against walls, and painted graffiti such as "Never again Stasi" and "Down with the SED."

The damage was actually far less than the million marks announced by the government but far more, psychologically, than the government can afford. For the first time since the beginning of their revolution, the Germans have resorted to violence. They have sacked the most feared fortress in the land, before television cameras that carried the scene into households everywhere. They have stripped the secrecy off the old police state and shown it for what it was, an insidious network of corruption and denunciation woven into the core of the Communist Party. And they have transformed the political situation by exposing the Party's fragile hold on power.

"Who Rules This Country Today?" was the headline on the Party newspaper in Halle on January 16. Modrow and the ministers? The Round Table? Or nobody? East Germany is drifting into dangerous waters, but this first shot of violence seems to have charged people with new energy. "Germans are supposed to obey orders, not to defy them," a young man in Halle explained. He cited the old saw: there will never be a revolution in Germany, because before storming the train stations the Germans will queue up to buy platform tickets. "We are having a revolution," he said proudly. "And we have stormed the Stasi."

PART III

FACES IN THE CROWD

THE STASI FILES

The most imposing building in Leipzig is also the most
impenetrable—or was, until it was taken by the
revolutionaries on December 4, 1989. It housed the
Stasi (the secret police, formally the Staatssicherheitsdienst); and when the Stasi set up shop in the middle
of the city, it did itself right. As a façade for its headquarters, it chose a splendid, nineteenth-century palace on the
Dittrich Boulevard opposite the German-Soviet Friendship House. Behind the palace it built a bunker the size of
a city block.

The bunker consists of thick, concrete walls, windowless on the ground floor, which rise seven stories to a roof

covered with antennae. The antennae are connected to an ultra-modern communications center deep in the bowels of the building, where the Stasi could eavesdrop on every telephone conversation in the city, 2,000 of them at a time. Records of the conversations were stored on tapes and entered into files—eight kilometers of files, according to one estimate, which is more than all the archives generated not just by Leipzig but by the entire duchy of Saxony over 800 years. Outside, the building is protected by turrets, spotlights, and a wall twenty feet high—twice as high as *the* Wall in Berlin. A sign on the wall says, "Strictly forbidden to smoke or strike a match within five meters." Another sign, freshly painted, hangs over the main doorway to the palace, which serves as an entry to the bunker behind it. It has a very different message: "Under the order of the citizens' committee and the government of the GDR, this building is under the safeguard of the city police."

Before last October, the people of Leipzig gave the Stasi building a wide berth. They referred to it fearfully as "the Round Corner," in allusion to its curved façade at the corner of the Dittrich boulevard and the Barfussgässchen. Many of them believed it was equipped with automatic cameras that filmed everyone who walked past. They would turn up their collars and cross the street in order to avoid being seen too close to its entrance. But every Monday evening from October 2 until the end of the year and well into 1990, the Leipzigers marched through the streets in huge demonstrations against the abuses of the Communist regime. Their route took them right past the Stasi building. As they streamed by, they often shouted "Reds out!" and "Stasi-Nazi!" But they avoided violence, and members of the local citizens' movement made sure there was no confrontation by linking hands to form a human chain in front of the entrance.

Before the demonstration of December 4, however, rumors had spread that the Stasi were burning their files in order to protect themselves and their informants. Some people claimed to have seen smoke rising above the antennae on the bunker. Others talked about files being trucked out at night to airplanes bound for Bucharest. By the time the demonstration that evening reached the Round Corner, the citizens' group had persuaded the Stasi to let them into the building in order to dissuade the demonstrators from taking it by storm. They declared it under occupation and formed a Citizens' Committee to guard its archives. The Stasi then melted away. Resistance would have led to civil war or perhaps even to a battle between the Stasi and Soviet troops stationed outside the city. So the Stasi disappeared and they have not been seen since, although the Leipzigers still expect to find them hiding behind every bush.

Having taken possession of the central symbol of the police state in their city, the members of the Citizens' Committee had to decide what to do with it. It was much more than a symbol, of course. It contained a labyrinth of offices, an arsenal of weapons, and above all a collection of very explosive files. Although the Stasi had indeed destroyed some material, they had left behind the great bulk of their records, which contained enough information to compromise almost everyone of any importance from the old regime and many of the leaders of the revolution.

A quick glance convinced the members of the Citizens' Committee that it would be a disaster to open up the files. Everyone would demand to see his or her dossier. Many would discover that a neighbor had been a spy and that he had reported a love affair of their wife or husband or their own liaisons with other neighbors' spouses, not to mention political and professional contacts that they would rather not have publicized. The Committee members may not have been pleased with what they found in their own files. In any case, they were a body that had constituted itself, no one knew exactly how, and they did not have a firm enough hold on legitimacy to dispose of the files as they liked. So they declared them closed and invited in some experts to sort through all the material scattered through the building and to put it under seal.

That is how Hans-Albrecht Grohmann got to have a look inside the lion's den. Herr Grohmann is an instructor in the History Department of Leipzig University. For years he has been trying to finish his dissertation on nine-teenth-century Saxony. Like many researchers, he keeps finding more material, and he cannot resist the temptation to look in the next box of documents. Who knows? It might contain an unpublished letter by Bismarck or an undiscovered diary of a coal miner. As a consequence of this addiction, he has never quite got down to writing. But he has acquired an unrivaled knowledge of the archives of the Saxon Ministry of the Interior—and so he was the ideal person to ask to look through the Stasi papers.

When the call came, Herr Grohmann could hardly be-lieve it. An invitation to peer into the inner workings of the most feared and secret organization of the state! Everyone had wondered how tightly it had wrapped its tentacles around the social order. Now he could find out. And I hoped I could find out from him. Aside from curiosity and voyeurism, I was moved by the desire to get some perspec-tive on what I would call Stasi consciousness—the feeling of being watched whenever you crossed a street and of being overheard whenever you made a phone call.

I encountered this consciousness everywhere I went in the GDR. Everyone I met had a story that seemed to illus-trate it. A museum director said that when he was plan-ning an exhibition of paintings, two Stasi agents turned up in his office. They informed him that the exhibition would have to include two pictures showing soldiers—GDR soldiers, depicted in a favorable light—or it would not take place. A housewife recounted that a Stasi spy in her apartment building had denounced her for letting her daughter wear Western blue jeans. A professor said he knew that one of the students in his seminar was an undercover agent for the Stasi. But which one? He could not tell, and he was dying to find out by inspecting his file at the Round Corner.

Other visitors to the GDR had the same experience. One woman told me about getting lost in her car a few miles from Potsdam several years ago. She stopped to ask directions from two peasant women talking in front of their houses. "Potsdam?" they said, looking at her incredulously. "No idea." She knew that anyone living so close to such an important city had to know where it was. Her East German friends later explained that the women must have been afraid to be seen talking with a Westerner and may even have thought she was a Stasi agent in disguise. The sense of an all-knowing, all-pervasive, secret presence is also illustrated by Stasi jokes, which became a fad a few months after the Stasi began to be dissolved and had to find employment in the civilian sector. Many were said to have become taxi drivers. So according to the most widely repeated joke, when you took a taxi, you only had to tell the driver your name; he would already know your address.

Were these stories figments of the collective imagination, or were they rooted in reality? Herr Grohmann ought to know. He was willing to talk, he said. But he could not divulge any personal details, because he was bound by his professional conscience to respect the secrecy of the files. He poured two glasses of beer and sat back in his chair, looking out the window at the smog-filled street. Like most of the East German academics I knew, he lived in a slum.

Yes, the stories were exaggerated. "Stasinismus," as people called it, should not be confused with the "Stalinismus" of the Soviet Union. Many Leipzigers had no file at all, and many of the files were full of boring, bureaucratic trivia. A typical dossier consisted of five to thirty pages: first, a cover sheet explaining the purpose of the investigation (to provide clearance for permission to travel, to check out denunciations, to verify suspicions about contacts with Westerners); then an account of the subject's private life accompanied by cross-references to other files; then an "ABV" report (a report by the neighborhood police officer or *Abschnittsbevollmächtigter*); then a report by the Party agent in the subject's place of employment; then miscellaneous reports by spies, each of whom was identified by a code number rather than by name; and finally a summary with a report of a decision (to be allowed to travel, to be incarcerated, to be investigated further).

Herr Grohmann found the quality of the language far inferior to what he had read in the nineteenth-century files. The grammar and spelling were sometimes faulty, the phrasing full of bureaucratic GDR jargon—words like "politically negative conduct" for dissidence. Throughout the reports he sensed a general spirit of misanthropy and distrust. The Stasi did not pay much attention to ordinary workers, but they concentrated on everyone who came into contact with different segments of the population and especially with Westerners. The fattest dossiers concerned writers, actors, artists, professors, street musicians, cabaret performers, and people married to foreigners or with relatives in West Germany. Also, for some reason—curiosity? prurience?—the Stasi were particularly interested in the competitors in the Miss Leipzig beauty contests.

What appalled Herr Grohmann above all was the prevalence of denunciation. Everyone seemed to be eager to supply the secret police with information on his neighbors. A neighbor's daughter wore a cross on a chain around her neck. A neighbor's son cut his hair in a style that seemed to be punk. Neighbors received mail or phone calls (those few who had phones) from *drüben* ("over there," i.e. West Germany). What the neighbors failed to come up with on their own initiative was supplied by the Stasi's spies. They were everywhere, looking inconspicuous, because the Stasi often hired people who already occupied ordinary jobs in the workplace. The most effective spies were those who had the most contact with the public—train conductors, cleaning women, priests, and teachers.

Teachers were especially good at identifying *Stinos (Stinknormale DDR-Bürger)* who watched Western television—the kinds of alienated East Germans who were known as "those who emigrate to another country every evening at 8 o'clock." The regime gave up on policing television habits in the 1980s. But before then it sent out agents to see whether T.V. antennae were oriented toward the West, and it particularly relied on kindergarten teachers. There were two children's programs, one from the East and one from the West, which featured the Sandman. The West German program always ended at the children's bedtime with some remarks about what the Sandman would bring for their dreams. By asking the next morning what the Sandman had brought, the teachers could find out whether a family watched Western television, and the information would go into its file at the Round Corner.

Spies did not receive large payments, sometimes a retainer of 400 marks a month, more often piecework wages for individual reports. Many did not work for the money but merely in the hope of getting a higher pension when they retired. Many were forced into it. The Stasi could put you in prison without trial; and they could hold you there indefinitely unless you agreed to spy for them. They could refuse you permission to travel if you balked at supplying reports on your co-workers or neighbors. And balking could be taken as a sign of a "politically negative" attitude. Once such symptoms were entered in your file, you might never get ahead in your job or never get a chance to move into a larger apartment or to buy a car. And if the Stasi had something on you, they could blackmail you into spying. Spies spied on spies. The whole system kept escalating, and in the end all of the GDR seemed to be honeycombed with denunciators and secret agents. The Stasi were a cancer eating away at the fiber of society.

How far had the disease spread? Herr Grohmann cautioned against the melodramatic view according to which, as the saying went, "Wherever three persons meet, one belongs to the Stasi." But in fact, his exposure to the documents tended to bear out much of the Stasi folklore. One document indicated that the GDR planned to have one Stasi informer for every ten adults in Leipzig by 1994. The archives uncovered in the Stasi's national headquarters in East Berlin were equally stunning. All the information collected in provincial centers like Leipzig was stored in gigantic computers in Berlin. In 1985, Erich Honecker had approved a plan to develop a computerized file on every citizen in the GDR's entire population of 16 million souls. By 1989, the Berlin headquarters already contained 6 million files crammed into 100 kilometers of storage space. Modern technology and Prussian thoroughness could hardly have gone further.

Herr Grohmann looked into the foam at the bottom of his beer glass as if he were trying to find the right word to describe his experience. "Staggering" (*verblüffend*), he pronounced. The "Stasinismus" of the East Germans' collective consciousness corresponded surprisingly well with

the practices of the secret police. But Herr Grohmann had
had to leave the Round Corner after only two weeks in the
Stasi files. He was a member of the Communist Party, and
the Citizens' Committee decided that it could not entrust
Communists with such sensitive material. So it sent him
back to the nineteenth century.

He said he was happier there, but he was not sure that
he could keep his job in the university. Party members are
no longer welcome in the educational system, either, and
financial cutbacks may provide a pretext for the university
to slough off people like him. Still, Herr Grohmann had
learned to make a living as a joiner while working as a
young man in a furniture shop. He could take that up
again if he were forced out of the classroom. Meanwhile,
he was glad that his double exposure to the archives of the
nineteenth and the twentieth centuries had given him an
opportunity to assess the character of the GDR. It may
not have been a full-blown Stalinist regime, he said, but it
certainly was a police state.

COMPARATIVE PUB CRAWLING

The beer is the same: watery, foamy, and cheap (the equivalent of five or ten cents a glass, depending on the category of the pub, one through four, in the hierarchy of socialist beer-drinking establishments). The waiters are as rude as ever: you may supplicate for a table or stand at the bar, but don't get in the way and no back talk. The decoration hasn't improved: frayed tablecloths and lampshades with tassels in category two, dirty linoleum and peeling wallpaper in category four. What is it that makes the pubs in East Berlin seem changed?

I made a tour of them in mid-December 1989. Then,

having fully recovered, I came back for more in mid-May. Something had changed, but I couldn't put my finger on it. My drinking companions, Eike from West Berlin and Alfred from East Berlin, said it was the *Wende* (the events at the end of 1989). But everyone attributes everything to the *Wende* now, even the weather. True, a pub crawl feels different when the weather is friendly. In May we had already stopped by a half dozen establishments before the sun began to set. In December it had been dark for hours before we had our first glass. The drizzle, the pollution, the dilapidation of Prenzlauer Berg—a working-class district, where we did all of our crawling—created the worst possible conditions for jollity. Yet it was jollier then. I would even say *gemütlicher* (cozier), if I could bring myself to use such a word, which clings like Lederhosen to the foreigner's preconceptions of the Germans.

Pubs in the Prenzlauer Berg are tiny spots of warmth and light in a cold and dismal world. They are neighborhood clubs, where the regulars all know one another and their beer arrives before they have to order it. The official hostility of the waiters creates a protective barrier against outsiders. Not that the waiters have to make an effort to be uncivil: rudeness goes with the trade, in fact with all the "service" industries in East Germany, where the servers are employed by the state and the customers are servile—if they wander in from outside the neighborhood. The insiders have their regular tables, their card games, their familiar ways of dunking sausages in mustard and gobbling up *Boulettes* (spicy meatballs).

We were only half outsiders in December, because at that time our group included two locals—Monika, known in the Prenzlauer Berg as "the princess" of the district's Bohemian fringe until she smuggled herself into West Berlin four years ago, and Horst, a short, bald painter, with a beard like an Old Testament prophet, who lived in a nearby loft—aside from Eike and myself. Monika gave me instructions about how, as a foreigner, I should confront an East Berlin pub.

First, don't seat yourself. Wait until a waitress gives you permission to sit down.

Second, occupy the right amount of chairs. If you are in a group of five and there are only four chairs at the table, do not take a fifth chair from another table or modify the disposition of the furniture in any manner.

Third, don't ask for special favors. Should there be "reserved" signs on all the free tables, don't expect to get one. You will only get grief.

Fourth, if you want food with your beer, take what you can get and don't ask questions. You are there on suffrage, by the grace of the workers.

We did in fact order some food at our first stop, the Café Burger, an establishment in category three: potatoes, cabbage, and pork (I think it was pork, but I couldn't really tell) with gravy for four East German marks (less than fifty cents at the current rate of exchange). Monika liked the place, because it is one of the few pubs where a woman can drink by herself without being disturbed. "Officially everyone is equal in the GDR," she explained. "Most women work. They generally get the same pay as men, and they do well in some jobs, like judgeships. But the machismo is unbearable. Women are commonly called girls (Mädel)."

I asked whether it was true that immigrant workers from Africa and Asia were not allowed to bring their families to the GDR. Monika did not know, but she had heard that the GDR had written a remarkable clause into a treaty with North Vietnam: if a worker was joined by his wife and she had a baby, the mother and child would be shipped back to North Vietnam. There are a great many workers from Vietnam, North Korea, Mozambique, and

Angola in East Germany, but they live in separate settle-
ments, sometimes within the factory grounds. They never
came to pubs like this one, which was a watering place for
workers from the Prenzlauer Berg and intellectuals from
Democracy Now, one of the citizens' groups that sprang
up in October.

I wondered whether I might find some Vietnamese at
our next stop, the Café Mosaik, because Horst said it was
a favorite place of the *Asis*. It turned out, however, that
Asi meant *Asoziale* in GDR-speak, and an asocial person
belonged to a specific category in GDR law: someone suspect, who did not have a regular job and would probably
never get one, because *Asoziale* had been stamped on his
identity card and entered in his police file. Horst had
nearly become an *Asi* himself. He did abstract paintings,
and he did not belong to the official artists' association (the
Verband Bildender Künstler Deutschlands), which controls all access to galleries. He could not sell his pictures
himself, because the state does not permit a free market
for art. But he had some friends in the theater, and they
found him a job painting scenery for three days a week.
Also, he had recently sold some pictures for West German
marks through a dealer in Munich, so he felt relatively
secure—but also angry. On October 2, he had participated
in a protest meeting of 200 artists and writers. They signed
a petition demanding a public discussion of public questions, notably the flight of refugees across the Hungarian
border.

That sounded rather innocent to me, but Horst explained that in the eyes of the regime it was as seditious to
demand the right to free discussion as it was to demand
the right to free elections: no issue could be separated
from the others without unraveling the entire web of oppression that had kept the East Germans quiet for forty
years. That is why one of the slogans from the November

demonstrations—"Widerrede ist nicht Widerstand" (Talking against is not resistance)—was so provocative, although it sounded so mild. But now, in December, everyone was talking back and everything was falling apart. He only hoped that the Stasi would also collapse.

In fact, a Stasi office stood right across the street from the Café Mosaik, and the pub seemed to thumb its nose at it: *Asis* mocking Stasi. Our fellow drinkers included the East German variety of punks in a setting that seemed to be everywhere hair—hair sprouting from heads in strange shapes and colors, hair beneath chins, hair under arms. We were surrounded by T-shirts and tatoos. Even the waiters looked undercombed and underdressed. When they unloaded the glasses from their trays, they picked up the rhythm of the hard rock music blaring from a juke box. Monika said that she sometimes danced with them.

She had organized a dance herself, in her own apartment overlooking the Helmholtzplatz, on the night before she escaped to the West. It was a good-bye party for her friends, although she did not dare to let them know it. Instead, she provided plenty of beer and loud music and danced until early in the morning. A Stasi car circled around the block, but no one was arrested. Now Monika had a good job and a nice apartment in the heart of West Berlin. This was her first time back to her old neighborhood. By stationing herself across the street in the Helmholtzplatz, she could see into a window of her former living room at a spot where she had placed an antique cupboard. It was gone now. Monika said nothing, but stood and stared.

Our last stop—I skip the relay stations, street corner pubs from category three or four, the beer usually at 35 pfennig (about a nickel) a glass—was at the Keglerheim, nicknamed the Fengler. Many of the pubs had neighborhood nicknames, I don't know why and can't say what this

one meant: by now things had begun to blur. But I can
clearly remember the hostess planting a kiss on Horst's
bald pate. She was seventy-five years old and had seen a
great deal of political struggle in the neighborhood. Her
pub was a bastion of the Social Democrats in the 1930s. A
few doors down the street was a Communist pub, and on a
corner across the street from it, a Nazi pub. There were
brawls every night after closing time. As soon as the beer
began to flow again after the war, the Fengler became a
meeting place for dissidents from all over the GDR. To
get in, you had to stop at a chain rigged up inside the door.
If your looks satisfied the hostess, she would unhook the
chain and direct you to a table or the bar. Before the
Wende, drinkers were not permitted to stand more than
one row deep at bars. But at the Fengler they stood five
rows deep and talked politics.

There didn't seem to be much politics in the air when
we arrived. The clientele was mostly young, in jeans and
sweaters. Some of them played billiards in an adjoining
room. Most simply talked, in the full-throated, East Berlin
manner, with broad gestures and table banging and none
of the studied coolness of young adults in the Western half
of the city. By now I was feeling something suspiciously
close to *Gemütlichkeit.* Eike bought me a Korn, a local
kind of schnapps, and I don't remember the rest. . . .

That was in mid-December. Eike and I returned in mid-
May in order to see if the mood had changed (ah, research!), but we may have spoiled our sample, because we
took another guide, Eike's friend Alfred. Alfred is a warm
and sympathetic type, but he has spent too much time in
pubs—and also in prisons. We picked him up in his room
on the sixth floor of a tenement building off the Lychener
Strasse. I have seen slums in New York and Newark and
Philadelphia but nothing like a really broken-down tene-

ment several courtyards deep in the Prenzlauer Berg district of East Berlin. The linoleum was peeling off the floor, the plaster off the walls, and the skin off Alfred's cheeks, which were already lit up by alcohol. He slept on a mattress that looked like an open wound and that lay on the floor by a pile of brown coal and an unhinged stove. He ate off a formica table he had fished from a junk heap. And he cooked from a burner fed by a frayed wire, which tapped electricity from the communal toilet, half a floor below. Alfred apologized for receiving us in such squalor. The police had cleared out his furniture during his last prison term, he explained, and he had had to live off the street. He was an *Asi*.

We climbed over the rubbish on the stairs and in the courtyards to the street, where we found still more rubbish gathered in huge piles every thirty or forty yards. People had abandoned their apartments when they migrated to the West. Others had moved in after them and had tossed the articles they did not want onto the street. Old couches, chairs, broken bric-a-brac lay in heaps, soaked through by the rain so thoroughly that they formed a single, sodden mass and blended into the pavement. The pavement itself lay in broken slabs that looked like the discarded remains of another era, the turn of the century, when the Prenzlauer Berg was lined with imposing façades and well-appointed sidewalks. Now the buildings seemed to suffer from leprosy. Balconies, friezes, stucco work of all variety had dropped off, and you could see the ends of steel beams sticking through the outer walls. The deterioration had been as bad in December, but it was far less visible then. The cruel light of the setting sun in May exposed every detail of the neighborhood's pathology, and the rubbish heaps added a new element: a reminder that much of the population had tried to escape from the disease before it leaked from the walls into their lives.

There were bright spots, of course. In December, the pubs themselves provided warmth and light. Unlike New York, where the streets give off light and the bars stay dark, East Berlin sinks into shadow by four o'clock in the winter, and its inhabitants gather in pubs to get away from the gloom. In May, however, they drink for the sake of drinking; and when I returned to the Prenzlauer Berg, it was possible to see the first glimmer of Westernization in the way they downed their beer. The Budike on Huseman-strasse offered draft Dortmunder with "Danysnack," American-style fast food, in place of curried sausage and *Boulette*. Farther down the street, the 1990 had turned itself into a hangout for West Berlin yuppies, who spent West German marks for West German beer in a fake Gay Nineties setting saturated with Western pop music. The entire Husemanstrasse had been gussied up to evoke an imaginary Old Berlin, with antique phonebooths and quaint lampposts. On the other side of the Kollwitzplatz, the Westphal offered hard rock and political punk that might have come out of London. And a few streets away, the Alternative Café duplicated the "alternative" (counter-cultural) scene in Wedding, just across the bor-der in West Berlin: everyone in the place was young and dressed in black, the women with bandanas tied around their foreheads, the men with earings and ponytails.

We sampled all these spots but spent most of our time in old-fashioned, working-class pubs like Zum Schusterjun-gen and Das Loch. Alfred told Stasi jokes that he had picked up as a newspaperman in the 1960s and 1970s. In those days, he said, you didn't joke casually in pubs. You made sure of your neighbors and kept your voice down. He knew: he had been arrested once in Das Loch ("The Hole," as it is known in the neighborhood; I never learned its proper name) for telling a joke about Erich Mielke, the former head of the Stasi, and a parrot. It didn't sound seditious, or even very funny, to me, but Alfred said you had to develop an ear for such things.

He had picked up most of his repertory in the *Wochenpost*, a mass-circulation weekly, where he rose to the rank of deputy editor-in-chief. You could not reach such a position without being a stalwart member of the Party. Alfred had been a good Communist since his early youth, when the disasters of the war had made him fiercely antifascist. After high school, he had volunteered for the army, worked for a military newspaper, and transferred to the *Wochenpost*. His job there involved vetting as well as editing copy, because editors were held responsible for the ideological import of everything they put into print.

Alfred had no objections to the Party line. In fact, he had applauded the construction of the Wall. But he never developed much capacity for self-censorship; and when he failed to blue-pencil a story that compared retirement pensions in the GDR unfavorably with those in West Germany, he got in trouble with the authorities. He went on to publish letters to the editor from retired people, who said they could not live on 300 marks a month. More trouble. Worried about the rising tide of public opinion, the government decided to raise pensions by 60 marks in April. Alfred ran a story, which announced that the increase would take place three months earlier, in January. The government caved in and advanced the date to January, but it also sent Alfred to jail, for five months, without a trial.

Upon his release, he learned that he had lost his job, but he found another one on a less important paper. By then he must have been spending a good deal of time in pubs, although I can't be sure, because I heard only Alfred's side of the story, and it came in installments that became cloudier as we progressed from pub to pub. For some reason, the second job evaporated, and Alfred eventually

found himself working as a corrector in a government
printing shop. One day he received the proofs of a government directive to all newspapers and district offices of the
Party calling for a general campaign to get more work out
of the miners in the brown coal pits before winter set in.
Seized by an irresistible graffiti impulse, Alfred scribbled a
remark in the margin about how ministers ought to spend
some time in the coal pits themselves. The proofs fell into
the hands of a Stasi agent in the shop, and Alfred went
back to jail, this time for six months.

Two more prison terms followed, interspersed with increasingly lowlier forms of employment—in the post office, on the railroad—until at last Alfred sank into the
category of the *Asis*. In the end, he supported himself by
scavenging for empty bottles—in the private sector, as he
put it. He must have emptied quite a few himself, but he
said that he made more than he consumed in drink. On a
good day he could collect ten marks in deposits for bottles
that he fished out of garbage cans and trains stopped in
stations at the end of the line. It was enough to live on, and
you never knew what might turn up in the streets of the
Prenzlauer Berg. The rubbish heaps grew greater every
day.

THE TRABI
AND ITS TRAINER

Werner Hartwig and Jörg Engel are taking a coffee break in the back room of their body shop in East Berlin. "Did you hear the one about the Trabi and the zebra?" asks Werner. Jörg is already smiling. Jokes about Trabis (Trabants, the tiny, two-stroke–engine automobiles that fill the streets of the GDR) are popular everywhere in East Germany and especially among garage mechanics. "The Trabi meets the zebra in deepest Africa. 'What kind of an animal are you?' the Trabi asks. 'A horse,' says the zebra, 'And what are you?' 'A car,' says the Trabi.' " Jörg and Werner burst into laughter.

The joke does not seem funny to most Westerners, but it is hilarious in an East Berlin garage. Jörg follows it up: "How do you double the value of a Trabi?" "I give up," says Werner. "Fill its tank," says Jörg. More laughter, and it is Werner's turn. "A man goes to order a Trabi. 'Fine,' says the distributor. 'You can have it exactly fifteen years from now. Do you want to pick it up in the morning or the afternoon?' 'I don't know,' says the man. 'Which would you recommend?' 'The afternoon,' says the distributor. 'That's when the repair man will be here.' "

Jörg told me that the joke was uncomfortably close to reality. East Germans often have to wait a generation for a new car; and when they get it, they can't be sure it will hold together. That's why he has so much business. He has seen Trabis in amazing states of disrepair, some of them so eaten away by rust that they have broken in half, some so smashed up that they would go straight to the junk yard in any other country. Not here, however, because if you have to wait fifteen years for a Trabi, you will do anything within your power to keep it alive.

Jörg and Werner have performed amazing feats of surgery in their tiny shop, working with antique welding equipment and hand tools that a West Berliner would disown. They improvise spectacular amputations and transplants, not because they want to show off their skill but because their customers are desperate and their suppliers incompetent. All spare parts come from a central dispensary run by the state. For two and a half years it has failed to supply them with any rear sections of the Trabi body; so they have cobbled together rears, using bits and pieces from junk yards and their own collection of dismembered bodies. A few years ago, the central supplier sent all left fenders to Dresden and all right fenders to Berlin. Jörg and Werner had to work with what they received, making the crooked straight and the rough places smooth, even though the end product occasionally listed to one side or another.

Bravura car repairing exists everywhere in East Germany. It continues a tradition of skilled craftsmanship that was nearly destroyed by the state's attempt to force heavy industry on the proletariat in the 1950s and 1960s. In 1966, soon after he had completed his advanced training in metalwork, Werner had a chance to buy a small body shop from the widow of a friend. But the authorities refused permission, explaining, "We don't need body shops; we are building socialism." In 1976 they announced a new line: craftsmanship was to be favored, and Trabis had to be repaired, because they were breaking down on a mass scale. With the help of a loan from the Volksbank, Werner set up shop on his own in a broken-down back courtyard in the Köpernick district of East Berlin. His work force consisted of himself and one helper—Jörg, who had trained as a welder and worked in the construction industry, although cars were always his first love.

The little business might be considered an enclave of capitalism, except that it was completely controlled by the state. Werner had to conform to state quotas for productivity—buying parts, billing customers, and paying Jörg according to official directives. Although he could work after hours on his own, he had to pay so much tax on the extra income that it was not worth it. In fact, he explained, he would have felt completely trapped within the system if it had actually worked. But it was a complete farce. While he complied with everything required of him on paper, he really did business according to an entirely separate system: barter.

How did bartering work? Werner gave me a long look and then smiled.

Suppose you come to me now, in June, and you say you must have your car repaired. I say, "Impossible; we can't

do anything before next April." Then you say, "But that is
a disaster, because I need to use the car to carry a load of
two-by-fours to my grandmother's house in the country."
"Oh, I say, you have two-by-fours? Maybe we can repair
the car in December." "That's too bad, you say, because
before then I must use the car to bring back some pork
that my grandmother plans to slaughter." "Oh, I say, you
will have some pork? Maybe we can repair the car in July."
"Still too long to wait, you say, because I plan to use the
car to haul a load of strawberries." "Okay, I say, it's a deal.
I'll do the job next week, and you pay the set price in East
marks along with a load of wood, a dozen pork chops, and
twenty boxes of strawberries."

Werner said he had once repaired a car door for a case
of bananas, and one of his best customers was a butcher
who always paid in steaks. A while ago Jörg took all the
dents out of a badly damaged body for a load of parquet.
He didn't need a new floor in his own apartment, but he
kept the parquet sections piled up in his living room until
he got a chance to trade them toward a computer. He was
a computer nut, and computers could only be had outside
the official economy, by means of barter. But you had to
barter hard. Customers would tell you anything to get
their cars repaired. They always had a wife who was preg-
nant and needed to be driven to the hospital or a father
who was susceptible to heart attacks. "One hand washes
the other; that's how the system works," said Werner.
"You exchange things for things. Money is no good."

Of course, barter had its disadvantages. Aside from the
inconvenience of having all sorts of unwanted goods ac-
cumulate in your apartment, you might run into a confidence man. If he found out that the major part of your
business never went through your books, he could
threaten to denounce you to the police. Blackmail was a
technique favored by the Stasi when they wanted to sink

their claws into someone. But how could you tell who worked for the Stasi? In bartering it was best to restrict yourself to networks of people you could trust.

Foreigners found it difficult to understand the system, because they did not appreciate the importance of the Trabi to the people of the GDR. To us, all Trabis were the same, but East Germans detected endless nuances among them—like Bedouins assessing camels and Eskimos discussing snow. True, a typical Trabi did not look like much, but it often cost 15,000 East German marks, well over a year's salary for most people. Secondhand Trabis were frequently more expensive than new ones because they could be purchased right away. Indeed, the wait for a new Trabi was so long that people sometimes sold their place on the list, and spare parts were so scarce that Trabi owners spent a great deal of time scavenging for them. If they appeared in the shop with the parts, they stood a far greater chance of getting their car repaired. Werner and Jörg frequented junk yards themselves. With luck, they could patch together a whole new car. "Out of two make one" was their motto.

In short, the car mechanic occupied a strategic place in a barter economy where the supreme object of value was the humble Trabi. "The mechanic is king," said Werner with a touch of pride. He claimed that car repairmen lived better and were more respected than doctors and lawyers. There were only forty body shops and hundreds of thousands of Trabis in East Berlin, he explained. Every boy dreamed of becoming a garage mechanic. They came into the shop all the time, asking about the possibility of an apprenticeship. Not that he could help them. Such things were decided by people with pull inside the Party, and they dispensed about a hundred apprenticeships to their favorites among a thousand or so candidates each year.

Did that mean that skilled workers enjoyed a position on the top of the heap and that the so-called land of workers and peasants really was a paradise for the proletariat? Werner could not find anything good to say about the government or the Communist Party. He did not dispute the worthiness of socialism, but he denied that it had ever been practiced in the GDR. Instead of distributing wealth, the apparatchiks creamed off everything for themselves and left ordinary people to cope as well as they could by developing networks outside the legal system.

Hence the importance of car repairmen. "It's like a spiderweb," Werner explained. "The mechanic sits in the middle and pulls all the threads." As an example, he cited the case of a friend who had spent three days trying to find some paint for the renovation of his apartment. Finally, he gave up and came to Werner for help. By pulling strings, Werner was able to get the paint in half a day. Now the friend is waiting for an opportunity to do him a good turn. That was how he and Jörg became a team: they performed little services for one another; the trust between them grew, especially after Werner helped Jörg procure a refrigerator; and ultimately they decided to share the same shop, more as friends than as employer and employee. "One hand washes the other," Werner said once more.

And both of them wash the Trabi, I thought to myself. Why did East Germans spend so much time scrubbing and polishing their miniature cars and then turn around and make fun of them in jokes? Werner said his customers treated their Trabis like spoiled children. Having waited many years for a Trabi to arrive, everyone in the family would clean it, fit it out with gee-gaws, collect spare parts for it, and devote a large portion of their income to its maintenance. The Trabi was their most important possession, their supreme luxury. And yet when they talked about it, they used a host of pejorative expressions like "asphalt bubble" *(Asphaltblase)* and "plastic tank" *(Plastepanzer)*.

The poor Trabi is always the butt of jokes in East German cabarets. In its spring show in 1990, the Distel cabaret of East Berlin featured the unveiling of the latest model outside a Trabi factory. It looked exactly like the models from all the previous years, except it had a "VW" badge on the radiator. Volkswagen had announced plans to build engines for Trabis in the GDR, which East Germans had greeted with remarks like, "You can't make a race horse out of a pig." The Distel players made the most of this situation. One of them, impersonating a sales representative, announced that the new model included 800 improvements. "Think what the old one was like!" commented another, dressed as an assembly-line worker.

The East Germans pour so much scorn on the Trabi that it is hard to understand their love for it. But such contradictions belong to their daily life. They are even incorporated into their language by means of a special verb: *hasslieben* (to love-hate). One evening in Leipzig I was given a lift in a Trabi by an attractive young woman. "Is this your first ride in a Trabi?" she asked, dewy-eyed, as if it were the first kiss. She stroked its dashboard fondly as it drove off, bucking, coughing, and spewing exhaust in the air. Another time, in Halle, a friend offered to give me a tour of the city in his Trabi. As he put it into reverse in order to pull out of the parking space, the gear shift came out of the steering shaft. He sat there waving the shift in the air as if it were the drumstick of a chicken and said, laughing, "Damned Trabis." Then he fumbled under the hood and we pushed the car onto the road. We spent the rest of the day seeing the sights in second gear, without a shift.

Such reactions would be unthinkable in West Germany, where a man's relation to his car is a serious business—perhaps more serious than his relations with his wife, if he drives a Mercedes or a BMW. To watch the Mercedes streak down the left lane of the Autobahn at 100 miles an hour, while the Trabis put-put along at 50 in the right is to see two worlds go by unknown to one another. Shut inside his metal box, each driver catches a glimpse of the other for an instant and keeps to his own course at his own speed. It's hard to avoid thinking of them as the two Germanys, one super-modern, hard-driving, serious, and fast; the other archaic, inefficient, absurd, and slow, but with a lot of heart.

The hare and the tortoise also come to mind. But it would be a mistake to take a sentimental view of the two cars and the societies they embody. The Mercedes will win. In fact, it had already won by November 9, 1989, and a half year later Daimler Benz won approval for plans to transform the Potsdamer Platz—the busiest crossroad of old Berlin, which had degenerated into a huge vacant lot by the foot of the Wall—into a gigantic Mercedes showroom. In March the waiting time for Trabis dropped below ten years. In May you could buy them on the spot. And in July nobody would touch one. The East Germans abandoned the Trabi and flocked to the secondhand car lots in West Germany, where they bought everything in sight.

To Werner and Jörg the decline and fall of the Trabi is no tragedy. They can mend fenders on Mercedes. Indeed, they expect business to improve, because East and West Germans are constantly smashing into one another when they drive into the unfamiliar half of the newly united country. But anyone who saw the first Trabis venture into West Berlin after the fall of the Wall will never look at one without a tinge of emotion. They are expensive, dangerous, uncomfortable, noxious, ugly, loud, smelly, and slow. And when I see one, I cannot help but say to myself, "Trabi, ich hassliebe dich!"

THE DIRTIEST
CITY IN EUROPE

G etting to Reinhard Becker's office is like going to the
moon. You orbit around Berlin, set a course for
deepest Saxony, turn off at the first scent of sulphur, and land in another world. It actually looks
like a moonscape: mile after mile of desolate terrain without a sprig of green, the ravaged remains of the brown coal
industry. Almost all the energy of the GDR comes from
brown coal, an inferior grade that produces far less heat
and far more pollution than the bituminous, "hard" coal
familiar in the West. The East Germans gouge brown coal
from the surface of the earth in gigantic, open pits, and the
pits extend for miles around the city of Bitterfeld, where

Herr Becker works as the town councilor for environmental affairs.

The environment in Bitterfeld is reputed to be the dirtiest in Europe, although there are other contenders in the industrial wastelands of Czechoslovakia, Poland, and Romania. Bitterfeld bases its claim not only on the coal dust from the mines and the coal briquette plants linked to them, but also on the waste produced by sixty-five factories that encircle the town. Each year they discharge 40,000 tons of dust and 90,000 tons of sulphur dioxide into the air and 70 million cubic meters of liquid waste, much of it poisonous, into the rivers of the region. The rivers turn bright yellow, brown, or red, according to fluctuations in the chemicals dumped in them. Most of the dumping comes from Chemiekombinate Bitterfeld (CKB), a vast industrial complex, which produces all sorts of films, paints, and pesticides under the motto, "Environmentally favorable products through environmentally favorable production."

You see the smokestacks of CKB jutting into the smog as you approach the town, and under them, on rooftops, window ledges, free surfaces everywhere, West German flags. It is an extraordinary sight—or was one in darkest January at the beginning of the election campaign: the flag of one country hoisted over the factories of another, an emblem of capitalism unfurled over the productive forces of socialism. As you enter into Bitterfeld, another message greets you from a sign at the city limits: "Bitterfeld. Environmental Emergency Area."

You see signs everywhere after you park the car in a mud flat near city hall and walk toward Herr Becker's office on the Ratswall. The Christian Democratic Union has covered the main square with posters proclaiming, "No socialism, never again." In a nearby park the CKB has erected a billboard with a picture of a spotless factory topped by a smokeless smokestack. The main caption reads, "Everyone is talking about the CKB, a firm with a good and a bad reputation. But chemistry belongs to our life, and we cannot make our way in the future without it." The small print explains that the firm employs 17,500 workers and exports 4,000 different products to 60 countries.

By now your eyes are beginning to sting. You notice that the eyes of everyone around you are ringed in red. When you ask directions from a young man, he points toward the Ratswall and adds, as if in explanation, that Bitterfeld is hard on sight. "It's not so bad today, but when the wind blows from the west, where the Mühlbeck pits are located, you have to clean your glasses every five minutes. You need glasses with windshield wipers."

A young mother pushing a baby carriage says she is worried. Two of her friends have babies in the hospital: "Bad lungs. But what can you do? It's no good to close the windows and keep your child inside. The air is everywhere." A grandmother at the banana stand (Western bananas for three West marks or ten East marks per kilo) insists that she feels fine despite thirty-eight years of residence in Bitterfeld. But when her daughter's baby developed an intractable skin rash, her daughter decided the GDR was hopeless and emigrated to West Germany.

The Bitterfelders are friendly and eager to talk about their air and water. Shoppers at the banana stand (bananas are still exotic in the GDR, so the stand functions as a town pump) say that they have learned to be wary of local produce. The ground is poisoned. Pollution has ruined 10 percent of the arable land in the GDR. In industrial regions the smog is so thick that it has stunted the production of vegetables and flowers in greenhouses: the sunshine can't get through. Last year the output of greenhouse tomatoes, cucumbers, and peppers dropped by

15–20 percent; and 30 percent of the flowers grown in greenhouses had to be thrown away.

The people of Bitterfeld seem to have an insatiable appetite for flowers. According to some housewives lined up outside a florist's, flowers add color to houses, and the houses need it. The acid in the air eats through the paint and corrodes the brick on the outside of the buildings. On the inside there is coal dust everywhere. It seeps under the windows and is tracked in on shoes, for it also covers the sidewalks. In order to heat their apartments, many tenants have to lug coal from heaps dumped on the sidewalks in front of the buildings. It is so cheap that no one bothers to steal it and so dirty that no one can escape its effects. A young mother says that she keeps her windows closed and washes her curtains once a week, but it is a losing battle. Her son developed a severe cough and had to be sent to Czechoslovakia to clear his lungs. Whole classes of schoolchildren are evacuated regularly for cures in seaside retreats. The rate of bronchitis among children is twice that of other areas in the GDR, and skin disease is rampant.

A pharmacist on duty in a nearby drug store says that the city does not have a single dermatologist. According to a recent report, it needs 223 doctors. It now has 47, and they might leave at any moment for better pay and better working conditions in West Germany. Doctors are doing so all over the GDR, but they are especially beleaguered in Bitterfeld, where life expectancy for men is five years less than in other parts of East Germany. The men often work in factories built in the 1920s, breathing in fluoride and phosphate gasses that escape from rotting pipes. They get good wages: sometimes 2,000 marks a month, with bonuses for the especially dangerous jobs, as compared with 1,000 marks or less in other industrial areas. So they don't complain, but they often go lame or come down with cancer. It is hard to say how bad the situation really is, explains the pharmacist, because there aren't many reliable statistics. For fuller information, you had better see Herr Becker.

So at last you do. From the intersection of Lenin-Strasse and Marx-Strasse, you cross over a small park named Green Lung, and you reach the Ratswall, a narrow street lined with crumbling brick houses. One of them has a sign: "Wasserwirtschaft and Umweltschutz" (Waterworks and Environmental Protection; at first glance, I misread *Umweltschutz* as *Umweltschmerz,* environmental/world pain). Behind the door, up a flight of stairs, bent over a desk in a dingy room sits Reinhard Becker. He appears to be in his early fifties and very much a politician: short, plump, jolly, a glad hand, and a quick tongue, he takes charge of the conversation and steers it in the direction he prefers. He knows better than to pretend that Bitterfeld is anything less than a catastrophe. Instead, he fixes the guilt firmly on "them" in Berlin.

"They take everything," he says, banging the table with his fist. "Everything goes to Berlin. We produce 8 percent of the country's wealth, and we get next to nothing in return." Before the *Wende* in November, "they" refused to let him publish information about the damage to the environment. Now he realizes his information isn't adequate, although the basic problem is clear. Bitterfeld lies at the center of an urban network woven around the coal pits. The region (Kreis) has been continuously mined since the mid-nineteenth century. Nearly half its surface area of 454 square kilometers has been dug up; so the beds of its rivers have shifted, and its whole topography has changed. Toxic wastes have been discharged into the water since the 1890s, when the chemical industries moved in. By the 1980s, the CKB dumped so much, everything from salt to mercury, that the authorities at the provincial

(*Bezirk*) level gave up trying to monitor it and settled for collecting fines, which amount to 20 million marks a year.

Herr Becker could not provide statistics on the state of public health. When it comes to fine points of chemistry and the esoteric issues of environmental sciences, he admits he is out of his depth. He is a water and parks man. He began his career in municipal government thirty years ago by concentrating on rivers. Bitterfelders have a bad habit of dumping old cans and remains of bicycles in a brown stream that runs by the "Green Lung." Herr Becker fished them out—so effectively, he explained, that he kept getting re-elected to higher offices. Of course, he was a member of the Communist Party, and there were no other candidates. But he managed to develop a not inconsiderable expertise in getting traffic directed, trees planted, and drinking water provided (it comes from sources at a safe distance in the Harz Mountains, but the pressure is so low that many faucets work only at night).

"Ecology" is a term that reached Herr Becker rather late. When it did, he had risen to the rank of municipal councilor, one of twelve elected officials who run the city's life in cooperation with the mayor. As he describes it, the machinery of government worked quite effectively before the *Wende*. The councilors got together, decided what needed to be done, and did it. Not that their life was easy. You should not imagine a municipal councilor as someone who sits on his *Sitzfleisch* and reads *Neues Deutschland* all day. When a tree fell in a park, Herr Becker had to be there. Worse, he had to find a way to remove it—no easy task since his work force consisted of four men without a chain saw. Despite inadequate funds—200,000 marks for environmental improvement—he managed to get 250 trees planted last year. He had hoped to reinforce the banks of the stream by the "Green Lung," though there was no prospect of shutting off the sewage pipes that feed into it. Garbage, in general, is a problem for Herr Becker. The West Berlin government solved its garbage problem the easy way—by buying the right to dump it in the GDR: 40,000 tons were dumped near Bitterfeld last year. But Herr Becker does not have an adequate supply of East German marks, not to mention "real money," as West marks are known in the GDR, and he needs three garbage trucks desperately. What can he do? Everything ground to a halt after the *Wende*.

The *Wende* did not hit Bitterfeld especially hard: a few thousand people turned out in the streets in November, well after the massive demonstrations in nearby Halle and Leipzig. But the mayor and councilors had to resign, mainly, it seems, because the townspeople believed that the results of the municipal election held last May had been falsified by "them" in Berlin. Herr Becker decided to stay on as a temporary employee, tending the parks and garbage, until the elections in May 1990. He won't run again. "There is no respect anymore," he explains. "A city councilor used to be somebody. Now we have a Round Table running things in Bitterfeld. They summon me every week. 'Why is the river so dirty?' they ask. Imagine it! There are housewives at this Round Table!"

But do not think that Herr Becker has much sympathy for the old regime. He associates it with the iniquitous North, the evil world of "them" in Berlin. That he could be "them" to the people of Bitterfeld seems never to have occurred to him. On the contrary, he has adopted some of the language of the citizens' movement that overthrew him. He describes the rule of the Communist Party as a "tyranny," and he is the first to deplore its effects on the environment.

Herr Becker's notion of the ideal municipal government derives from West Germany, which he imagines as decentralized, supremely professional, and full of technological marvels. A short while ago he visited Bitterfeld's "sister city," Marl, a center of the chemical industry in Hesse, West Germany. "It was wonderful," he said. "Spotless. The sidewalks are clean, the steps are clean, the roofs are clean. The stucco is all in place, and it's painted with bright colors. Local services are paid for by local taxes. The man in charge of parks has fifty people working under him. If a tree blows over, he pushes a button, and in ten minutes the tree is gone." The municipality of Marl is sending Herr Becker some sophisticated equipment, so he can measure the density of phosphates and fluorides in the air—gasses undreamt of in his philosophy when he first began to pull old bikes out of Bitterfeld's riverbeds.

What will become of Herr Becker, and hundreds of similar town officials throughout the GDR? His answer, in a word, is "unemployment." "We lost our legitimacy," he explains. But he sees no need to apologize for his many years in charge of the environment of "the dirtiest city in Europe." He has done pretty well himself. Two of his three children are grown up, and he expects he will find some sort of job in the future. After all, he, too, grew up in Bitterfeld, and he has done so many favors for other people that they will find a way to help him. Other small-time city politicians have suffered far more: "They believed in Marxism, and in November their whole world fell apart. Many were driven to despair, many wound up in the hospital, or worse." What is "worse"? Soon after the opening of the Berlin Wall, there were reports of two or three suicides of East German officials.

You leave Herr Becker's office wondering about the dimensions of the revolution in East Germany and about the disparity between his understanding of the situation and what really exists, etched in the façades of the buildings and the faces of the people passing by. Until he is turned out of his office by the town council to be elected in May, he will continue with business as usual, as if a few more trees planted in the "Green Lung" could actually stop the spread of bronchitis.

In order to get some other readings of the situation in Bitterfeld, you make two more stops. First, in the office of the local newspaper, the *Mitteldeutscher Zeitung*, a reporter confirms your suspicion that the town councilor for environmental affairs has little effect on what goes into the air and water of the city. Such things are determined far above Herr Becker's head, at the level of the Party's first secretary for the region. The Party boss handles all important questions in conjunction with the minister for industry in Berlin and the factory directors, who are also Party men and care about nothing except reaching production quotas. According to the reporter, life in Bitterfeld will get worse before it gets better, once the GDR is swallowed up in the West German economy. Most of the local industries will collapse, and unemployment could run anywhere from 3,000 to 15,000. But it will not include Reinhard Becker. His friends will look after him, and, anyhow, small-time politicians have a way of surviving big-scale changes in governments.

Second, in the office of Bitterfeld's Citizens' Movement (Bürgerinitiative Bitterfeld), an angry young woman says that Becker is nothing more than a Party hack. He has no professional training, no understanding of environmental science, and no respect from the people of the town. He and the other members of the old town council will never be loyal to anything but the Communist Party, and they will never be able to learn from their mistakes. Bitterfeld must have a new generation of leaders, if it is to save its water, earth, and air.

Air, earth, and water. The struggle for survival in Bitterfeld has been reduced to the most basic elements. As you drive off through the smog, West Berlin looks like an oasis in an industrial wasteland, and Western Europe appears to be a thin band of brightness on the edge of a world extending eastward through endless shades of gray.

EVENINGS
WITH THE OLD GUARD

L eipzig, Halle, Jena—great names. A professor cannot
hear them without a sense of awe. They summon
up the modern university as we know it now and as
the Germans invented it more than a century ago.
So I felt a quickening of the pulse when the train pulled
into Halle, my main stop on a lecture tour of the southern
GDR in January.

The pulse skipped another beat or two when I learned
that my first stop in Halle was to be dinner with the president. Not that I find university presidents especially imposing. I know one or two of them in the United States,
and their main attribute is superior housing. They live in

palaces, furnished like museums and administered like the headquarters of multinational corporations. What would the palace of Halle's university president look like? I put on my best tie.

The president (actually rector) was a chemist, Horst Zaschke, who greeted me at the front door in his shirt-sleeves. He apologized in advance for the roundabout route to the dinner table, but he promised it would be worth it, because he had recently killed a pig. We took an elevator to the fifth floor, crossed over a landing, walked down a hall, climbed a stairway, walked down another hall, and arrived at last at his apartment. It consisted of five rooms, just right, he explained, for a man with a wife and three children. As two of the children had grown up and moved out, he had room for a study with a small library. It opened onto a balcony, where Herr Zaschke led me to admire the view: immediately before us, a half dozen high-rise apartment buildings, giant cement boxes exactly like his, and beyond them the smokestacks of factories surrounding downtown Halle, whose lights glimmered faintly through the smog.

We had a glass of beer in the living room–dining room, a small but comfortable space furnished in varieties of *Plaste und Elaste* (GDR German for synthetic materials of a plastic and rubbery character), with a television set and knick-knacks that Herr Zaschke had brought back from his travels. Frau Zaschke, their youngest son, and his girl friend joined us, and we repaired to the dinner table. I had never seen so many kinds of sausage spread out on a single board: Mettwurst, Knackwurst, Bratwurst, Leberwurst, sausage from every conceivable part of the pig, from the brain to the trotters, grilled, smoked, and raw; and interspersed amidst it, platters piled high with potatoes, pickles, and raw onions.

Herr Zaschke explained proudly that he came from a

family of farmers in Thuringia. Once a year they gathered together to butcher a pig. It took them all day, because they transformed every centimeter of it into sausage of one kind or other and they allowed plenty of time for gossip and drink. He had just returned from this year's ceremony, so he was pleased to be able to offer me the full spectrum of Thuringian butchery. I was very touched, and tucked in with a good appetite, eating my way from the animal's guzzle to its zatch and watering it all down with excellent Thuringian ale.

When we paused to catch our breath, Herr Zaschke offered some remarks on the experience of running a university in the midst of a "revolution," as he called it. He had had no difficulty with the students. As in Leipzig and other places, they had formed a student council to defend their interests, but they bickered among themselves and they were not fundamentally opposed to the old regime. Indeed, they benefited from it. There were only 10,000 of them, all carefully selected, all sure of a place somewhere in the state administration or the state-run industries after their graduation. The small minority of graduate students in subjects like my own already knew where they would be professors. For in education, as in everything, the GDR worked by planning rather than by competition. No, the students were not activists. They had never occupied a building or even participated much in the street demonstrations, although Halle was a hot spot in the protest movement.

Professors were another matter. He had a faculty of 1,500. Almost all had been members of the Communist Party before September, but 1,000 had turned in their Party cards, and nearly everyone had a grievance of some kind. A faculty personnel committee was attempting to cope with the complaints. But another committee was debating basic changes in the university's structure. They might abolish "sections" (large administrative units, one of which, for example, covered all foreign languages and literatures) and create something similar to American-type "departments" (smaller units, such as German, English, and Romance languages) or even revert to the old, nineteenth-century "faculties." Meanwhile, no one knew whether authority was invested in the former section chairmen, or deans, or future department heads, to say nothing of the cells of the Communist Party.

Before the revolution, there had been a Party secretary responsible for the university. He transmitted orders from the Party hierarchy, and he had to approve of all important decisions by Herr Zaschke, who was a good Party member himself, of course. But the secretary had just resigned, and the Party was in chaos. Instead of leaving Herr Zaschke with freedom to maneuver, the power vacuum made it impossible for him to plan—and what was a rector without a five-year plan? He couldn't even be sure of his budget for the next semester. Normally, he also cleared all plans with the mayor, who in turn worked closely with the Party secretary for the region *(Bezirk)*. If he had to construct a new laboratory, they would sit down together and talk it out, with their elbows on the table. The mayor could not only unfreeze credits, but he could also provide construction workers and building material, which were desperately scarce in the GDR. Now, however, the mayor was besieged by citizen activist groups who had created a local Round Table. No one knew exactly where they came from, but they had power. They spoke for the public and lobbied for special interests. Herr Zaschke regretted that he had not had the foresight to seize a seat at the Round Table himself, so that he could defend the interests of the university. But he was grateful that he still had access to the mayor and that the mayor was still in office, unlike the mayor of Leipzig, who had been forced to resign because of the rigging of the municipal elections last May.

Despite the bleakness of the situation, the rector saw some bright spots. Indeed, his eyes lit up when he described the state of the Stasi. After the local branch of New Forum had occupied Stasi headquarters, they had ceased to be a power in the city's affairs. Not only had they withdrawn their spies from the university classrooms, they had also abandoned a magnificent building, the most modern and best equipped in all Halle. Stasi headquarters had more space than all the sections of the university combined. Herr Zaschke had just been through it. It had lecture halls, seminar rooms, laboratories, a library, sports facilities, a barber shop, and so many offices that he could give one to each of his professors. All he needed was the keys. The university could move right in; and if it ever expanded, it could take over the garrison of the Soviet army next door.

True, the Soviets did not live as well as the Stasi, but their barracks would do for students, who were desperately short of housing, and the drill grounds could be converted into soccer fields. Although Herr Zaschke could not predict when the Soviet troops would pull out of the GDR, he was sure it would happen before the Americans left West Germany. Would I like to make a bet on that? The rector's eyes twinkled. East German universities were going through hard times, I knew, but there was hope if their affairs remained in the hands of good Communists like Herr Zaschke.

My hopefulness faded the next morning, when I began to look around the city. The problem was not simply that Halle was polluted, more polluted than anything I had ever seen (I had not yet been to Bitterfeld), but it was collapsing. I saw a building collapse myself, just a few yards from where I gave my first lecture. One moment it was a structure, the next a heap of bricks. It was an impressive sight: an imposing townhouse, which had been inhabited for centuries, suddenly reduced to rubble. But the citizens of Halle did not seem to notice. They saw such things every day, or perhaps walked past them without really seeing. On nearly every street in the heart of the old city were piles of brick and stone that had once been buildings. Some of them had held up against the elements since the Middle Ages, right through World War II, but the neglect of the last few decades had finally done them in. They had become state property, and the state did not bother to patch their roofs and replace their drains. So the walls cracked and the roofs caved in and eventually whole structures heaved over.

I passed hundreds of ancient houses poised on the brink of collapse. One particularly fine Renaissance building with a carved stone gateway and a courtyard sheltering a spiral staircase had a plaque on the wall. It said that Friedrich Schleiermacher had lived there when he was a professor at Halle. I thought of friends in America who had devoted years and years to the study of Schleiermacher's thought, and I imagined an emergency rescue campaign: phone calls, faxes, $100 from every philosopher in the world within a week. But it was hopeless. The building would not make it through the winter. Halle would not make it—not the ancient university town, though something would survive, something made of steel and concrete like the high-rise apartments where the rector lived on the edge of the city. I could begin to understand the bitterness in his fantasy of moving the entire university out of every crumbling building into the bright and roomy citadel of the secret police.

I also began to understand the anger behind a demonstration I attended that evening. *Beton Sozialismus* (concrete socialism) was the target of the fiercest placards, and

"Our city is collapsing" was the loudest chant in the streets—except for the cry that was beginning to drown out everything else in the GDR: "Germany, a united fatherland." Again and again the speakers denounced socialism and what it had done to their city. In demanding protection for the environment, they were not trying to save the dark Teutonic forest. They wanted decent air and housing in the middle of Halle. And it was clear that the only way they thought they could get what they wanted was by unification with West Germany.

After the demonstration, I went to dinner with three professors of literature in the Haus der Wissenschaftler, a kind of faculty club. When I mentioned my astonishment at the modest way in which the rector lived, they said he had no choice. If he used his influence to get a better apartment, he would be denounced as a *Privilegierter* (someone who enjoys special privileges). Resentment of a privileged class of Party members had been simmering for years in the GDR, but it boiled over in early December, when the top men in the government were arrested for corruption and pictures of their luxurious homes and hunting lodges appeared in television sets throughout the country. Waves of outrage continued to spread as local scandals broke. In Halle, the president of the regional council (*Vorsitzender des Bezirksrats,* a position roughly comparable to a state governor in the United States) had been arrested for abuse of office following revelations about his hunting lodge. The regional Party secretary had been forced to resign, and there was talk of more heads rolling.

I said I could understand the resentment of flagrant abuses, but a larger apartment for the rector of the university did not strike me as excessive. What was the dividing line between ordinary people and the privileged? Apartment size, said the professors. There were other criteria—

access to cars, permission to travel—but apartments were the main thing. You could measure the distinction between the privileged and the nonprivileged by the number of square meters in their apartments. An extra room was a sure sign of an apparatchik.

What about income? I asked. The professors laughed. Everyone had roughly the same salary, they explained, but that didn't matter. What counted was access to things, especially scarce things, like living space in Halle, and access came through influence—in the Party. To illustrate the point, they told me about their own apartments.

I will refer to them as Colleagues A, B, and C, because I don't want to use their real names and they often addressed me as "Colleague Darnton." (East German professors move from "Herr Professor" to "Colleague" once they get to know you, and from "Colleague" to "Comrade" at meetings of the Party.) Colleague A explained that they were senior professors and Party members but definitely not members of the privileged class. She had the best apartment of them all: three rooms in a new building for 98 marks a month (hardly $10 at the current rate of exchange), heat, water, and electricity included. But she had a husband and a child. Colleague B lived alone and had two rooms for 38 marks, including heat and water. Colleague C, a distinguished professor of literature, also lived alone in two rooms. He paid 30 marks (about $3 a month), heat and utilities included, but his apartment house was in terrible condition. He would gladly pay three or four times that amount for a third room, because he had no place to put his books. If enough people moved to the West and if he pleaded hard enough, he might someday get a three-room apartment, on grounds of professional need.

But he dared not press the point. An extra room would mark him as a *Privilegierter,* and he was already a marked

man. This he explained to me after the others had left and
he had paid the bill: 40 marks, or about $4, which was
more than his monthly rent, for a three-course meal with
beer for four persons. A year ago someone had denounced
him within the Party organization of the university for
spending too much time in "NSW" countries, i.e., countries of the "nonsocialist way" *(nichtsozialistischer Weg)*.
Although he was no *Reisekader* (someone, usually a high-
ranking Party member, permitted to travel in the West), he
had been allowed to attend a few conferences and to make
a research trip to West Germany in 1988. Evidently he had
aroused the jealousy of a comrade-colleague, so he needed
to be especially careful. Not that he would be thrown in
jail: I shouldn't think that Stalinism in the GDR was anything like the brutal variety developed by Stalin himself in
the Soviet Union. But he might not be allowed to travel
anymore, and he could not bear the thought of being cut
off once again from the West, especially from France.

His love of France went back to 1945, when he was sent
there as a young and bewildered prisoner of war. He was
treated well, learned the language, and returned to Germany fired up with a passion for French literature and a
hatred of fascism. While studying for his doctorate, he fell
under the spell of Werner Krauss, an authority on the
French Enlightenment and a hero of the Communist resistance. Like many intellectuals of his generation, Colleague C joined the Party out of conviction. His faith held
through the darkest days of Stalinism, even after his closest friends were accused of deviationism and disappeared
into a prison camp. When they returned ten years later, he
and they accepted their punishment as a necessary measure to maintain Party discipline. A group of them within
the university pushed for reforms in the mid-1970s, when
the system began to loosen up. They had fierce arguments
with the hard-liners, and they rejoiced at the advent of

glasnost and perestroika. But when the regime turned against perestroika, they began to turn against the regime—inwardly, in the privacy of their consciences, for they never broke with the Party and never would.

Then the revolution hit. They did not support it, but they did not oppose it, either. And when they got a chance to speak their minds in debates within their Party cells, they argued for some kind of democratic socialism. Who, I asked, were "they"? "You will meet them at dinner tomorrow night," replied Colleague C. And I did—a dozen of them, all professors in their sixties, the old guard of what was left of Communism in the University of Halle.

Judging from the way they fell on the beer bottles lined up on the table, they were old friends who had been through many battles together. One of them mentioned seeing a placard in yesterday's demonstration with a picture of Honecker in the striped costume of a prison convict. That was going too far, he protested, in a tone of mock seriousness and then lit up with a smile. Another professor wondered aloud whether anything could ever stop the emigration to West Germany. There was so much loose cash to be picked up there! A neighbor of his had emigrated last month, just packed his bags and disappeared with the wife and children. Yesterday he returned on a visit—in a new car, which he had bought on the installment plan with the unemployment payments that he was already receiving in the West.

Everyone had stories about how the *Ossis* (East Germans) were playing the system of the *Wessis* (West Germans). They told of husbands and wives who pretended to separate so that she could run their household in the East while he collected unemployment in the West—800 DM a month, or about four times the wages of a worker in the GDR. He would come home on weekends, his pockets full

of Western currency, which went a long way in a city like
Halle. In fact, he could use the money to buy up cheap
GDR goods and sell them back at an enormous profit in
West Germany, notably to the Turks who frequented the
Polish market of West Berlin. More ambitious Ossis could
exploit the West German desire for vacation cottages in
the GDR, a promising field for underhand entrepreneurs
because Wessis were not permitted to acquire East German real estate, except through inheritance. If you or your
family had a place anywhere near Berlin, you could adver-
tise in the West Berlin *Tagesspiegel,* indicating only that
you had something for sale in the "suburbs." A Wessi
would recognize the code and come with a contract, which
would commit you to give him the use of the property
during your lifetime and to leave it to him after your death
in return for a pile of West marks.

My dinner companions recounted these stories to one
another in the manner of sick jokes, and found them very
funny; but they made me feel uncomfortable, for they all
suggested that the sickness was located in the East German economy. Or was it in socialism itself? I wondered,
when the conversation shifted to socialist jokes:

Question: What is socialism?
 Answer: The most difficult mode of transition from cap-
        italism to capitalism.

Question: What is the definition of capitalism?
 Answer: The exploitation of man by man.
 Question: What is socialism?
 Answer: The reverse.

I had heard them before. They seemed to represent a
variety of gallows humor which had spread throughout
Eastern Europe. But here, amidst the old guard in Halle,
they sounded particularly grim.

Many bottles later, Colleague D pulled his chair up next to mine. I had heard that he was the dominant figure in the Party organization of the university and that he had argued for the total dissolution of the Party during the national meetings held at the height of the crisis in December. I can't remember his exact words, but they went more or less like this: "Socialism is dead, finished. It was never anything more than an illusion, anyhow. As a philosophy, it is far superior to capitalism, but as an economic system it does not work. And there is no compromise between the two systems, no middle way. Forty years of experimentation with a planned economy have ended in failure. Socialism is dead."

I looked around the room and saw only old men, bitter, drunk, and broken. They would not rally to the West. They would remain in Halle, slowly collapsing, like the buildings. For they had nothing to hold them up; they believed in nothing. Colleague D leaned over and looked hard into my face: "Two systems have competed for almost a half a century," he said. "Which has won?" He gave the answer in English: "The American way of life." A smile was on his lips, and in his eyes a look, not of hostility, but of hatred, pure hate.

WHAT IS
LITERATURE?

Looking back, everything seems clear: the connection between literature and power in the GDR can be seen as a struggle of good guys against bad guys. On the one hand, writers and their allies among the intellectuals; on the other, censors and the apparatchiks of repression.

Despite its simplicity, there is a great deal to be said for that view. For the last twenty years, many of the best-known writers in the GDR sniped at official orthodoxies, while the state prohibited their books or drove them out of the country. Until recently, the works of Freud, Nietzsche, Schopenhauer, Max Weber, Kafka, and many giants

of twentieth-century literature could not be found in East
German stores. And every book that did appear had
passed through an elaborate censoring mechanism under
the direct control of the Central Committee of the Communist Party. Writers seemed to be struggling to spread
enlightenment, censors to prevent revolution, just as in the
eighteenth century.

So when the revolution broke out, exactly 200 years
after the French Revolution, the intellectuals took charge
of it. Writers and actors organized the supreme demonstration of November 4, which precipitated the collapse of
the regime. While nearly a million demonstrators cheered
them on, Christa Wolf, Heiner Müller, Stefan Heym, and
Christoph Hein lectured the government about its abuse
of power. Five days later, the Berlin Wall came tumbling
down, and people began to talk about Christa Wolf as the
next president of the GDR. Where could one find a better
example of the intelligentsia seizing power, except in
Czechoslovakia, Hungary, Poland, and—who knows, perhaps some day?—the Soviet Union?

But Christa Wolf did not become president of the GDR.
East Germany has no Václav Havel. Its intellectuals disappeared from the scene almost as soon as the Wall fell,
and some of them, notably Stefan Heym, did not hesitate
to say they were sorry it had fallen. Not that one can
accuse the writers of being *Wendehälse* (turncoats or trim-
mers, a favorite expression for people who switched sides
after the revolution). On the contrary, they generally favored maintaining socialism and an independent GDR at
the very moment when the rest of the population swung
behind the campaign for unification with West Germany.
In mid-November, when the cry of the crowd shifted from
"We are the people" (Wir sind das Volk) to "We are *one*
people" (Wir sind *ein* Volk), the writers dropped out, and
they have remained on the sidelines ever since.

In many cases, this loyalty to the old regime expressed a genuine commitment to socialism and a horror of the sort of consumer society where books are bought and sold like toothpaste. But it also coincided with the writers' self-interest. Although they might refer to themselves as "intellectual workers," they often looked like *Privilegierte*, members of the privileged class, to the general population. They had good apartments, permission to travel, and an assured income. The official Writers' League (Schriftstellerverband) dispensed a vast amount of state patronage. Its members could be sure that they would never go hungry, for it could always find them work—editing classic German texts or writing catalogues for exhibitions or producing volumes to celebrate an anniversary or a theme sponsored by the Ministry of Culture. In 1989 state grants to writers came to more than 2 million East German marks.

None of the cultural industries under the old regime was governed by the marketplace. All were supported by the state. In the case of the book trade, the Communist Party owned nearly all the printing presses, and the government apportioned the entire supply of paper. Government officials also supervised sales in bookshops and set book prices, which were remarkably cheap—usually eight East marks (roughly a dollar at the prevailing rate of exchange in late 1989) for a hefty, hardcover novel and a few pennies for a paperback. Publishing houses played an intermediary role in this process, but all seventy-eight of them were owned, directly or indirectly, by the state. The Ministry of Culture appointed their directors, who were always members of the Communist Party and were always held responsible for the books they published.

Their responsibility remained more ideological than commercial, however. The Ministry of Culture made sure that the publishing houses stayed solvent. It had to, because it controlled their access to paper and printing, limited their prices and press runs, and often paid them direct subventions. As they were protected from the pressure of the market, they could keep their lists free of Western-style, fast-food books—exercise manuals, soap-operatic sex, and other varieties of what they called *Trivialliteratur*. They could afford to be high-brow and high-minded, and also to pay writers decent advances, along with royalties that usually ranged from 10 to 15 percent. In some respects, such as copyright law, the writers fared better in the GDR than they did in West Germany or the United States. If they were unlikely to get rich quick from a best-seller, they did not fall victim to publishing strategies built around blockbusters.

The system left no room for private enterprise, little for freedom of opinion, but plenty for making compromises. For example, it forbade writers to publish books that did not pass the censorship, but it looked the other way if they published them in West Germany—provided they received official permission. It did not allow them to make money from sales in the West, but it made exceptions to the rule if they turned three-quarters of their royalties over to the Ministry of Culture. And once the shock had been absorbed, it often permitted East German publishers to produce home editions, usually in small printings of less than 10,000. Stefan Heym tried to get round this system when his novel *Collin* produced a sensation and a great deal of revenue in West Germany. He was condemned to a 15,000-mark fine for failing to share his wealth with the ministry. But the public covered the fine by stuffing money into Heym's mailbox, and ever since then the "Heym Law" on Western royalties has remained a dead letter.

Other episodes did not have such happy endings. The one that most shook the publishing world was the imprisonment of Walter Janka, the director of the Aufbau pub-

lishing house, in 1957. A militant Communist since the
early 1930s and a veteran both of the Spanish Civil War
and of Nazi prison camps, Janka had tried to rescue one of
his most eminent authors, George Lukács, during the
Hungarian revolution of 1956. The government encour-
aged him, because everyone assumed that Lukács, as
Hungary's most eminent Marxist intellectual, would be a
target of the revolutionaries rather than a victim of the
Soviet troops who were coming to suppress them. In fact,
however, Lukács supported the uprising; and by support-
ing Lukács, Janka exposed himself to the charge of
counter-revolutionary agitation. The charge was fab-
ricated in the GDR Ministry of Culture, which was looking for victims in the campaign to wipe out all opposition
to the rule of Walter Ulbricht. Many of Janka's friends
knew he was innocent, but they also knew that he had
dared to publish such un-Stalinistic authors as Thomas
Mann and Ernst Bloch, and that his editions of Lukács
were being withdrawn from the bookstores and pulped.
No one among all the writers and publishers of East Germany dared to speak out. Janka was condemned to five
years in the deadly prison camp of Bautzen. When he was
released, a diseased and broken man, he withdrew into
silence. He did not break his silence until October 28,
1989, when his account of his experience, *Schwierigkeiten
mit der Wahrheit (Difficulties with the Truth,* published in
West Germany at the end of 1989), was given a public
reading in the Deutsches Theater.

By that time, Stalinism seemed to be a thing of the past.
The last wave of repression against authors occurred in
the 1970s. Wolf Bierman, whose razor-sharp ballads had
wounded some powerful sensibilities, was forced into exile
in 1976. Although he was not allowed back into the GDR
until last November, 172 writers had protested against his
expatriation; and they were not persecuted for doing so. In

1978 the dissident Rudolf Bahro received a three-year prison sentence for publishing his attack on Stalinism, *Die Alternative*, in West Germany without permission. But when he promised to emigrate to the West, the authorities released him, and they have not imprisoned any authors since. By the 1980s most East German writers seemed to have made their peace with the regime and to have found a fairly comfortable place for themselves in the *Nischengesellschaft* (society of private niches or corners) that grew up within the old Stalinist structure.

Readers, too, seemed to be fairly satisfied, as far as one could tell from observing their behavior in bookshops. To be sure, the shops looked sad in the 1970s, when they seemed to contain little more than biographies of Brezhnev and the works of Marx-Engels-Lenin. But things brightened in the 1980s. Although it was still impossible to find anything by Nietzsche—except in certain cafés in Leipzig and East Berlin, where tattered, old copies circulated under the tables—a wide range of German literature appeared on the shelves. When customers entered bookshops, they commonly took large plastic baskets and then filled them to the brim, like Westerners in supermarkets. They formed long lines before the cash registers, reading from their baskets the way Americans nibble from the food heaped into their shopping carts. They read their way home in busses and subways. And once home, they read through the evenings and brought their books back for more reading at work.

Work does not engage much energy or imagination in the GDR. Most offices and factories have twice as many employees as they need, and most of their employees work half as much as they are supposed to. They take breaks to do their shopping. But there is such a limited range of consumer goods available in the shops that they often settle for a book—a book rather than a newspaper or a magazine because until November 1989, periodicals contained more propaganda than news. Many people watched television, even in the so-called Valley of the Clueless (Tal der Ahnungslosen) around Dresden, where Western broadcasts did not penetrate. But the book was the favorite medium under the old regime. Despite the upheavals of the last fifty years, East Germany remained an old-fashioned society, closer in some respects to Wilhelminian Germany than to the West Germany of today. People had plenty of time, and they spent it with books, which provided them with escapist fantasies and traditional *Bildung* (education, cultivation.)

Such, at least, is the view of the East German publishers I have consulted. They report that they could have sold far more books than they produced, because the demand seemed to be insatiable, at least in fields such as current fiction and classics, as opposed to Marxism-Leninism. They usually printed new novels in editions of 20,000, more than the press runs of much fiction in the United States today. In 1989, the GDR produced 625 works—a total of 11.5 million copies—in the field of East German fiction and belles-lettres alone. That included a good deal of poetry and high-brow essays, which would not sell in the West. East Germany's total output of books from 1945 to 1990 came to 215,000 titles and 4 billion copies—a remarkable amount for a country of 16 million people. Just how those millions absorbed the books is another question. But everyone in the literary trades seems to agree on one point: before the revolution, the GDR was a *Leseland* (reading country)—or rather, as Christoph Hein put it, a *Buchleseland* (book-reading country).

All that changed after November 1989. When Dietmar Keller, the last minister of culture from the old regime, made a speech at the last Leipzig book fair before the election of March 18, 1990, he sounded as though he were delivering an elegy: "In these days when people reflect about the cultural identity of the GDR, and when they ask themselves what our country can contribute to a united Germany, they will cite its literature, its publishing industry, and its good reputation as a *Leseland*."

From January 1, 1990, censorship ceased to exist and subventions began to dry up. From November 10, 1989, newspapers and magazines started to cover the news without being muzzled by the "Agitation and Propaganda" section of the Communist Party's Central Committee. Even television freed itself from the censor—and also began to broadcast commercials. Theaters ceased to be filled because the public could now get its politics straight, from the press rather than from inuendoes on the stage. And the press came increasingly from West Germany, notably from the four giant conglomerates, Springer, Gruner and Jahr, Burda, and Bauer, which by March were selling seventy-three different newspapers and periodicals in the new, wide-open market of the GDR.

How did the writers react to this situation? Three hundred thirty-seven of them gathered together at a special congress of the Writers' League in March 1990. They did not celebrate their role as the intellectuals who mobilized the people during the heady moments of the previous fall. Still less did they confront the Stalinist episodes in their more distant past. Instead, they dumped their previous president, Hermann Kant, a hard-line member of the Central Committee of the Communist Party, and reorganized themselves as an interest group. The dominant theme of their discussions was: How can we survive in a literary system based on open competition in the marketplace?

Not that writers in the GDR have always avoided questions of principle. They discussed all the issues raised by the practice of literature in East Germany at a congress in

November 1987. This was the last time that the literary
system of the old regime appeared in full dress before the
public and the first time that it was publicly attacked from
within its own ranks. Erich Honecker, accompanied by
half the members of the Politburo and the top officials in
the Ministry of Culture and the Cultural Division of the
Central Committee, greeted the writers as "trustworthy
partners and fellow militants of the working class and its
Marxist-Leninist Party." Soon afterward, in a work
group, Christoph Hein attacked the state censorship as
"outmoded, useless, paradoxical, hostile to humanity,
hostile to the people, illegal, and punishable." A donny-
brook followed. Writers, publishers, journalists, and Party
leaders went at one another in a general battle over what
literature in the GDR was and what it should be.

Nothing was resolved, of course. Nothing is today. But
the experience of the GDR in the last two years suggests
that literature involves a great deal more than inspiration
on the part of authors and understanding by readers. Between author and reader there exists a vast system for
producing and distributing the printed word. That system
has varied enormously from time to time and place to
place. The ideal time and place to study it is when it falls
apart, for then you can catch some glimpses of its inner
workings. Of course, it helps to have an insider as a guide.
Just after the collapse of the literary old regime in East
Germany, I was lucky enough to have two—two censors
from the Publishing and Book Trade Administration
(Hauptverwaltung Verlage and Buchhandel) in the Ministry of Culture. Their testimony is important enough to
warrant a chapter to itself.

THE VIEWPOINT
OF THE CENSOR

Ninety Clara-Zetkin Strasse, East Berlin, the entrance on the left, past a porter's office, up two flights of stairs, down a long corridor, and through an unmarked door: the Sector for GDR Literature. You have arrived at the central nodal point in the nervous system around which literature is organized in East Germany, the office of the censor.

Strictly speaking, censorship did not exist in the GDR. It was forbidden by the constitution. That did not prevent the new regime from abolishing it at the end of December 1989, however, and its abolition did not mean that the army of censors who filtered manuscripts through the ma-

chinery at Clara-Zetkin Strasse ceased to exist. Two of
them, Hans-Jürgen Wesener and Christina Horn, showed
me around the premises on June 8, 1990.

Herr Wesener poured the coffee. We were sitting in the
main office for East German literature, a drab room furnished in plywood and plastic like most of the offices in the
bureaucratic wasteland of the GDR. They no longer vetted books, Herr Wesener assured me. They tried to help
the publishing houses put their affairs in order while preparing for the onslaught of the market economy in July.
Not that many of them would survive. Literature, as it had
existed under the old regime, was doomed.

But was there any reason to regret the old system? I
asked. Didn't it involve state control, ideological policing,
and all the fettering of thought summoned up, in a word,
by "censorship"? Herr Wesener and Frau Horn exchanged looks. Clearly there was a great deal to be explained to this foreigner.

Censorship exists wherever there is a selection process
in the production of literature, they explained. Most of it
takes place in the heads of writers, and what the writers
fail to cut usually gets filtered out by editors in publishing
houses. The censors in Clara-Zetkin Strasse actually elim-
inated very little of the literature that reached them—on
the average, a half dozen of the 200 to 250 manuscripts
that they approved each year in the field of current East
German fiction.

Formally, they never censored anything at all. They
simply refused to give books an official authorization
(*Druckgenehmigung*). Herr Wesener handed me an authorization, a small printed form with his signature on the
bottom. It looked unimpressive, until he explained that it
alone could unlock the machinery of the publishing industry. For no printer could accept a work that was not
accompanied by a *Druckgenehmigung*, and virtually all

printing houses were owned by the Communist Party. Was it fair to say, then, that the process of authorization *(Genehmigungsverfahren)* and censorship *(Zensur)* came to the same thing, and that the GDR had actually developed an air-tight system of censorship, despite the provisions of its constitution?

Frau Horn admitted as much, although she did not feel happy with the term "censorship." It evoked too many negative associations in the minds of the uninformed and gave them a bad reputation. In fact, she thought that by authorizing books she had promoted them. Many of the manuscripts that she shepherded through the bureaucracy would never have appeared in print had she not removed phrases that were certain to provoke the wrath of the Central Committee of the Communist Party. A censor had to be familiar with the sensitivities of the men at the top of the Party and to have an ear for language that was likely to offend them.

For example, authors who spoke of "opponents of Stalinism" were sure to get in trouble. She made them say, "contradictors of their era." Those who made explicit reference to the 1930s might kindle suspicions that they were alluding to Stalin's purges. So she changed "1930s" to "during the first half of the twentieth century." A phrase such as, "The air is unbreathable in Bitterfeld," was suicidal for an author. It had to go, as did any use of the word "ecology," which enraged some top Party leaders. "Critical" was another dangerous word. It suggested dissent. When Frau Horn saw a phrase like "a critical discussion of Soviet history during the 1930s," she changed it to "a discussion of early twentieth-century history."

For even "Soviet" could be seen as a provocation, at least after 1985, when everything that came out of the Soviet Union looked suspicious to the Central Committee in the GDR. Back in the 1960s, the censors had to beware of all things American. Kurt Hager, the chief ideologist of the Central Committee, had opposed the publication of a translation of *The Catcher in the Rye* on the grounds that Holden Caulfield should not be allowed to serve as a model for socialist youth. (They eventually got the book past the Central Committee, and it had a great success among young readers, even though Hager thought that East German youth was supposed to admire "winners," like their Olympic stars, rather than "losers" like Holden.) But after the advent of Gorbachev, the Soviet Union became by far the most delicate subject that crossed their desks. In fact, glasnost and perestroika remained taboo in the GDR until the "October revolution" of 1989.

All this sounded fascinating but also puzzling. Did the censors understand their task to be the protection of society against corruption and sedition or the protection of authors against the ire of the Central Committee? And why did the Central Committee loom so large in their work? Frau Horn and Herr Wesener exchanged another glance, and Herr Wesener said that he had better begin at the beginning.

I should understand that he and Frau Horn were committed to two causes, literature and socialism. They had both studied German at the Humboldt University in East Berlin; and like many students, they had hoped to pursue their literary interests by working in the Ministry of Culture. Soon after the Publishing and Book Trade Administration (Hauptverwaltung Verlage and Buchhandel) was established in 1963, they found themselves doing what I would call censorship. They did it willingly, because they believed that the GDR, unlike West Germany, was committed to certain values: socialism, humanism, anti-fascism, anti-racism. They thought it right to keep books like

Mein Kampf out of the country. They were good Party members, and they sympathized with the Party line at the height of the Cold War, even when it took the form of slogans such as, "No co-existence in the realm of the spirit. Truth is indivisible."

But they felt a tug at their loyalties in the 1970s, when socialism in the GDR seemed to be increasingly indistinguishable from Stalinism in the Soviet Union. They rallied to the liberal wing of the Party and argued for reforms during inter-Party debates. They were appalled by the rejection of glasnost and perestroika in 1985. And when the protests of 1989 came to a climax in the gigantic demonstration of November 4, they joined the crowd calling for a peaceful revolution. By then, they had come to identify with the authors whose works they had to censor, and they saw their own work as aimed against their ultimate superiors—the leading members of the Central Committee, known in the censorship office as "them."

I had heard a lot of talk about "them" before. Everyone I met from the administration of the old regime had struggled against "them" as an undercover liberal within the Communist Party. If I had had the opportunity to interview Honecker about what went wrong, I am sure he would have answered "them." But Herr Wesener and Frau Horn did not seem to be especially intent on justifying themselves. They were trying to explain how they did their job and how censorship operated in the GDR until its abolition only six months ago. Far from challenging the system, they accepted its basic premises and did everything they could to make it work. But what were those premises?

"Planning," said Herr Wesener. In a socialist society, literature had to be planned, like everything else. He handed me a copy of the current plan lying on his desk. It was an extraordinary document, seventy-eight pages long, entitled, "Thematic Plan, 1990: Literature of the GDR." It listed every work of fiction that was to appear in East Germany in 1990, and it was accompanied by an even more interesting document, a "thematic plan evaluation" *(Themenplaneinschätzung)*, which provided a general account of the year's fiction for the consideration and approval of the Central Committee. I felt a little dizzy, holding a year's output of "literature," for a year that had not yet ended, within my own two hands. To help me get my bearings, Herr Wesener and Frau Horn gave me a tour of the institutional context in which "literature" took place, and then took me through all the stages of the process that is censorship.

The organizational chart below is my version of the bureaucratic machinery in the Clara-Zetkin Strasse, which processed all East German books before the revolution. Enrich Honecker, as general secretary of the Communist Party, and Kurt Hager, as head of the Central Committee Secretariat for Ideology, set the general line of cultural policy. In principle, it passed through the Politburo and down the line of command within the government. In practice it was usually transmitted through the Cultural Division of the Central Committee to the Publishing and Book Trade Administration in the Ministry of Culture, and Honecker and Hager often intervened directly in the work of the literary bureaucrats. The Publishing and Book Trade Administration consisted of four divisions. Two of them concerned the economic aspects of literature: the allotment of paper and printing facilities, subsidies, pricing; and the general supervision of publishers and booksellers. The other two concentrated on the supervision of the literature itself, one specializing in nonfiction and one primarily in fiction. The fiction division was split into five sectors, one of which handled current East German literature. Frau Horn ran it, working with

THE CONTROL MECHANISM
FOR LITERATURE IN THE GDR

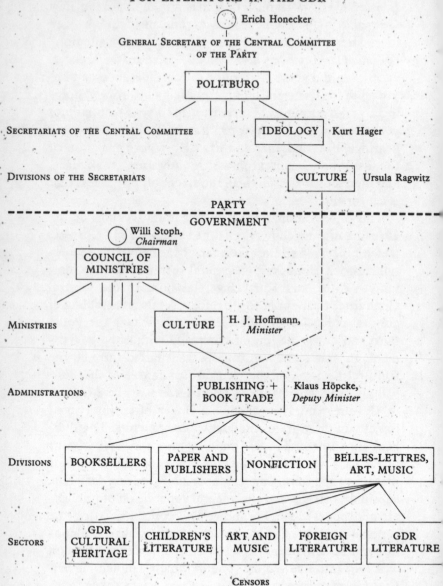

◯ Erich Honecker

GENERAL SECRETARY OF THE CENTRAL COMMITTEE
OF THE PARTY

POLITBURO

SECRETARIATS OF THE CENTRAL COMMITTEE   IDEOLOGY Kurt Hager

DIVISIONS OF THE SECRETARIATS   CULTURE Ursula Ragwitz

PARTY
GOVERNMENT

◯ Willi Stoph,
Chairman

COUNCIL OF
MINISTRIES

MINISTRIES   CULTURE H. J. Hoffmann,
Minister

ADMINISTRATIONS   PUBLISHING +
BOOK TRADE Klaus Höpcke,
Deputy Minister

DIVISIONS BOOKSELLERS | PAPER AND PUBLISHERS | NONFICTION | BELLES-LETTRES, ART, MUSIC

SECTORS GDR CULTURAL HERITAGE | CHILDREN'S LITERATURE | ART AND MUSIC | FOREIGN LITERATURE | GDR LITERATURE

CENSORS

five other specialists *(Mitarbeiter),* whose functions included censoring. Herr Wesener directed a similar team in
the sector of foreign literature.

It may be that some books began as a twinkle in an
author's eye. But in the GDR many were commissioned by
the Ministry of Culture, and many were arranged by contract between publishers and authors. About two years
before a publisher expected to put out a book, he would
submit a project for it to the Publishing and Book Trade
Administration. In one of the offices at Clara-Zetlin street,
an employee located at the bottom of the organizational
chart would reduce the project to an index card. Herr
Wesener had thousands of the cards in his files. He pulled
one out, a printed form on cheap, gray paper with twenty-
one rubrics: publisher, author, title, press run, and so on,
all of them squeezed onto a surface 14 centimeters long
and ten centimeters high. Someone had filled in the rele-
vant information and, on the back, had written a short
paragraph about the general nature of the book—a translation of a volume of lyrics by the Czech poet Lubomír
Feldek, which was proposed for publication in 1990:

> Thanks to his ironic and laconic verses, the author has
> made a name for himself beyond the limits of the Czech
> language. He is a sensitive observer of social processes,
> which he is able to evaluate from a committed point of
> view. This would be his first appearance in the GDR.

Once it had accumulated a year's worth of dossiers and
index cards, the office began to prepare a plan. The leader
of each sector would bring together representatives of the
Writers' League (Schriftstellerverband), publishing
houses, book stores, libraries, universities, and the Ministry of Culture in a committee known as the LAG
(Literaturarbeitsgemeinschaft) in the case of the fiction

sector. The LAG would approve every book proposal, rather as an editorial board does for publishing houses in the West, except that it spoke for all segments of the literary industry and had a sharp eye for ideological issues.

Back in their offices, Frau Horn and Herr Wesener would incorporate the committee's decisions and its general observations into drafts for the plan. The plan itself was an important, secret document, which went before the Central Committee. It had to be prepared with care, by means of consultations among the specialists in all the sections and mutual criticism of drafts. In the end, the plan was the responsibility of the deputy minister for publishing and the book trade, Klaus Höpcke. Höpcke had to defend it before the Cultural Division of the Central Committee and anyone else in the Party, from Honecker on down, who might be offended by a book.

The Party's Cultural Division consisted of about fifteen ideologists directed by Ursula Ragwitz, who, I gathered, was something of a dragon. Once a year, Höpcke would take the plan from each of his five sectors and march over to "Culture" in the Central Committee, where he would do battle with Frau Ragwitz. The censors could not tell me how much blood was shed in these encounters. All they knew was that Herr Höpcke would return with decisions, always verbal and never with any accompanying explanation: Stefan Heym is out next year; Volker Braun is in, but only with an edition of 10,000; Christa Wolf stays, but only with a reprint of a work that appeared in West Germany last year.

Herr Wesener and Frau Horn then had to relay the decision back to the publishers. "This was the hardest part," Herr Wesener explained, "because we could never give any reasons, when there was trouble with a book. All we could say was 'Das ist so.' 'That is what they decided.'" There were ways of getting around "them," how-

ever. When the Central Committee put off an edition of
Doctor Zhivago, the staff at Clara-Zetkin Strasse came
back with a report that a complete edition of Pasternak's
works was about to be published in West Germany. In
order to protect the GDR market from clandestine im-
ports, they persuaded the Committee to permit *Zhivago*
right away. They always left about forty places in the plan
for GDR fiction free, so that they could squeeze in late
proposals and have some room for improvisation. If they
knew a book would be "hot" ("hot" was a catchword used
in the office in opposition to "quiet"), they left it out of the
plan and slipped it in afterward. Of course, they always
had to get clearance from someone in the Central Committee. But they could take late proposals to individual
members and thus avoid the group dynamics in which the
members of the Cultural Division tried to outdo one another in demonstrating their militancy by turning down
books.

Finally, with Klaus Höpcke's help, they got to know
some of the quirks of Frau Ragwitz and her group. They
phrased the plan in a way that would flatter the preferences of certain individuals while avoiding their "aller-
gies"—for example, the unacceptable terms mentioned by
Frau Horn, "critical" and "ecological." Their basic technique was to hide difficult books in a mass of unprob-
lematic ones and to disguise the difficulties by neutral
wording. Although the ideologues in the Cultural Division
were wise to such tricks, they could not easily spot
unorthodoxies in a document containing hundreds of plot
synopses and thematic overviews.

When a particularly difficult proposal came to her office, Frau Horn would draft its entry for the plan herself,
after consulting several veteran co-workers. They would
begin with the question, "How much heat can we permit
in the plan?" If a book looked too explosive for the current

climate of opinion, they would postpone it for a year or two. "Let some grass grow first," they would say to one another. But after putting their heads together, they usually came up with a formula that seemed likely to get past Frau Ragwitz, who in the long run desired nothing more than "quiet" herself. Newcomers could not be entrusted with "hot" items. It normally took them two years to learn the ropes—and above all to master the basic principle of the GDR bureaucracy: always keep your mind fixed on the positions above you in the pyramid, and always bend with the force of centralization.

I began to think that Frau Horn spent more time censoring the documents produced in her office than the books themselves. But she assured me that she also blue-penciled literary texts. Once the project for a book had been incorporated in the plan and the plan had been approved by the Central Committee, she notified the publisher, who notified the author, who completed the text. The publisher then sent the text to another writer or literary scholar for a critical review, and produced a report of his own. Both reports came to her office along with the final draft of the book, and she kept them on file in case there should be a difficulty anywhere within the Central Committee, which could demand to see the text and the surrounding documentation at any time. At that point she began to exercise censorship in the strict sense of the term—a line-by-line vetting of a finished work.

How did a censor go over a novel or a collection of essays? Did she tick off items from a questionnaire or work from an established protocol? Frau Horn explained that she paid special attention to certain "sensitive points," such as defense, protest movements, church dissidents, and references to the Soviet Union. She never allowed statistics about environmental conditions or provocative references to the Berlin Wall. But she no longer worried about topics like crime and alcoholism, which used to be taboo, because such things were deemed to be nonexistent in a socialist society. In general, she went by her instinct: censorship was a matter of *Fingerspitzengefühl* (tact and sensitivity).

It also seemed to be matter of protecting one's own skin, although the censors described it as if it were above all an attempt by them to promote freedom by taking liberties wherever the system left them some room to maneuver. When asked if they could get burned by permitting something too hot, they explained that their procedures had built-in safeguards. They could justify their decisions by the reports they received from the publishers; they diluted their responsibility by spreading it out among their colleagues; and they were always covered by their boss, Klaus Höpcke.

They also covered him. They understood the pressures on his office, which served as a funnel for all the books produced in the GDR each year. If the Central Committee was unhappy with what went on in the office, it did not need to punish Höpcke personally. It could cut his allotment of paper. Paper was scarce in East Germany, and he had to find enough of it to supply the entire book trade, despite the competing claims of newspapers, magazines, and many other industries. Because they sympathized with Höpcke's endless struggle for paper, the censors tried to help by keeping things quiet and by diverting the noise away from him. On a few occasions, they even approved difficult texts without informing him, so that he could plead ignorance if he were summoned before the Central Committee. Herr Wesener signed the authorization to print Christoph Hein's outspoken novel, *Der Tangospieler,* and kept the decision to himself, in order to provide his boss with what was known in Watergate Washington as deniability.

Höpcke seems to have been something of a hero to his inferiors and also to many of the publishers and writers whom I met in East Germany. They described him as a hard-boiled, hard-line journalist who took over the Publishing and Book Trade Administration in 1973 with the worst possible ideas about imposing order on intellectual life. But the more time he spent battling the Party bureaucracy, the more sympathy he developed for independent-minded authors. By the 1980s, he had become an expert at slipping unorthodox books past the Central Committee. Two of them nearly cost him his job. Günter de Bruyn's outspoken novel, *Die neue Herrlichkeit*, caused so much offense at the top of the Party that it had to be withdrawn from bookstores and pulped—only to be reprinted with Höpcke's blessing once things had quieted down. *Hinze-Kunze-Roman* by Volker Braun produced an even greater scandal, because it dealt with the relationship between a high Party member and his chauffeur. Höpcke had tried to smoothe its way by phoning his friends in the press and warning them to soft-pedal its attack on apparatchik privileges. He even wrote a review of it himself. But it was denounced within the Central Committee as an "intellectual bomb." Höpcke was called on the carpet and given a formal censure. He managed nonetheless to hold on to his position by taking the blame and bending with the wind. And a few years later, at a meeting of the East German PEN organization in February 1989, he supported a resolution condemning the arrest of Václav Havel in Czechoslovakia.

Höpcke's courage won so much respect among some East German authors that in the debate about censorship in the Writers Congress of 1987, both sides claimed him as one of their own—a "partner," as several of them put it, rather than an opponent of literature. They simply disagreed on what literature was, or should be. To Hermann

Kant, the president of the Writers' League and a member
of the Central Committee, literature was a social system,
involving the Party, the Ministry of Culture, publishers,
booksellers, reviewers, and all the other institutions me-
diating communication between writers and readers. To
Christoph Hein, it ought to be a writer–reader affair, and
the intermediary bodies impeded communication: they
were so many instances of literature "behind closed
doors"—or, in a word, censorship.

To the actual censors, people like Herr Wesener and
Frau Horn, the "closed door" variety of literature belonged to their daily work. And no one made it work better, in their opinion, than Klaus Höpcke. He operated
within the intersecting circles of politics and culture,
where everyone knew everyone else. If he thought a book
might cause a scandal, he prepared its reception by well-
placed phone calls to his former cronies in the press. Book
reviewing hardly existed in the GDR, but books were
mentioned in newspapers and sometimes on the radio or
television. Höpcke knew how to determine the *way* they
were mentioned, and to keep them from being mentioned
at all. He could do wonders over drinks or dinner in apartments (the political elite knew better than to meet in restaurants, where the walls might contain listening devices
and the waiters might be agents of the Stasi). It was a
matter of knowing how to "speak through the flowers"
(durch die Blumen reden), a game of suggestions and in-
nuendos, which everyone knew how to play, because
everyone had an interest in keeping it going, even the
members of the Central Committee.

The game proceeded smoothly as long as the players
could keep it to themselves. Occasionally, however, there
was outside interference, usually in the form of an article
in the Western press about some heresy that everyone in
the East had managed not to see. Then the Central Com-

mittee had to sit up and take notice; Höpcke had to take action; and the book had to be pulped or the author expelled from the Writers' League, as happened to Stefan Heym and a half dozen others in 1979. But no one would be sent to a prison camp. In fact, there was even a play element in the repression. When the Stasi mounted a twenty-four–hour watch outside Stefan Heym's house, he brought a tray of coffee to them in their trucks.

The game also worked because the players constantly changed places. A top censor in the Publishing and Book Trade Administration often became a director of a publishing house or a journal or even turned into an author and an officer in the Writers' League. The career of the current minister of culture, Herbert Schirmer, typified the way paths crossed within the cultural-political elite. He began as a bookseller, took up cultural journalism, shifted to a publishing house, worked for a while as a free-lance critic and writer, moved into museum administration, and finally, having cultivated the right people in the Christian Democratic party, rose through regional politics to the top position in the Ministry of Culture in the coalition government formed by the CDU in March 1990. Of course, the Communist Party determined the pattern of all such careers before the revolution. But the patterns have survived the change of regime. The bureaucracy is still in place, and most of the bureaucrats are still at their desks, including Christina Horn and Hans-Jürgen Wesener. They no longer censor books, but they oversee literature, working with publishers and worrying about the onset of the open market.

Open markets have constraints of their own, of course. GDR authors often speak of "censorship" when they describe the commercialization of literature in Western systems driven by the profit motive. In their view, the publisher is the censor, and he desires nothing more than to suppress good literature in order to get rich on trash. Planning looks more rational to them, not merely as a way of allocating resources but as an agency of *Bildung* (cultivation). To its defenders, therefore, the literary system of the GDR derived its strength from what they took to be the good, old-fashioned, Prussian qualities of culture and thoroughness. Those were precisely the qualities that made it so oppressive, in my view. By mixing socialist doctrine with the Prussian bureaucracy, the East Germans had created a perfect system for stifling literature while at the same time persuading themselves that they were stimulating it.

But then I was an outsider. Perhaps it was impossible for me to get inside the censor's way of understanding censorship. As I walked away from the Clara-Zetkin Strasse, it seemed to me that there was no escape from the system for someone who accepted its premises. Planning and Prussianism left little room for maneuver. But well-intentioned bureaucrats like Herr Wesener and Frau Horn made the most of what there was, and they succeeded in getting some remarkable books to readers. In fact, there was not one system, but two: a formal structure, where planning ruled supreme, and a human network, where people bent the rules. I knew which I preferred, but I also realized that nothing was simple in that strange world on the other side of the Wall.

THE REVOLUTION
IN A VILLAGE

I t's not quite true that there is nothing to do on a Saturday night in Laucha. The village has two pubs. But
one of them, a *Ratskeller* under the sixteenth-century
town hall, doesn't get many customers. It is a state-
run operation, and the state—a remote presence mediated
through municipal, district, and regional councils—had
the bad judgment to hire an outsider as bartender. He
slams the beer mugs on the tables, complaining loudly
about being forced to work in a hick town where there isn't
so much as a movie house. The other pub is only a room in
a boarding house on the edge of town, and it is monopolized by a few old men who play cards.

If you must have some excitement, you can take a bus to
Naumburg, fifteen miles south. Naumburg has cafés, beer
served from stands in the marketplace, and even a few
skinheads. To the north lies Halle, the capital of the region *(Bezirk)* and a far-off, wicked city in the eyes of the
people in Laucha. Laucha itself is a sleepy little town,
quite typical of village life in the GDR: population 3,000,
two policemen, one baker, two butchers, a state-run general store, and a privately owned grocery. Most of its
inhabitants work in a nearby cement factory, in a food-
processing plant, or in the cooperative farms in the surrounding country. On Saturday nights, they stay home,
drinking beer and watching television.

They do not go to church on Sunday mornings. The
church itself is an imposing structure from the fifteenth
century, when Laucha was a prosperous farming and market town, far more important than it is today. The
church's spire still dominates the village, and its bell
strikes off the hours, a reminder of better days, when Laucha had one of the few bell-casting foundries of northern
Germany. But its roof leaks; the plaster is flaking off the
walls; and it remains damp and cold through most of the
year. When the faithful attend service—twenty or thirty
persons, most of them old women clustered together in the
front pews—they seem to be crushed by the emptiness of
the building and the weight of the past. From October to
June, they meet in a cheerier, well-heated room in the
vicarage.

Laucha's pastor, Christoph Müller, does not consider
services in the vicarage as anything more than a strategic
retreat from the building he hopes to fill someday. He has
seen it full twice, on October 22 and November 5, when
the church served as the center of the revolution in the
village.

"Revolution" may not be the appropriate term, for

there was no dramatic change in Laucha's power structure during the autumn of 1989. Laucha hardly has enough power to be structured. Like all municipalities in the GDR, it is ruled from Berlin. It has a mayor, a town council, and six municipal employees. But it doesn't raise its own taxes or determine how it will spend the money that dribbles down to it from the central government. The mayor, Helmut Lauterbach, dribbled down himself—no one is quite sure how. He arrived at Laucha's *Rathaus* two years ago, a *Diktat* imposed on the villagers from Berlin. He was elected, of course, but the people of Laucha have developed a jaundiced view of elections. On election day, they say, "I am going to fold, not to vote" ("Ich gehe falten, nicht wählen"), meaning they will check the names on the ballot, fold it, and put it in the ballot box without any illusion that they are participating in a democratic process.

The ballots carry nineteen names for the nineteen part-time town councilors, who in turn select one of themselves as mayor. All the candidates are chosen beforehand by the Communist Party (SED) and the puppet "bloc parties." None of them is opposed. A good Communist puts an x in the box next to each of the names on the ballot without bothering to use the voting booth in the corner of the room. Less-than-perfect Communists may enter the booth and strike names off the ballot; but if they do so, they know that their own names will go down in the files of the secret police, thanks to the Stasi observers posted near the booths. Nonetheless, at the election held in May 1989, many people strode bravely into the booths and struck off Herr Lauterbach's name. That did not prevent him from being elected by a thumping majority, of course, but it confirmed the common conviction that elections are rigged.

It also predisposed people to respond when the atmosphere changed throughout the GDR last autumn. The strongest response came from one of the mildest citizens of Laucha, the pastor's wife, Annemarie Müller. Frau Müller never had the slightest interest in politics before September 1989. After marrying Herr Müller twenty-seven years ago, she devoted herself entirely to her family and the Church. All three of her sisters also married pastors. They had grown up in a strict, Lutheran household, where in the evening they would pray together over *Abendbrot* (a light meal, commonly composed of soup, bread, and sausage) and read the Bible. The father, a fairly prosperous farmer, made sure they received a good education. Annemarie studied theology at Naumburg with the intention of becoming a pastor herself. But then she met Christoph and gave up her vocation in order to marry him. The Church did not allow married women into the priesthood until the 1970s, when the number of pastors declined so drastically that it needed to fill hundreds of parishes. By then Frau Müller had four children. While raising them and working part-time with the elderly in her husband's parish, she took correspondence courses and finally was ordained in 1985.

Now Frau Müller serves as the pastor in four small villages in the farm country surrounding Laucha. She goes from church to church in an old Trabi. A typical Sunday service involves only four or five old women—no choir, no organ, no sermon, really, but rather a conversation about the ways of God and man before the celebration of the sacrament and a hymn intoned by a few scratchy voices. A burial will bring out fifty people, but Frau Müller knows she is not reaching much of the population. She rarely meets young people, except by chance when she calls on an ailing grandparent. It is not that Marxism has conquered the younger generation, but rather that the entire society, down to the smallest village, has been secularized.

Such, at least, is Frau Müller's view. She does not see herself as locked in a fight to the death with the government. On the contrary, she accepts the position adopted by the General Synod, known as "the Church in social-ism," which allows the clergy to voice criticism without fundamentally challenging the socialist order—but which does not fill the churches on Sundays.

The churches filled to overflowing in the autumn of 1989, however, and Frau Müller found herself leading something that looked like a revolution. It all began at a special service held by all the clergy of the district *(Kreis)* in the town of Freyburg, seven miles from Laucha, on September 17. As often happens in the GDR, the service ended with some general prayers in which members of the congregation come forward and ask for divine intercession in difficulties faced by the entire group. But this time the prayers were political. The congregation, led in some cases by distraught young children, asked for the opening of the GDR's borders, the right to travel, and the release of imprisoned dissidents. Taken aback by this welling-up of political consciousness, one of the pastors suggested that all interested parties meet on the following Sunday in the priory of Thalwinkel, a neighboring village.

Twenty-two people turned up, an impressive number in view of the fact that political meetings were considered to be illegal at that time. Everyone present wanted to get information about "citizens' initiative groups," quasi-underground organizations that were said to be spreading throughout the country. Frau Müller had learned about one of these groups during a visit to a sister in Halle, and she circulated copies of a statement—crudely typed and mimeographed on ratty paper—which described its aims:

We are forming a political arena for the entire GDR. In it, citizens from all walks of life, occupations, parties, and

groups will be able to participate in the discussion of this
country's most vital social problems. To identify this general initiative, we have chosen the name

New Forum.

We call upon all citizens of the GDR who want to collaborate in the alteration of our society to become members of
NEW FORUM.

The manifesto did not make specific political demands.
It did not need to. To call for a general discussion of social
problems was in itself seditious in September 1989. By distributing such material, Frau Müller took a step in the
direction of a revolution and became a founder of New
Forum in her area.

She did not do so all at once, however, and her fellow
pastors did not provide unanimous support. In addition to
her husband, only three of the ten pastors in the region
(Bezirk) were willing to collaborate with her. They met in
different vicarages each week, reinforced by friends and
sympathizers. At first they included only the core of the
regular congregations, but then the group was joined by
ordinary citizens who were fed up with the government—
workers from the cement factory, technicians from small
industries, nurses, sales clerks, auto repairmen, electri-
cians, some farmers, and a few teachers. Twenty-two
people turned up for the meeting on September 24,
forty-three on October 8, and after that more than Frau
Müller could count.

When the group could no longer fit into the community
rooms of the vicarages, the Müllers invited it to meet inside the church at Laucha. They did not make a public
announcement of the meeting, but news of it spread by
word of mouth; and when it began, at 8:00 P.M. on October
22, for the first time in their lives the Müllers saw their

church full. The pews were crammed with 600 people, all of them angry. Herr Müller opened the discussion by asking everyone to remain calm and to speak their minds frankly—after giving their names and place of residence. People in the GDR do not like to identify themselves publicly. They assume that any public meeting will be infiltrated by undercover agents of the Stasi, and they are especially timid in Laucha, where "civic courage is not a strong point," according to Herr Müller. But once the villagers began to speak out, he found it difficult to restrain them. One person after another rose to his feet and denounced the domination of the village by the Communist Party. "The Communists up there are devouring our substance" (Die Kommunisten da oben fressen uns weg) was the main theme of the remarks, as the Müllers later reported them. Several speakers also deplored the deterioration of the local economy and environment. (Some of them work in the Buna chemical factory near Halle, one of the worst pollutants in the GDR.) After two hours of heated discussion, the meeting ended with common prayers, many of them political. A large number of the protestors lit candles as they walked out of the church. They marched to the town hall nearby, left the candles blazing on its steps, and returned quietly to their homes.

In its form, the protest meeting followed the model that had been developed a few weeks earlier in Leipzig: prayers in the church and a candlelight procession in the streets. The clergy took the lead in calling for an avoidance of violence, and the town's two policemen stayed out of sight. By the time it reached Laucha, the Leipzig model had proved its effectiveness, for the authorities had backed away from their threat to crush the demonstration in Leipzig on October 9; similar demonstrations had occurred without bloodshed in several other cities, and so the Müllers did not expect a miniature Tiananmen Square

to explode in their village. They remained worried, nonetheless, because the political temperature continued to
rise. It neared the boiling point on November 4, when
almost a million people took to the streets in East Berlin.
On the following day, far away in the deep south of the
GDR, the citizens of Laucha gathered for the largest
meeting that had ever occurred in their town.

This time the church could not contain the crowd. The
protestors spilled out into the main square and listened to
the speeches from a loudspeaker system that had been
rigged up from the chancel. Uncertain about how to react,
the mayor and his duo of policemen decided to remain
invisible. The authorities in Nebra, the administrative
center of the district, dispatched a paddy wagon full of
police, but it stayed at a safe distance; and once again the
meeting proceeded peacefully. There were more angry
speeches, more calls for free elections and the right to free
travel, and another candelight procession.

On November 6, Herr Müller was summoned to appear
before the district president at Nebra. The president read
him a lecture about the need to maintain order and objected to the inflammatory language used at the meeting.
To drive the point home, he quoted some of the protestors' remarks, word for word. Herr Müller was taken
aback but not completely surprised, because he had assumed there were Stasi agents in the crowd. He replied
that he could not control the mood of the people and that
it had to have an outlet. In retrospect, he said he found the
district president and the mayor of Laucha to be surprisingly conciliatory—as if they sensed that power was already beginning to shift and they felt more threatened
than he did.

The decisive shift occurred three days later, when the
Wall was opened in Berlin. Despite their geographical and
cultural distance from the capital, the people of Laucha

followed the events of November 9–12 on radio and television and drew the appropriate conclusion: the GDR could no longer be run as a police state. Once authority had collapsed at the center, they were able to seize control of their affairs at the periphery.

By this time, Frau Müller had come a long way in organizing a local chapter of New Forum. She, too, had to be discreet. A Stasi agent lived just across the street, and she knew her phone was tapped. Pastors always had tapped phones and spies in their congregations. "We decided not to be afraid long ago," she explained to me two months later. "They can get you when they want, and you can't live your whole life in worry." Besides, the system had already meted out some of its most effective punishments in the indirect, nonviolent manner typical of the GDR. None of the four Müller children had been admitted to a university, although all of them had done well in school. The sons and daughters of pastors are often excluded from higher education in East Germany. They belong to a special category, the *Sonderlinge* (peculiar), which is subject to a highly restrictive admissions quota, unlike the children of workers and farmers. Within Laucha itself, all the Müllers remained *Sonderlinge,* cut off from the rest of the population by an invisible barrier of fear.

Not that the town is run by terror. Everyone knows that real power is concentrated in the Communist Party, especially at the district and regional level, and in the Stasi, which has six agents in the district as well as an undetermined number of paid informers. But no one worries about being carried off to a Gulag Archipelago. The only person who recently disappeared is a drunk, who received a year and a half in prison for painting a swastika on a wall. Nonetheless, the villagers avoid contact with the pastor. They say hello to him in the bakery or post office, but they do not invite him into their homes, and very few of them attend church.

It must be said that Herr Müller looks somewhat severe, if not forbidding, and he occupies a highly visible position in Laucha. As the only public figure in the only independent institution of the town, he stands out in opposition to Herr Lauterbach and the *Rathaus*. But Frau Müller is a warm, engaging person with a ready smile, soft blue eyes, and hair swept up in a bun, which gives her a grandmotherly appearance, although she is only fifty-one. (Women in the GDR often look ten years older than their counterparts in West Germany, where cosmetics are a major industry, hair is commonly dyed, and middle-class faces are often *gelifted*.)

In late October, Frau Müller began sounding out some friends in the village about the possibility of founding a chapter of New Forum. Her sister in Halle provided her with more information, including another crudely mimeographed circular entitled *Neuesforum* (no. 1, 1989), which described the character and goals of the organization. It explained that New Forum was founded at a meeting of thirty dissidents at Grünheide on September 9–10. They did not intend to create a political party or an underground resistance movement, but rather to take advantage of provisions in the GDR constitution in order to open up "a legal, political field of activity." In practice, this meant forming local groups that would develop their own programs and exert pressure on their town and district councils. As the circular explained,

We have no offices, no telephones. . . . We do not want to have a centralized structure. The local groups [*Basisgruppen*] should be as independent as possible. They should be formed in neighborhoods, . . . where people can get to know one another and decide what concerns them most, both in local and national politics. People should get together who have common interests, such as public education, the economy, or the environment. But they should not form elite groups. They should not create closed circles of specialists who prescribe what is to be done for the rest of the population.

This sounded good to Frau Müller. She liked the emphasis on democratic decentralization, local initiative, and action. For the handout insisted that New Forum was no discussion club. As an example of what the local chapters could attempt to do, it urged them to stage demonstrations before their town halls and to demand an investigation of the last local elections. Frau Müller saw a perfect target in Herr Lauterbach and the *Rathaus* standing diagonally across from the church in Laucha's main square.

At the next demonstration, on November 19, she invited everyone interested in founding a chapter of New Forum to attend a meeting in the vicarage. By this time the opening of the Wall and the collapse of the Council of Ministers and the Politburo in Berlin had made the villagers ready to stop demonstrating and start organizing. But they did not want to create an elaborate structure. Instead of electing a president and a slate of officers, they chose a council *(Sprecherrat)* and split up into small groups, where they discussed electoral, economic, and environmental questions. The group discussions led nowhere, however. At the end of the year, Laucha's New Forum consisted of only a dozen activists, half of them women. They included a cook, two teachers, a biologist, a pastor, a secretary, a mechanic, a cemetery custodian, a truck driver, a laboratory technician, a carpenter, and an apprentice. Everyone else seemed to be too worried about the economic situation to become involved in politics.

Nevertheless, the twelve set to work, reading up on the legalities of local government and discussing ways to make the most of the election issue. Since December 7, New Forum in Berlin had joined other citizens' groups and forced the government to negotiate with it at a Round Table. Other Round Tables sprang up in district centers and town halls throughout the country. So Frau Müller and her colleagues demanded one for Laucha. On January 8, for the first time, they confronted Herr Lauterbach at a round table in the *Rathaus*. According to the minutes posted outside the House of the Young Pioneers (a Communist youth group), they had begun with a general indictment: "Confidence in the work of the town council has been damaged." Then they demanded to know what the town's budget was and what last year's expenditures had been. No one had ever seen a municipal budget in Laucha. The mayor considered it his own business, but he bent with the wind: he was on the side of the citizens, he replied, and would gladly keep them informed. After a great deal more talk—accompanied by a stony silence from the representative of the SED (Communist Party)—all the participants of the Round Table agreed to continue their discussions at another meeting two weeks later. Meanwhile, Frau Müller and her friends began to prepare for the local elections, which were only four months away, and the Stasi agent who lived across the road from the Müllers decided to take early retirement.

Such was the "revolution" that had occurred in Laucha by mid-January, when I arrived for a brief visit. It was not a spectacular affair. No bloodshed, no storming of citadels, no transformation of a power structure. Its well-mannered demonstrations, miniature New Forum, and modest Round Table make it look like a Lilliputian version of the great *Wende* that had swept through the rest of the country. Everything arrived in Laucha two or three weeks late. Everything passed through intermediate stages in Halle or Leipzig or Freyburg. Even communications from New Forum in Berlin were relayed in a haphazard manner by means of personal contacts. New Forum itself rejected everything that smacked of centralization or of a clearly articulated structure. As an organization, it resembled the committees of correspondence of the American Revolution more than the Jacobin Clubs of France. But it hardly had an organization at all. It merely provided an occasion for people like Annemarie Müller to find their voice.

When Frau Müller spoke out, she used the gentlest tones, in language befitting a "peaceful revolution" *(friedliche Revolution),* as the people of the GDR like to describe it. But she stood her ground; and when the municipal election takes place, it seems likely that she will drive Herr Lauterbach from the *Rathaus.* If so, can one speak of a "revolution" in Laucha? The word is so overused these days—we have "revolutions" in women's wear and in the tactics of football—that it has nearly lost its meaning. But a significant shift of power occurred at the village level in Laucha, even if it was determined from outside and if it did not produce an immediate upheaval in the town hall. It had to do more with the way people think than with the power that comes out the barrel of a gun. But collective attitudes, or *mentalités* as the French call them, have a power of their own, the sort of thing that expresses itself in everyday behavior in the street. After November, Herr Müller found that people no longer crossed to the other side of the road when they saw him coming. They greeted him openly and engaged him in

conversation, and Frau Müller found herself talking about
village affairs in homes that had been closed to her before
the opening of the Wall. Doors and walls opening everywhere—that is what happened in Laucha. Fresh air in
place of fear.

PART IV

"WE ARE ONE PEOPLE"

INVENTING POLITICS

February 2, 1990

The revolution in East Germany has had so many turning points that it makes the head spin, but the turn taken at the end of January seems to be decisive. Prime Minister Hans Modrow advanced the date of the parliamentary elections to March 18 and announced that until then the government would be run by a coalition of all the major political parties. The Communist Party (SED) has renounced its monopoly on power in fact as well as in principle, and it did so with the blessing of Mikhail Gorbachev, who not only endorsed Modrow's moves during a hurried meeting in Moscow but also gave qualified support to the prospect of German reunification.

To many outside the GDR, this turn of events will appear healthy. Modrow made it sound catastrophic. When he described the state of affairs to the East German parliament on January 29, he seemed to be announcing the end of the world. He confessed that his government could find no way to stop emigration to West Germany, which threatens to cripple key sectors of the economy. Strikes were breaking out everywhere, workers demanding impossible pay increases, the state's budget teetering toward bankruptcy, production falling, crime increasing, and local administration grinding to a halt. "Radicalization" had gone so far that all sorts of public institutions were receiving bomb threats. Fear was seizing the entire apparatus of the state, and he could not guarantee the safety of ordinary citizens. In short, the GDR stood on the brink of chaos, and it could be saved only by the formation of a "government of national responsibility," a coalition of all the major political groups, which sounded something like a Committee of Public Safety.

Modrow is not given to apocalyptic pronouncements. He has a slow, deliberate way of speaking, which makes the ponderous manner of Helmut Kohl seem light. In fact, some say that Modrow has adopted Kohl's style, although the two men look so different—Kohl could eat Modrow for breakfast—that the comparison seems ludicrous. Modrow often begins statements with long, Kohl-like windups, such as "I take it as a presupposition that. . . ." And when he delivers, his rhetoric sounds so unrhetorical that it rings true. "Here is a man of substance," those on the receiving end are supposed to say to themselves, "not a politician."

But Modrow is a politician, the only one in the GDR who enjoys both respect and visibility among the population as a whole. In only a few weeks as prime minister, he

made himself into East Germany's elder statesman. Before
the November revolution, he was relegated by the old apparatchiks to the position of first party secretary in Dresden. While they grew fat in their hunting lodges, he lived
in a modest apartment and ultimately joined in one of the
demonstrations. Then, in desperation on November 8, the
Party called on him to head the government, where he has
ruled as the embodiment of virtue and solidity, the ultimate *Spiessbürger (petit bourgeois)* in the so-called land of
workers and peasants.

The look and manner of Modrow is of more than anec-
dotal importance, because the whole country is awash
with symbolic transformation. In fact, most of the violence mentioned by Modrow has taken place on the symbolic level. The workers and peasants may be packing
their bags for resettlement in West Germany, but they are
not lobbing Molotov cocktails into town halls. As far as I
could tell during a quick visit to the GDR in early February, they were going about their business as usual, and if
anything with more spring in their step—perhaps because
of the withering away of the police or some unseasonably
springlike weather.

But there are ferociously anti-Communist graffiti everywhere. Karl-Marx-Stadt announced that it would resume
its old name, Chemnitz. The Communist Party itself is
debating another name change in the hope of expunging
its Stalinist past. Having traded in its old title, the SED
(Socialist Unity Party) for a double-barreled name, SED-
PDS (Socialist Unity Party–Democratic Socialist Party),
it now proposes to call itself simply the PDS. It also
removed its emblem—a fifteen-foot, multi-ton monstrosity showing two clasped hands—from the façade of its
headquarters in East Berlin. The operation took three
days and left an open wound on what once appeared to be

an impregnable bastion. Photographers made the most of it, especially as the insignia had been a pet project of Erich Honecker, the former Party chief.

Honecker himself has become little more than a symbol. At age seventy-seven, after three cancer operations, he looks like a dead man. He tottered out of the hospital, visibly disoriented, on the day that Modrow announced the new coalition government, and he was promptly put under arrest. In the flurry of medical bulletins and the flash of the photographers' lightbulbs, one could not avoid the impression that the surgeons were keeping him alive so that he could stand trial for corruption. Honecker has come to personify the evils of the old Party just as Modrow embodies the virtues of the new one, and the SED (or SED-PDS or PDS) needs to bury its past by condemning its former leader and his closest associates. As Hans-Jürgen Joseph, the prosecutor-general, explained to parliament, "We have a historical duty to bring to justice the main culprits for violations of the constitution, for our economic chaos, for the muzzling of the people and systematic violation of human rights." Translation: the Party needs a scapegoat.

It could hardly do better than Honecker, who occupies a peculiar place in the East German imagination. He is now hated with an intensity that can barely be imagined in the West. Turned out of his house in the luxurious colony for Party leaders in the Wandlitz section of Berlin, he has taken refuge in the rectory of a Lutheran minister in Lobetal, north of Berlin, while he awaits his trial. A Church spokesman said that it had received twenty-two threatening phone calls in one morning from people who were furious that it had given asylum to "a pig."

That is the sort of violence that Modrow deplored in his speech of January 29. He warned parliament against "growing social tensions, which the existing political structures are increasingly unable to control." But the problem resides more in the political structures themselves than in the social order. Modrow is so much a politician, however incorruptible, that he may mistake the collapse of his own party for the disintegration of society. To a man who has devoted his life to the Party in a society where the Party has monopolized all forms of politics, the end of the Party must look like the end of the world.

But the end is near, at least for what remains of the old SED. The Party's name changes are symptoms of a deep discontent within its lower ranks. When one talks with its members in private, they say that time and time again they have failed to reform it from within and are now determined to dissolve it altogether in order to create a social democratic party like those in Hungary, Poland, and Czechoslovakia—or, more to the point, West Germany.

However, the Social Democrats (SPD) of West Germany have spawned a brother party in the GDR, which is also called the SPD, and it is emerging as the most powerful new party in the entire country. In fact, so many new parties have sprung up in the GDR that one could say the East Germans are recreating politics. Instead of a system of conflicting factions within a single, leviathan party, they have produced a whole spectrum of political organizations. At least two dozen parties are fielding candidates for the March 18 election; and if one counts splinter groups, the number of players in the new political game would come to well over fifty. Indeed, the East Germans are not just playing a new round of an old game, they are inventing the game itself, with a new set of rules: that is the chaos that horrifies Modrow. The East Germans have not had any experience with a free, multiparty system since Hitler seized power in 1933. Will they be able to improvise one in time to establish an effective government after March 18?

Revolutions may open up unprecedented possibilities

for change, but they cannot wipe the slate clean and produce totally fresh beginnings. The new politics of the GDR are shaped by the situation inherited from the Communist old regime and by two other factors: relations with the Federal Republic of Germany to the west and with the Soviet Union to the east.

Consider the situation in the last week of January, when the critical turn was made. At the beginning of the week, Modrow declared that the government's authority had eroded so seriously that he needed to form an emergency coalition ministry with the nine major opposition parties. The parties had been advancing ever greater demands for a share in the government's decisions since they began negotiating with it at the Round Table in early December. Now they began to negotiate among themselves about whether they could afford to say no. At the same time, the four bloc parties who had ruled for years in collaboration with the SED began to consider whether they should leave the current ministry. Every party inside and outside the government had to weigh two basic considerations: on the one hand, the attraction of assuming power and responsibility in a moment of crisis; on the other, the danger of contamination from the Communists. The balance tipped at a different angle in different cases, depending on the particular strengths and weaknesses of each group. The bloc parties had worked hand in glove with the SED for so long that they seemed likely to be wiped out in an anti-Communist backlash at the elections. One of them, the Christian Democratic Union (CDU), announced on January 24 that it would withdraw from the government—and then withdrew its withdrawal two days later. On the same day, January 26, the opposition groups said they would accept a coalition but only under stringent conditions: Modrow and the other ministers would have to cut their alignment with the SED and turn over all the key posts to the opposition.

By January 28 Modrow had extracted a promise from the other bloc parties to remain with the SED and the CDU in his government, and he began a seven-hour marathon negotiation with the opposition parties. At midnight, they reached the crucial decision to advance the election from May 6 to March 18 and to govern the country together as a coalition until that date.

Then everyone fell to squabbling. The SPD's partners at the Round Table accused it of precipitating an early election in order to take advantage of its relatively advanced stage of organization. And the CDU lamented that its ties to the SED were depriving it of support from the Christian Democrats in West Germany. At this point, the parties' Western connections began to become crucial, owing to three main factors.

First, reunification with West Germany had emerged as the overwhelming desire of the electorate, except for a few fringe groups on the far left. Second, each of the new parties needed money and equipment, which could be legally supplied from affiliates in the West, according to a revised draft of the new electoral law. And third, the configuration of power in West Germany itself shifted after Oskar Lafontaine won a striking victory for the SPD in the state elections in the Saarland on January 28. Lafontaine is certain to lead the SPD in the general elections in West Germany in December, and he now looks like a strong threat to Hermut Kohl and the CDU. So there are really two campaigns under way, each influencing the other.

The parallels can be seen best by examining a chart of the main parties contending the elections in West and East.

BERLIN JOURNAL   228

The Main Parties in the
West and East German Elections

West Germany

Green Party
Social Democratic Party, SPD
Free Democratic Party, FDP
Christian Democratic Union, CDU
Christian Social Union, CSU (affiliated with the CDU)
Republican Party

East Germany

Communist (or Democratic Socialist) Party, SED-PDS

Christian Democratic Union, CDU ⎫
Liberal Democratic Party, LDPD   ⎬ Bloc Parties
National Democratic Party, NDPD ⎪
Farmers' Party, DBD   ⎭

Social Democratic Party, SPD   ⎫
Free Democratic Party, FDP   ⎪
Democratic Social Union, DSU   ⎪
New Forum   ⎪
German Forum Party, DFP   ⎪
Democratic Beginning, DA   ⎬ Opposition
Democracy Now   ⎪   Groups
Initiative for Peace and Human Rights ⎪
United Left   ⎪
Independent Women's League   ⎪
Green League   ⎪
Green Party   ⎭

How can so many competing and overlapping factions ever settle down into a coherent political system? A Western observer instinctively sorts them into the familiar categories of left, center, and right. But those divisions do not necessarily make sense to the East Germans. In the GDR, the Communist Party is commonly identified with the defense of the status quo or the "old regime." The four bloc

parties, which have rubber-stamped Communist directives for decades in the parliament, appear as reactionary
front organizations. And the new parties—or "groups"
and "movements" as they sometimes call themselves—do
not fit into any pre-established pattern.

New Forum, the most prominent opposition group,
identifies itself as a grass-roots movement that is neither
left nor right. An offshoot of it, the German Forum Party
(DFP), says it wants to be a "popular party of the middle."
But the middle keeps shifting, if you follow the groups
clustered around Democratic Beginning (Demokratischer
Aufbruch), another group formerly linked with New
Forum that is moving back and forth between an alliance
with the Free Democrats on the one hand and the Christian Democrats on the other.

Unclear, yes; unsettled, certainly; but not at all unim-
portant—the jockeying for position among the parties and
groups is laying the foundation for a new political order.
Of course, the landscape continues to be cluttered with
the remains of the old order. In fact, you can still hear
echoes of the 1920s in some of the political talk today. The
LDPD is considering changing its name to LDP in order
to disguise its recent past as a bloc party by evoking its
long-term origins in the Liberal Democratic Party of the
Weimar Republic. Count Otto Lambsdorff, the secretary-
general of the Free Democratic Party in West Germany,
recently said of East German politics, "It has begun like
Weimar, but it must not end like Weimar."

Lambsdorff spoke from experience, because, like the
leaders of the Western CDU, he has been combing
through the political confusion in the East in order to put
together a coalition that would strengthen his party's position in the West, and in the united Germany that lies just
over the horizon. The Social Democrats have no problem:
they have thrown all their weight behind the Social Demo-

cratic Party of East Germany, which has no compromising past as a bloc party and already seems to have taken the lead in the election campaign. But the West German FDP and CDU face the same dilemma: their sister parties (the LDPD and CDU) already exist but as partners of the Communists in the bloc-party system of the old regime, and they are competing for support among the same assortment of new political groups, whose hatred for the bloc parties seems stronger than their desire to win the election.

Victory is crucial to the older and more professional politicians in the West, however, because whatever party wins in the GDR in March is certain to improve the chances of its sister party in West Germany in December. Moreover, tension is growing between the partners in the West German government—the CDU and the FDP—and between their leaders, Chancellor Helmut Kohl and foreign minister Hans Dietrich Genscher. If no party wins a majority of seats in the Bundestag in December, the FDP might well desert the CDU and form a government with the SPD. So in searching for allies in East Germany, the CDU and the FDP are competing against one another, and the election campaign in the East has become a battlefield of the campaign in the West.

While scouting for a partner for the FDP in East Germany, Lambsdorff found that the LDPD opened its arms to him and that it offered many advantages: an organization, offices, money, newspapers, and a membership of 100,000. But its past was polluted. And the new FDP, though pure, included only about 2,000 members, all of them amateurs.

Similarly, the marriage brokers of the West CDU found the East CDU to be well endowed but tainted, while the CSU, the DA, and the DFP seemed willing to be wooed but not to cohabit with a former bloc party. In each case, the tension is concentrated in an area of the political spectrum that a Westerner would label as center-right. But Western labels may be misleading or meaningless to people in East Germany, and the entanglement of acronyms and initials is enough to bewilder anyone in the East or West. One cartoonist pictured a campaign worker painting a sign on a wall which ran:

DPSPDSPDSPDSPDSPDSPDSPDSPDSPDSPDSPD

It was a joke about the overlapping initials of the Social Democratic and formerly Communist party and the general unintelligibility of the campaign, but the Christian Democrats made the most of it by printing a variation in the form of a stop sign in their campaign literature:

By playing games with the letters, the CDU (Christian Democrats) suggested the SPD (Social Democrats) was indistinguishable from the PDS (new Communist party), which in turn was the same thing as the SED (old Communist Party)—a low blow, especially as the CDU itself could be accused of fellow-traveling with the SED.

A similar game could be played with the initials of the parties negotiating with the Free Democrats. By presenting itself as the LDP, the LDPD hopes to win the support of the FDP (West), even though the FDP has its eye on the FDP (East) and the DFP. Electioneering has turned into tongue-twisting.

Whether voters can follow it all, or care to, is another question. They may well get lost in the forest of symbols and the underbrush of party initials. Instead of worrying about the new politics in the East, many continue to climb into their Trabis and drive west, voting with their wheels. The statistical count varies, but it came to about 400,000 last year; and unless the political and economic situation improves, it may well reach a million in 1990—a vital 6 percent of the population, since the emigrants are mainly young and skilled. Unification is becoming a *fait accompli* by the interpenetration of the political parties and the emigration of the East German population.

It remains a crucial question of principle, nonetheless, because the relations of East and West Germany are embedded in the relations of the Eastern and Western powers. Therefore, as soon as he had announced the formation of his emergency coalition, Modrow flew off to Moscow. Here, too, his *Spiessbürger* bearing may have done him service. He arrived on Gorbachev's doorstep looking earnest and exhausted and clutching his briefcase like a messenger boy. Nothing could have been further from the Soviet caricature of the West German as a fascist-revanchist-man-eating monster. Gorbachev then made the pronouncement: German unification was not in itself objectionable. It was a question that "history would decide." Gorbachev had made a similar remark to Richard Weizsäcker, the president of West Germany, three years before, giving history "a hundred years" to make up its mind. Now he declared that it was about to take its decision, which meant in effect that his own mind was made up.

Gorbachev's benediction may save the East German
Communists from a disaster in the election, because they
were the only important party that had not rallied to the
cause of unification, which is the most popular cause in all
the other platforms. On February 1, therefore, Modrow
was able to announce his own plan for a "united German
fatherland" (*Deutschland einig Vaterland,* a phrase stolen
from the opposition demonstrations). In some points, it
coincided with the ten-step plan proposed by Chancellor
Kohl last December, but in one respect it had a curious
resemblance to a proposal made by Stalin in 1952: a united
Germany would be established as a neutral power, with its
present boundaries, in the midst of Europe.

The same proposal twenty-eight years later had a completely different meaning, for the context had changed,
and meaning in politics as in poetry depends on context as
much as content. No one, Modrow included, expects West
Germany to withdraw from NATO. But everyone understood that Modrow, Gorbachev, and Communists everywhere had now accepted the inevitability of German
reunification.

Will that be enough to rescue the Communists on
March 18? No one can say, because history is moving
faster every day, and it has plenty of time to change its
mind in the next six weeks.

CAMPAIGN TRAILS

March 3, 1990

Now that the East German politicians are rounding the bend for the last dash to the election on March 18, they sometimes ask a puzzling question: Whatever happened to New Forum? The movement that precipitated the revolution in October, and that looked like an East German version of Solidarity in November, was nowhere to be seen by the end of February. The latest polls give it 3 percent of the vote as against 53 percent for the Social Democratic Party (SPD), 13 percent for the Christian Democratic Union (CDU), and 12 percent for the former Communist Party (PDS). What went wrong?

The answer to that question is the story of the East
German revolution itself, which began as a popular uprising against a Stalinistic regime and now is settling down to
party politics, Western-style. Although New Forum is
running a slate of candidates, it insists it is a "citizens'
movement," not a party. Either way, it has been squeezed
out of its leading role by the course of events.

The difficulties of New Forum could be read in the
faces of the delegates to its campaign convention in
Schwerin on February 23. They looked like a group of
college professors attending a convention of the Modern
Language Association—except that there were so few of
them: barely a thousand bunched into one end of a hall
that held 8,000. They did not raise hell. They did not even
raise their voices. They addressed their head candidate,
Jens Reich, a very nice molecular biologist from East Berlin, as "Herr Professor."

The convention consisted of nothing but speeches and a
modest supply of campaign literature—poorly mimeographed handouts distributed from three card tables near
the entrance to the hall. There were no other props—no
videos, no photographs, no glamorous public figures, no
posters, no campaign buttons, no slogans, no bunting,
no funny hats or fol-de-rol of any kind. New Forum has
trimmed off its radical fringe. Its most colorful characters
have drifted into left-wing splinter groups such as the Independent Women's Association, the Green League, the
Green Party, the United Left, the Humanistic Party of
Germany, and the Free German Youth.

A few thousand members of those groups paraded
through East Berlin on February 22 chanting "GDR, our
motherland," a feminist-leftist-anti-unification reply to
the refrain of the center right, "Germany, a united fatherland." But no one seemed to listen, because virtually everyone following politics in the GDR was concentrating

on the conventions of the major parties, and all those parties favor unification with West Germany.

Hence the dilemma of New Forum. It began last October in East Berlin as a protest movement directed against
the worst abuses of the old regime. By December, it had
established branches throughout the provinces and
seemed ready to take over the country. And by mid-January the government had conceded everything it demanded: the right to travel freely, the end of the
Communist Party dictatorship, and the calling of free
elections. But the very success of New Forum made its
platform look outdated. In February it found itself campaigning for what it had already accomplished, while the
other parties had taken up a new set of issues: not merely
whether East and West Germany should unite, but how
unification should take place—quickly, by means of an
Anschluss (annexation), or deliberately, with protection
for the social welfare system left over from the regime that
had been abolished.

The delegates who gathered to launch New Forum's
campaign from Schwerin seemed to be stuck in an earlier,
more idealistic phase of what they referred to as "our
peaceful revolution." Their speakers summoned up the
heroic days of the October demonstrations as if they had
occurred years ago. They looked backward rather than
forward and to the East rather than the West. Instead of
invoking the prosperity of West Germany, they cited the
example of Solidarity, and the delegates reserved their
warmest applause for a deputy sent by Lech Walesa.

When the speakers left the podium, they did not disappear into smoke-filled rooms. They mingled with the delegates in the corridors, sipping soft drinks and talking
political philosophy. They actually came from three "citizens' movements"—New Forum, Democracy Now, and
Initiative for Peace and Human Rights—which were

sponsoring a common slate of candidates in a coalition called Alliance '90. But they seemed less intent on winning votes than on preserving a peculiar East German identity, which they said had been forged in the demonstrations last autumn. They could not define this identity, but they described it as a heightened political consciousness directed against the authoritarianism of the East on the one hand and the consumerism of the West on the other.

Despite the coalition's poor prospects for the election, Professor Reich sounded satisfied with the state of things. "We achieved our goals in November," he explained in an interview. "We defeated Stalinism and forced the government to call free elections. But we have no illusions about winning them. We do not seek power; we do not want to take over ministries; we will operate from the outside and keep the politicians honest. I am not a politician myself."

He certainly did not act or look like one. In his acceptance speech, he derided the political professionals, who struck poses and fed promises to the little red eye of the television camera. But he could not avoid the cameras himself. They pursued him mercilessly; and as he repeated the same answers to the same questions, in broadcast after broadcast, he looked as though he would rather be anywhere but there, wilting under the arc lights in a tweed coat and a knit tie.

The other speakers sounded the same themes. They identified themselves as doctors, teachers, ministers, scientists; and they spoke out for human rights, social welfare, the environment, and the family. They had little to say about unification with West Germany, except that it was a threat to low rents, cheap consumer goods, and full employment. "We are neither left nor right," they insisted. "We represent the interests of humanity."

It was all very high-minded but not satisfactory to some of the delegates on the floor, who staged a small and well-

mannered revolt at the end of the evening. "There were
thousands of people with us in the streets in October and
November," one delegate protested. "But they have left us
now. We have lost our momentum." "We have lost touch
with the people," said another. "I can see it in this hall. I
can hear it in the pubs. You say you won't use slogans, but
a few slogans might be of some help." "There were 150
members of New Forum in my region a few months ago.
There are 30 now," complained another. And so it went,
until the chairman called a halt, and the last speaker tried
to arouse some enthusiasm with a keynote address on the
victories won during the heroic days of the "October Revolution."

A cluster of red and blue balloons was supposed to be
released from the ceiling at the climax of his speech. But
someone missed the cue. When the balloons floated down,
most of the delegates had disappeared into their Trabis
and were driving off through the smog toward a very uncertain future.

Three days earlier, Chancellor Helmut Kohl had come
from Bonn to open the campaign of another coalition, Alliance for Germany, from the cathedral square in Erfurt.
An East German CDU politician introduced him as "the
chancellor of our German fatherland," and the crowd of
130,000 East Germans roared back, "Helmut! Helmut!"
When at last the waves of sound receded, the basso pro-
fondo of the chancellor boomed out over a magnificent
amplifying system brought with him from the West: "We
will shape the future as one people in one Germany."
"Germany a united fatherland!" shouted the crowd, waving hundreds of West German flags, which had been generously distributed.

Kohl was making the first of six campaign speeches that
he was to deliver in the next four weeks. By mid-February

his backers from the Federal Republic had already spent a million marks in the East German campaign. They had set up offices in all fifteen electoral regions and had distributed 25 tons of posters and pamphlets. Since Kohl himself will be standing for re-election in West Germany in December, he is really campaigning on two fronts. For the political professionals from Bonn, reunification is already taking place: it is marathon of photo opportunities and T.V. spots for the same party on two sides of the same nation.

As he looked out over the sea of black, red, and yellow flags, the chancellor made three points: unification, prosperity, and the danger represented by the SPD. Above all, he paid tribute to "the splendid social order of the market economy," which had brought West Germany to the top rank of the European powers, thanks "not only to the industry of 60 million citizens . . . but also to the basic conditions established by Conrad Adenauer and Ludwig Erhard." If only such conditions could be created in East Germany, "We will build a flourishing land together." Provided, of course, that the voters kept the SPD out of office. Not only did the Social Democrats understand nothing about economics, they had a long history of collaborating with the Communists (Kohl was alluding to the forced fusion of the old SPD with the Communist Party in 1946). The conclusion was clear: vote CDU, and "Long live our German fatherland!" "Germany a united fatherland!" boomed the crowd in reply, and the campaign was launched.

The hoopla surrounding Kohl was so deafening that you might have thought he was the candidate. While he worked the crowd, the actual candidates, the three leaders of the parties that make up the Alliance— the East CDU, Democratic Outbreak, and the German Social Union— remained discreetly in the background. Their names appeared in small type under the main headline of a party poster, which announced the arrival of Kohl as if he were the Messiah: "Federal Chancellor Helmut Kohl Is Coming."

When at last he got a turn at the microphone, Lothar de Maizière, the candidate of the East CDU, seemed to have learned his lesson. He kept his message simple: "Progress and prosperity for all." Looking the cameras straight in the eye, he explained that he had only three wishes: that his children would no longer have to tell lies in school; that his wife would be the only one to listen when he telephoned her; and that the only persons to enter his apartment would be invited guests. To make a complete break with the old police state, East Germany should look West. The road to prosperity led toward immediate unification, without any of the dallying favored by the SPD.

The right, in short, is trying to outflank the left by sounding more eager for unification, more committed to a free market economy, and more militant against everything smacking of Stalinism. It is staging a Western-style media campaign, heavily televised and heavily financed from Kohl's supporters in the West, and it is making the most of its not-so-secret weapon, Kohl himself. Thanks to the weight of his office, his heavy rhetoric, and his sheer physical bulk, he embodies everything he proclaims: prosperity in a united Grossdeutschland.

But if it comes to a contest of personality cults, the SPD seems sure to win. It can import from the West the man who first championed "East Politics" twenty years ago and who has remained enormously popular in the GDR ever since. On February 24, Willy Brandt raised at least as much enthusiasm in Leipzig as Kohl had done four days earlier in Erfurt. At the East SPD's campaign convention there, he received a standing ovation after defining his formula for unification: "What belongs together will grow together." Then, before 100,000 cheering spectators in the Karl-Marx-Platz (as it is still called), he mixed another metaphor into his speech: "The train of unification is gathering steam. Now we must make sure that no one falls under the wheels. It is more important to prevent that than to assure the comfort of those who are traveling first class." "Willy! Willy!" roared the crowd, while a beaming group of SPD candidates nodded their approval.

"Willy Brandt is our idol," said one of the candidates, Ingo Richter, who leads the SPD in Rostock, East Germany, to Oskar Lafontaine, who is certain to head the SPD's campaign for the December elections in the West. Twelve days earlier, Richter and Lafontaine had stood on opposite sides of a crack that nearly split the alliance of the East and West parties. Richter announced that if he won the election, he would have the Rostock area by the Baltic coast apply for "immediate *Anschluss*" with West Germany—that is, membership in the Federal Republic as a constituent state, according to a procedure defined in article 23 of West Germany's constitution.

Lafontaine favors unification by means of gradual and carefully negotiated stages, which would lead to an entirely new constitutional order in conformity with a provision in article 146. According to rumors at the Leipzig convention, he had threatened to refuse to lead the West SPD in the December elections if Richter had his way. Richter didn't. At an emergency meeting in Bonn, Willy Brandt persuaded him to back down, and so the Social Democrats entered the campaign united on unification as an issue.

The Richter–Lafontaine episode went deeper than disagreement over constitutional niceties. It exposed an immanent division between the East and West Social Democrats on the future of Germany. So strong is the

Drang nach Westen (drive toward the West) in the East, that the politicians of the GDR are outdoing one another in advocating a quick fix with the Federal Republic. But the West Germans are now beginning to resent the pressure of emigration—100,000 settlers from the GDR have arrived since January—and to worry about the cost of unification.

In contrast to Kohl, Lafontaine has argued against accepting any immigrants who do not already have a job and a place of residence in the Federal Republic. He also has opposed a proposal of Ibrahim Böhme, the head candidate of the East SPD, for the introduction of the West German mark as the currency of East Germany by July 1. And in Leipzig he argued, to lukewarm applause, that the two SPD parties should make the two Germanys take the slow road to unification.

Fortunately for him, Lafontaine was able to enlist Brandt on his side of the argument, and Brandt made it look like a defense of social democratic principles: by unifying Germany slowly, an SPD government would defend the subsidies and social welfare legislation that protect East Germans from the worst abuses of a market economy.

In the end, therefore, the party adopted a platform favored by the leaders of the big brother party in the West. It promised, if it formed a government, to negotiate with Bonn for the creation of a "Council for German Unity," to be composed of representatives from both countries under the chairmanship of Willy Brandt. The council, working with commissions from both parliaments, would propose a constitution for a united Germany. And the constitution, if approved by plebiscites in the East and the West, would go into effect after the election of a common parliament. Meanwhile, steps would be taken to adjust the two economies, and parallel negotiations with the four victorious powers from World War II would integrate the united Germany in the European order, while guaranteeing its present boundaries, notably the Oder–Neisse line.

It seemed like a bold formula for change if compared with the situation when the SPD was founded only five months ago, but would it be enough to win the election, which was then only three weeks away? Most speakers at the convention decided to play it safe by ignoring their differences on unification and attacking their most important common enemy, the CDU. The East German CDU had cooperated with the Communists for years as one of the "bloc parties" in the parliament. So it was vulnerable to the same charge that it had leveled against the Social Democrats—of being soft on Communism. Stephan Hilsberg, the spokesman for the SPD executive committee, drew the loudest round of applause when he observed that the CDU "used to follow Honecker (the former leader of the Communist Party), now it is following Kohl."

Where does this sort of electioneering leave the PDS— that is, the party left over from the old Communist SED? It launched its campaign at the same time as the others, in a convention that met in East Berlin from February 24 to 25. Although it could not display any prominent personalities from the West, it made the most of its own leader, Hans Modrow, who as prime minister of the transitional government has established himself as the most popular politician in the GDR.

In fact, the convention turned into a personal drama focused on Modrow. Some newspapers had reported that he would not accept the nomination as the PDS's leading candidate and might even leave the party. Wolfgang Berghofer, the mayor of Dresden and formerly a close associate of Modrow, quit the party two months ago. Because Berghofer is considered clever, ambitious, photogenic, and nearly as popular as Modrow himself, his move suggested that any politician who wants to have a future in East Germany had better put as much distance as possible between himself and the PDS.

Were Modrow to resign, or even to refuse the nomination, the PDS would lose so badly on March 18 that it might never recover. He is its greatest asset. He has established a reputation for integrity in contrast to the old apparatchiks, who are now awaiting trial on charges ranging from corruption to treason. And the sympathy for Modrow has increased since he returned empty-handed and humiliated from a meeting with Kohl in Bonn on February 13. He had not crawled on his knees in order to beg charity, he reported to the opposition groups at the Round Table in East Berlin. If the East Germans were to unite with their wealthy, overbearing brothers in the West, they would do so with dignity and without sacrificing either their values or their identity.

That kind of talk goes down much better than campaign speeches in the GDR. The leaders of the PDS made it clear to Modrow that they did not expect him to campaign at all. He could concentrate on keeping the country together and directing the government—a role that also works quite well in winning votes. All he need do is say yes to the nomination. "Hans, you can feel how every member of this party depends on you," said Gregor Gysi, the party secretary, to Modrow before wild applause at the opening session of the convention on Saturday, February 24.

When at last Modrow rose to give his answer on Sunday evening, the delegates hung on his every word. He bent over his text, reading quietly and deliberately without a glance in the direction of the television cameras. And as he spoke the tension grew, because he listed all the reasons for him not to run: the party needed to make a new beginning with new leaders; his first responsibility was to the people, not the party; he was physically exhausted; and he needed to devote all his remaining energy to running the government during the critical weeks before March 18. Then, in a spectacular *non sequitur,* he announced that he could not disappoint hundreds of thousands of people: he would accept the nomination after all. The delegates whooped and cheered.

Modrow seemed to be the only thing worth cheering for at the convention. Gysi announced that the membership, which had stood at 2.3 million a year ago, had dropped to 700,000. That might be enough to bring in 12 percent of the vote, as the polls had predicted, but it seems likely that many members will continue to drift into left-wing splinter groups or the SPD. The party that once held a monopoly on power will almost certainly be reduced to a marginal role in the opposition.

But will it be able to play any role at all? Gysi announced that the PDS was ready to enter into a coalition, even as a member of the loyal opposition, but all the other parties have declared that they will have nothing to do with it. So the PDS has turned into a political pariah. Its opponents do not even campaign against it. They use it to insult one another; for they seem to base their strategy on the premise that the best defense is a good offense, and the most offensive weapon in this former Communist country is the charge of contamination with Communism.

If the campaign has demonstrated anything, it is the isolation of the former Communists in the PDS and the former revolutionaries in New Forum. The two political forces that had confronted one another at the beginning of the revolution have been relegated to the sidelines, and East German political life is conforming to a West German pattern. In fact, the West Germans seem to be taking it over. The campaign has been dominated by the media, personality cults, and a foreign variety of political professionalism imported from the Federal Republic. The home-grown parties contesting the election—thirty-five, at last count—have shaken down into three coalitions of the sort that can be found throughout Western Europe: a conservative group gathered around the CDU on the right, a social democratic group concentrated in the SPD on the left, and a small group of liberals in the middle.

The peculiar political identity of East Germany, as the leaders of New Forum understand it, seems likely to disappear in the common pattern of politics-as-usual. Or was that identity an illusion, generated in the heat of events last autumn? Revolutions never remain fixed in their heroic phase. The October revolution has disappeared from East Germany, and March may be the beginning of a Thermidorean reaction.

ELECTION RESULTS

March 19, 1990

E ast Germany just voted itself out of existence. Given their first chance in fifty-seven years to say what they wanted at the polls, the voters made the message clear: union with the Federal Republic, thank you, and the sooner the better.

The election was really a referendum on unification—not whether it should take place, but how, at what pace, and by whom. Since November, the East Germans had voted with their feet, pouring across the border at a rate of 2,000 a day. On March 18, they voted the same way with their ballots: for *Anschluss,* or immediate annexation to the Federal Republic.

Anschluss has a terrible echo to the Anglo-American ear. It summons up the annexation of Austria by Hitler in 1938 and the German expansion that led to World War II. But East Germany was not in an expansive mood on March 18. Instead of marching through the streets or tearing about in cars with horns blowing and fists waving, most people watched the election reports on television and went to bed. By 10:00 P.M. the streets of East Berlin were empty. Monday was a work day, and work was what everyone seemed to want—good jobs for good pay in the world that lay on the other side of the Wall.

A mild conclusion to a "gentle revolution" *(sanfte Revolution)*, as the events since last October are called in the GDR. There was little left of the excitement and idealism that pulsated through the body politic last autumn. The citizens' groups identified with the revolution nearly disappeared in the wave of votes for the conservative Alliance for Germany sponsored by Chancellor Helmut Kohl. At last count, Kohl's Alliance received 48 percent of the vote, and the citizens' groups that campaigned as Alliance '90 (New Forum, Democracy Now, Initiative for Peace and Human Rights) received 3 percent. The revolution is over.

But so is the old regime. The former Communist Party (PDS) did quite well (16 percent of the vote), considering its demoralized and discredited state last January. But it will be reduced to an isolated role in the opposition, because no other party wants to form a coalition with it.

All the talk on election night was of coalitions, especially of a center-left alliance between the CDU and the Social Democrats (SPD). But on the morning after, it looked as though the new regime would be governed from the center right. The SPD did so badly (21 percent of the vote, whereas the polls had given it 30–53 percent) that Kohl's East German allies seemed likely to form a government patterned after the West German model. With its partners—the German Social Union (DSU, a counterpart to the Christian Social Union in West Germany) and Democratic Beginning (DA)—the CDU controls 193 seats of the new, 400-seat parliament. If it forms a coalition with the Liberals, who got 21 seats, it would have an absolute majority; and it would be a mirror image of the coalition that rules in West Germany. Nothing could conform better to Kohl's prescription for uniting the two Germanys. Nothing could better represent the takeover of East German politics by the West.

Kohl's campaigning in the GDR certainly smacked of Westernization *(BRDierung,* in the slang used by his opponents in East Germany). At rallies in six GDR cities, he appeared before a total of about 800,000 persons, one fifteenth of the entire electorate. Advance men from the West CDU prepared his way, combining Western P.R. with what they took to be down-home GDR values. Thus one of the fliers distributed on glossy, West German paper in Rostock: "Once before, about 120 years ago, a chancellor unified Germany—Otto von Bismarck. Today it is Helmut Kohl who is bringing us unity."

The professionals knew how to prepare a personality cult, but they did not know whether it would take. "We are in *terra incognita,"* said one of them in Rostock. He had covered the town square in bunting and strung up a spectacular, high-tech public address system, but he confessed that he had no "feel" for the mood of the public. He could only adjust the P.A. system to the roar of the crowd. When a group of hecklers tried to drown Kohl out with boos and whistling, the aide turned up the microphone so that only Kohl could be heard, and after the rally he was none the wiser.

In most places, Kohl was received with cheers. But were the crowds celebrating him, the CDU, West Germany, or the fact that a West German chancellor was standing before them and proclaiming their place in a "united German fatherland"? A crowd of 150,000 had shouted "Helmut! Helmut!" at the climactic rally in Leipzig on March 15. But many of the same people had cheered just as loudly for former chancellor Helmut Schmidt of the SPD in the same city on the same day. A plane had circled overhead dragging a streamer that said, "Welcome Helmut!" No one knew which Helmut was intended.

The signals have been hard to read in the GDR, even for the East Germans. Almost none of them had ever voted in a free election, or seen a Western politician in the flesh, or responded to a pollster. Half of them did not know which way to vote a week before the election, according to the polls—and the polls themselves, from exotic establishments like Infratest in Munich, looked like overeducated guesses.

Of course there was a great deal of handwriting on the walls. One poster, spread all over East Berlin by a left-wing group, simply said, "NEIN." Its meaning, to East Berliners, was clear: stop the stampede toward unification with the West. So a right-wing group went around the city painting out the first *N,* and it became "EIN," an appeal for a united Germany ("Deutschland *ein*ig Vaterland," according to the most popular slogan on the right).

The best place to take the pulse of East Berlin during the last week of the campaign was the northwestern sector of Alexanderplatz, which turned into a kind of Hyde Park Corner. Instead of listening to orators on soap boxes, however, the East Berliners improvised one-on-one debates, surrounded by clusters of kibbitzers. The themes were always the same. "Forty years of experimentation with socialism is enough," one would say. "The only way to prosperity is over there" (*drüben,* a term for West Germany that makes it sound as though it lies somewhere over the rainbow). "Don't kid yourself," another would reply. "Capitalism means high prices, high rents, and high unemployment."

The second argument seemed to be gaining ground, at least in Berlin, on the eve of the election, and the former Communists of the PDS made the most of it. In a series of hard-hitting speeches, which came to a climax at a rally of 80,000 in Alexanderplatz on March 16, Gregor Gysi, the leader of the PDS, played on the public's fears of what unification would cost. He did not oppose union with West Germany in itself. He attacked Kohl's version of it, an "instant, forced merger of the two Germanys. That would be a total capitulation before the powers of capital. The West German constitution doesn't even recognize a right to work. It just says you can choose a job—if you can find one. It's the same with the currency union. It all sounds good, but don't let yourself be fooled. At West German prices, we will all be beggars."

A few months ago, when the Communists held a monopoly of power, that kind of rhetoric would have been dismissed as propaganda. But as the East Germans neared the election, they seemed to worry that it might be a prophecy. Forty years of indoctrination had left them with a genuine fear of the wicked capitalist world, which used to be located safely behind the "anti-fascist protection barrier" (i.e. the Wall) and now was offering to annex them. Moreover, they had a great deal to lose: cheap food, low rents, guaranteed employment, and a safe pension system.

True, those benefits were subsidized by a state-run economy that was so inefficient it kept the entire country far below the level of prosperity attained in West Germany. But Gysi made West Germany sound like a threat to the roof over everyone's head and the ground under everyone's feet; for West Germans once owned a great many of the apartment houses that are now state property in the GDR as well as a great deal of the land that is now farmed by cooperatives or collectives. The PDS made unification sound like expropriation.

But when the moment of truth came, on March 18, the prophecy of doom from Gysi, and the moderate variations of it from the Social Democrats, wilted before the Bismarckian appeal of Kohl. Seen negatively, the victory of the CDU was a rejection of everything that smacked of the old Communist system. Seen positively, it represented a commitment to Western democracy—or at least to West German prosperity. In either case, the triumph of the CDU in the East seems certain to strengthen the CDU in the West, where Kohl himself will stand for re-election on December 2. By the end of the year, the two Germanys will probably be ready for a merger under the banner carried by Kohl in the GDR: "Freedom, Unity, Prosperity."

So, after a period of considerable confusion, the ground has been cleared, and one can recognize the main outlines of a new political landscape. The East has come to resemble the West. In the process, something has been lost, something represented by the exotic undergrowth of little parties and citizens' groups that proliferated during the street demonstrations in October and November 1989. They claimed to speak for a "GDR identity" or a peculiar East German "political culture" as well as causes like feminism, environmental protection, disarmament, and homebrewed beer. The electoral law actually favored them, because it provided for proportional representation without a requirement for a minimal share in the vote, such as the 5 percent "hurdle" that a party must clear in order to hold a seat in the Bundestag of West Germany. As a consequence, a tiny party like the German Beerdrinkers' Union could win a place in East Germany's new Volkskammer (parliament) with only 0.25 percent of the vote nationwide.

This system provided a counter-balance to the weight of the CDU, SPD, and FDP (Free Democrats), who drew on their big brother parties in West Germany for funds, expertise, and media stars. The little parties prided themselves on having no analogues in the West. Their candidates did not have blow-dried hair, did not know how to catch the little red eye of the television camera, could not even get through a speech without stumbling. They crowded onto the ballot—twenty-four in all—some of them coalitions of coalitions, like Alternative Youth, which was composed of the Free German Youth, the Marxist Youth League, the United Young Left, and the Green Youth. But when the ballots were counted, they were flattened by the well-oiled party machines from the West.

The counting of the ballots and the balloting itself were important ceremonies throughout the GDR. At Local 650 in the Prenzlauer Berg district of East Berlin, a working-class neighborhood full of decrepit tenements, the electoral board supervised the "urn" or ballot box (actually a cardboard carton with a slit in the top) from seats aligned against the walls of a ground-floor room. There were seven on the board, representing as many different parties. When the voters arrived, they showed their identification cards, received a ballot, and walked behind a "booth" (actually a three-sided plasterboard screen that had been borrowed from a district in West Berlin). There they placed an x in a circle next to the name of the party of their choice, folded the ballot, and deposited it in the urn.

There was a solemn air to the whole business. When it came to counting the votes, at 6:00 P.M., a crowd gathered in the room. They merely wanted to watch, they said.

When they had voted in the municipal elections last May, many of them had spoiled their ballots in order to protest against the regime, but that had not stopped the electoral commission from announcing a stunning victory for the Communist Party. Now they wanted to see that every ballot was counted and accounted for.

The president of the board emptied the urn onto a table in the center of the room. The crowd drew close, fascinated, as the members of the board began the tally. There was some oohing and aahing as individuals spotted x's by the parties of their choice, until the president called for order. He announced the total vote: 1,087, about 85 percent of the local electorate, although he could not be sure because so many people had emigrated to the West. An onlooker said that he had noticed a ballot with two x's somewhere in the pile, so the board counted the votes all over again. At last the president read out the results: a solid victory for the PDS. No one applauded. Many people took notes. Mothers explained the process to their children, and one woman said that she had come all the way from Hamburg to see it with her own eyes. She had grown up in this neighborhood and had emigrated to West Germany before the Wall went up. "Now it is decided," she said gravely. "They have chosen freedom. There's no turning back now."

After the counting, the votes were put in plastic bags, which were locked into a suitcase. The president of the board then drove off with them, escorted by a policeman, to the central electoral commission in the Palace of the Republic. There the final tabulation took place under the eye of the commission's president, Petra Bläss, a twenty-five-year-old graduate student in German literature.

Perhaps the most important result of the election was not who won but the fact that it took place. For the first time since Hitler seized power in 1933, the East Germans

selected representatives of their own choice. By placing
x's in circles on small sheets of paper, they restored legitimacy in a country that had gone politically bankrupt—
even if the country itself should disappear in the embrace
of the Germans in the West.

THE RECOVERY
OF LEGITIMACY

April 7, 1990

When the deputies to the new East German parliament took their seats on April 5, they found themselves acting out a problem of political theory: How do you transfer legitimacy? There they were, making speeches and casting votes in the same building under the same constitution as their predecessors from the old regime, yet they thought they had made a revolution. The session opened with some remarks by their provisional president, Lothar Piche: "Forty years of a difficult course have in this moment come to an end." No one doubted that the old order had ended, but how could they begin a new one?

And why begin with Lothar Piche, an obscure deputy from the small and contentious German Social Union party? Unlike the Queen of Great Britain, who embodies sovereignty when she opens Parliament, he had only one qualification for the job of calling the house to order: he was the oldest available member of it, and not very old at that—sixty-three (the previous parliament, much despised as a rubber stamp of the Communist Party, had a one hundred-year-old deputy). Age suggests continuity with the past, but Piche declared a break with the regime that had tyrannized over the country for forty years, and he ended by invoking a higher authority: "May God protect our German fatherland." Those words would have been taken as a call for an insurrection or a sign of madness under the old parliament. They brought the deputies of the new parliament to their feet with a thunderous round of applause.

It is impossible to know precisely what chord Piche struck, but it may have gone back far beyond the forty years of Communist rule, beyond the twelve years of Nazism, even beyond the twentieth century, to a Lutheran past identified with German nationality. The revolution—or *Wende* (turn), to use the more modest expression favored by many East Germans—began in the Church, which was the only independent institution of any importance under the Communist system. Many of the new deputies are clergymen, including the leaders of several parties: Markus Meckel of the Social Democrats (SPD), Rainer Eppelmann of Democratic Beginning (DA), and Hans-Wilhelm Ebeling of the German Social Union (DSU). The largest party, the Christian Democratic Union (CDU), takes its Christianity seriously—a predominantly Lutheran Christianity, in contrast to the Catholicism of the CDU in West Germany.

A large proportion of the deputies began the day on

April 5 by attending a service at the Gethsemane Church, the home of the opposition movement in East Berlin. Ten minutes before the opening prayer, two busloads of deputies from the Democratic Socialist Party (PDS, previously the Communist Party) arrived, led by the party secretary, Gregor Gysi, a professed atheist. He explained that they wanted to pay tribute to the role of the Church in the renewal of democracy.

The former Communists looked uncomfortable in the pews, especially when the preacher took as his text, "Lord save me from false friends." But the congregation seemed to hear the words from the Bible as a reference to the secret police (Stasi), which, according to a recent article in *Der Spiegel,* may have employed one of every ten deputies as an informer under the old regime. The deputies therefore had to confront their own past as well as that of the GDR in general when they assembled in the Palace of the Republic. Each of them must clear himself before a parliamentary commission, which has full access to the Stasi files.

The issue of "Stasinismus" cast a long shadow over the creation of the new government. It, too, posed a problem of legitimacy, all the more so as it had become dramatized in the person of two of the country's leading politicians, Wolfgang Schnur and Ibrahim Böhme. Four days before the election, Schnur admitted he had worked for the Stasi and resigned as president of the Democratic Beginning party. In a recent interview with *Stern* magazine, he explained that he had begun by reporting on dissidents within the church. Then, as a founder of Democratic Beginning, he informed the Stasi of everything that went on within the movement. He continued to provide regular reports in secret meetings with Stasi agents until he emerged as a leader of Alliance for Germany, the coalition put together from Bonn by Chancellor Helmut Kohl.

After appearing regularly at Kohl's side in photographs
and television broadcasts, he was denounced by one of his
undercover contacts and pressured into making a confession by some of Kohl's aides. He disappeared into a hospital, a victim of a heart condition and of the contradictions
within the GDR.

Böhme's case was sadder, because he had been imprisoned for fifteen months by the Stasi after protesting
against the persecution of intellectuals, and he had seemed
to personify a new brand of politics in East Germany.
Young (41), articulate, and energetic, he acquired something of a Kennedy aura. During the election campaign,
he was one of the few candidates who could stride through
packs of photographers, seize a microphone, and work up
a crowd with well-turned rhetoric. Most of the pre-elec-
tion polls made him out to be the next prime minister of
the GDR. Even after his party, the SPD, received only 22
percent of the vote, he appeared as a key figure in the
negotiations to form a coalition government. But then he,
too, had to clear himself of accusations of collaboration
with the Stasi. He spent the weekend before the opening
of parliament frantically searching through the files in the
Stasi headquarters in East Berlin. It was a Kafkaesque
hunt through a labyrinth of codes and aliases—"Paul
Bongartz," "Dr. Rohloff," "Maximilian"—inside a moun-
tain of documents. In the end, Böhme broke down. A final,
crucial file could not be located. He resigned as leader of
the party and disappeared into another hospital, suffering
from exhaustion and an infection of the inner ear.

All the deputies had followed the unraveling of the political careers of Schnur and Böhme. Many of them must
have dreaded their own confrontation with the records of
the old police state. But their main item of business was to
found a new order, and they went about it with a mixture
of solemnity and good-humored amateurism that con-

trasted happily to the machinelike deliberations of the previous parliament. First they constituted themselves as a sovereign body by voting to accept the results of the election. Then they elected their own president, who was to serve in effect as speaker of the house. That occupied them for most of the afternoon, because they adopted an elaborate procedure, designed to keep everything open, democratic, and as different as possible from the rubber-stamping of the Communist era. There were five candidates for the presidency, including Hans Modrow of the PDS, the former prime minister. In nominating Modrow, Gysi smiled slyly and described him as a man who represented "the past, present, and future of this land." Because Modrow had just been voted out of office and the PDS reduced to a minority role in the opposition, that remark hit a collective funny bone and the deputies roared with laughter. It was the first time that anyone had laughed in the Palace of the Republic—or very nearly so, for a veteran West German reporter claimed that he had heard three jokes in twenty-five years of covering the old legislature.

When the ballots were counted, no one had a majority—another unprecedented situation, because most votes were carried unanimously under the old regime. So the deputies voted again. This time the winner was the CDU candidate, Sabine Bergmann-Pohl, a forty-three-year-old doctor and mother of two from East Berlin. Although Piche had forgotten to make a formal announcement of the tally and a formal offer of the presidency, Dr. Bergmann-Pohl made a short acceptance speech. She assured the deputies that she had passed her own examination in the Stasi archives and urged them to make a new political beginning by following a principle, which she quoted from the morning sermon in the Gethsemane Church: "The power of the rulers must not be misused."

The deputies spent most of the rest of the afternoon voting for six vice-presidents. Once again Modrow was a candidate, and once again he was defeated. He, Gysi, and a few other survivors from the former government seemed to disappear in the middle of the 400-member body. Their position appeared all the more anomalous in that the seating plan of the parliament did not correspond exactly to the political spectrum. True, the United Left party sat to the president's left, and the CDU sat to her right. But the PDS, which is trying to create a place for itself in the left opposition, occupied a no man's land in the middle, well to the right of the SPD and close to the Liberals and the right-wing DSU. The old categories do not fit into the new order.

That the newness involved something more than ceremony and seating plans became clear toward the end of the day, when the deputies began to tear apart the constitution. Some had argued during the campaign that the *Wende* itself had made the constitution obsolete and that insofar as the GDR had any constitutional order at all it was unwritten, as in England. No one took that argument seriously, but neither did anyone want to maintain the rules of the game devised by Walter Ulbricht and Erich Honecker. So, by a two-thirds majority, the deputies voted to strike out the preamble, which defined the GDR as a "socialistic state of workers and farmers."

They also abolished the Council of State (Staatsrat), which had acquired a reputation as a tool of authoritarian rule under Honecker. In doing so, the parliament wiped out the highest official position in the country, the presidency of the Council of State, which had last been occupied by Modrow. It will create a new office of state president; and until that is filled, Dr. Bergmann-Pohl will act as head of state. Her main activity had previously been the direction of the section on lung disease in the Charité Hospital of East Berlin.

From Ulbricht to Honecker to Egon Krenz (the Party chairman and head of state after the overthrow of Honecker last December) to Modrow to Bergmann-Pohl—a curious line of descent. No one expects it to extend much further, because all the members of the new parliament understand their main task to be the fusion of the GDR in the Federal Republic of Germany. But states cannot be turned on and off like light switches or blended together like the ingredients of a cake mix. They contain symbolic forms of power, which are charged with meaning in the collective consciousness of their citizens. The electing, praying, joking, and voting of the deputies represented an attempt to found a new order without breaking utterly with the old one. The deputies tried to preserve legitimacy and to create it at the same time, to work within a constitutional system while changing the constitution. Soon, however, they will have to go beyond this preliminary tinkering with symbols and confront the deepest contradiction of all: the need to preserve something peculiarly East German while the GDR is swallowed up in West Germany. How they can find a way through this dilemma should be clear in a matter of months, or perhaps even weeks. At the moment, it seems to be impossible.

POLITICS AND GUILT

April 17, 1990

O n April 12, at its second meeting, the Volkskammer
(parliament) got down to business—that is, to
politics—and at last the world had a chance to
observe parliamentary politicking, GDR-style.
Anyone who expected horse-trading, back-scratching,
and pork-barreling was in for a surprise: those notions
might work in Washington, or Rome, or Bonn; but not in
East Berlin, where the deputies struck such a high moral
tone that they were nearly incomprehensible to observers
from the West.

A Westerner in the Volkskammer feels like Alice in
Wonderland. Everything seems upside down or out of

place. Instead of being buttonholed in lobbies or filling backrooms with smoke, the deputies sit in their seats and listen to the debate. Many of them take notes. They behave like students in a lecture hall—or rather, since they keep their shoes on and wear their Sunday best, like a congregation in a church. Given the number of preachers among the deputies, the churchiness of the proceedings may not be surprising. It seems odd, nonetheless, that Rainer Eppelmann, a pastor who once spent eight months in jail for resisting the draft, should take over the ministry now known as "disarmament and defense." And no one would appear to be less suited for the role of political boss than the two main protagonists in the negotiations to form the new government, Markus Meckel (SPD) and Lothar de Maizière (CDU).

Meckel resembles an Old Testament prophet. A pastor metamorphosed into a foreign minister, he wears a full, black beard and looks distinctly uncomfortable in his new uniform, a dark flannel suit, which has replaced the blue jeans that he wore through countless protest meetings and street demonstrations since last October. By contrast, de Maizière, the new prime minister, appears completely buttoned up. He never says two words where one will do, and he carries a pained expression on his face, as if a political rally or a press conference were a form of penitence imposed on wayward flesh. He entered politics as a lawyer involved in church affairs, and he directed the affairs of the church as vice president of the general Protestant Synod (Synode des Bundes der Evangelischen Kirchen). De Maizière's tastes seem to be relentlessly high-brow, his bearing a product of Prussian *Bildung* (education, cultivation). He was a viola player until a nervous disorder forced him to abandon music as a profession. When asked in a recent interview which historical figures he most admired, he said without hesitating, "Bach and Mozart."

Such are the men who set the tone of the new politics in the GDR. They confronted questions of the kind that can be found in politics everywhere, questions about how to form a government and how to defend the pocketbooks of their constituents. But they handled them in a way that began to define the peculiar quality of political life in East Germany as opposed to that in the Federal Republic.

Two issues stood out immediately after the election: Would the CDU and the SPD be able to join in a grand coalition, and would the currency union take place at an exchange rate of one East mark for one West mark? The three parties in the Alliance for Germany (CDU, DSU, and DA), when supported by the Liberals, commanded an easy majority in the Volkskammer. But to prepare the way for unification with the Federal Republic, they needed to modify the constitution. To change the constitution, they needed a two-thirds majority. And to mobilize two-thirds of the deputies, they had to win the support of the SPD. The SPD, however, was still smarting from its defeat in the election. By remaining in the opposition, it could profit from every failure of the government to extract concessions from Bonn, and it could prepare the way for a comeback at the municipal elections of May 6.

That Bonn might not be quite so big brotherly as it had seemed before March 18 became apparent when the currency issue began to unravel. The central bank in West Germany recommended that the West mark be introduced into the GDR at a rate of 2:1 (two East marks for one West mark), except in the case of bank accounts under 2,000 East marks, which would be converted at 1:1. Chancellor Kohl refused to commit himself, but the East Germans thought he had already made a commitment during the election campaign. To them, the West mark stood for the prosperity they expected to achieve by union with the West. A 2:1 exchange rate would, in their view, halve their salaries and make them into half-citizens, victims of the economic takeover about which they had been warned by Kohl's opponents in the campaign.

In fact, when Kohl had made an issue of the currency union in a campaign speech at Cottbus on March 13, he had talked like politicians everywhere in the West—out of both sides of his mouth. He gave the impression that he favored a 1:1 rate without making an unambiguous endorsement of it. But the East Germans had never before encountered Western political talk. They thought a promise was a promise, and the depth of their misunderstanding was misunderstood by Kohl, because he had never before campaigned in the East. During the last half-year, the East Germans had developed a political tradition of their own, through mass demonstrations in the streets. So when the parliament convened, the East Germans took to the streets again: 100,000 in East Berlin, 70,000 in Dresden, 50,000 in Leipzig, and tens of thousands in Rostock, Cottbus, Halle, Magdeburg, and Gera. They carried placards with the same biting language that they had used against the Communists last fall: "A new beginning with an election fraud—not with us"; "2:1 wages is a mockery" ("2:1 Lohn ist ein Hohn"); "You wanted the whole cabbage [*Kohl*]—Now you've got the salad"; "Whoever burns us with Kohl will get a strapping" ("Wer uns verkohlt wird versohlt").

In short, the stage was set for a political confrontation, and the SPD was given exactly the kind of issue with which politicians make hay—Western politicians, that is. Oskar Lafontaine, leader of the SPD's sister party in West Germany, had already elaborated a grand strategy for the conquest of Bonn and eventually of Berlin, the future capital of a united Germany. Lafontaine calculated that Kohl would either keep his campaign promises, and the hasty cobbling together of the two economies would produce intolerable rates of inflation and unemployment; or Kohl would not honor what the East Germans took to be his word, and voters in the East would turn against the CDU, first in the local elections of May 6, then in the all-German elections expected to take place sometime in 1991. Either way, the SPD would reap the harvest that the CDU had sown.

But the politicians in East Germany, who were pastors and doctors and teachers only a few months ago, have not developed a hay-making mentality. After agonizing over the decision for three weeks, Meckel and the other deputies of the SPD finally agreed to join a grand coalition government led by de Maizière. That made them junior partners of the CDU—not a glorious role and not the one imagined for them by Lafontaine. But it gave them a chance to collaborate in the unification of Germany and to do so on their own terms. They got de Maizière to give them seven of the twenty-four ministries, to take a strong stand for a 1:1 exchange rate, to defend the GDR's social welfare system, and to commit the government to principles such as the right to work, which will not go down well with the CDU and its financial backers in the West.

True, the SPD agreed to negotiate for unification according to article 23 of the West German constitution—that is, by means of annexation rather than by the creation of a new constitutional order—but it surrounded that commitment with so many provisos that the final agreement between the SPD and the CDU-led coalition read like the Social Democratic platform. The document itself ran to fifty pages, more than the constitutions of the two Germanys put together. On April 12, a half hour before the parliamentary session began, the leaders of all the parties in the coalition gathered to sign it. There turned out to be so much to sign and so many signatories that the session had to be delayed. But at last the coalition strode into the main hall of the Volkskammer: East Germany had a government, and the government had a policy.

Not quite, however, because before taking office, the new ministers had to be sworn in, and the oath-taking raised a new problem, which gave the deputies their first chance to test the machinery of parliamentary government. How could a nonsocialist ministry, composed primarily of devout Lutherans, swear allegiance to a godless, socialist constitution? Despite the amputation performed on its preamble the previous week, the old GDR constitution contained much language that de Maizière and his colleagues could not stomach. They especially wanted to find a way around article 79, which made an oath to uphold the constitution a precondition for taking office. To do so, however, they needed to carry a resolution by a two-thirds majority; and to bring the resolution to the floor, they needed to modify the agenda, which they had failed to prepare correctly. Before long they found themselves entangled in a thicket of procedural difficulties. President Bergmann-Pohl attempted to cut them free by a ruling from the chair, but she was promptly accused of partisanship by some deputies on the left. Hard words were exchanged, followed by a walk-out, party caucuses, and two rounds of voting.

Through it all, the deputies lectured one another about the general principles of government. How could the CDU assume power by constitutional means while at the same time challenging the validity of the constitution? asked a philosopher from the Alliance '90 party. A radical from Democratic Beginning answered that since a revolution had occurred, the constitution did not really exist at

all—although no one would admit it. This view, which
echoed sentiments expressed in Paris in 1793 and in Saint
Petersburg in 1917, produced consternation. A moderate
from the SPD placated some consciences by arguing that
they could maintain the underlying structure of the constitution while ignoring its "socialist lyrics." And at last
the house agreed on a formula whereby the new ministers
would swear to uphold the "the justice [Recht] and laws of
the German Democratic Republic."

They did so, some of them adding "so help me God."
The whole business took up most of the day. But in the
end the GDR had acquired its first freely chosen government, and the government had learned how to translate its
command of seats into actual legislation. Although the
fumbling and the confusion seemed amateurish, they actually added to the authenticity of it all; for nothing could
have been more different from the parliamentary procedures of the old regime, where everything sailed through
the Volkskammer without any back-talk. The new deputies filled the air with talk—arguments, objections, reflections, questions, a whole gamut of rhetoric never before
exhibited in a parliament of the GDR.

They also took action on another item of business that
was equally incompatible with the politics of the old regime. In a resolution addressed to world opinion, they
declared:

The first freely chosen parliament of the GDR admits, in
the name of the citizens of this country, its share in the
responsibility for the humiliation, persecution, and murder
of Jewish men, women, and children. We feel sadness and
shame and acknowledge this burden of German history.

We ask the Jews of all the world for forgiveness. We ask
the people of Israel to forgive the hypocrisy and hostility
of the official policy of the GDR toward the state of
Israel. . . .

When the Americans made a revolution, they issued a declaration of independence. The East Germans promulgated a declaration of guilt. In doing so, they also took a step toward unification with West Germany, because they accepted their share in the common burden of German history: unification by guilt came before unification by means of the deutsche mark and the constitution. It was a strange way to found a new regime—one can imagine how it might look in some future psychohistory—but it certainly distinguished the new government from the old. When the Communists established the GDR in 1949, they rejected the notion that East Germany could be held accountable for any of the Nazi crimes. After all, they argued, the Nazis had tried to annihilate Communists as well as Jews, and de-Nazification was the first priority of Communist rule. Why should they pay reparations to Israel or agonize over history? All the guilt lay on the other side of the Iron Curtain, a *cordon sanitaire,* which protected them from being contaminated by the strains of fascism that had survived in the Federal Republic.

When the Iron Curtain parted, the East Germans suddenly found themselves in another landscape. They saw that they had avoided a confrontation with their past, while their fellow Germans to the West had raked it over in plays, films, books, and most recently in an impassioned debate among historians, the *Historikerstreit.* Then, with the lifting of all restrictions on free speech, some distressing symptoms began to appear in their half of Germany: a few swastikas were sprayed on walls, some monuments to the Soviet dead were defaced, a great many hostile comments were aimed at Poles, foreigners in general, and especially "guest workers" from Vietnam and Africa. These incidents might represent a repressed current of fascism bursting into the open, but more likely they were a flailing out against official values, a breaking of taboos.

Taboos were being shattered all over Eastern Europe—statues of Lenin dragged from pedestals, hammers and sickles cut out of flags. On April 13, the Soviet government admitted that one of the most terrible atrocities of the war, the massacre of 7,000 Polish officers in the forest near Katyn, had not been committed by the Nazis, as it had always maintained, but by Stalin's secret police. The Soviet confession of guilt was meant to open the way for reconciliation between the Soviet Union and Poland, just as the East German confession was aimed at the restoration of diplomatic relations with Israel. But their combined effect produced a blurring of the distinction between Stalinism and Nazism, which represented opposite extremes in the old East German orthodoxy.

The ideological blurring had actually begun to spread through the GDR last winter, when activists occupied the offices of the Stasi (secret police) and the tyranny of the Stasi began to be presented as if it were a continuation of the work of the Gestapo. "Stasi-Nazi" was an important theme of the street demonstrations and the election campaign. Then, as the campaign ended, the whole country had its nose rubbed in the dirt of its Stalinist past. In early March a retired forester and an old farmer took two East German historians to the site of a mass burial ground at Fünfeichen, near Neubrandenburg. They had witnessed cartloads of corpses from a Soviet prison camp being dumped in unmarked graves from 1945 to 1948. The Germans had used Fünfeichen as a camp for prisoners of war, most of them Soviets, and the Soviets converted it into a camp for Germans, most of them Nazis. Most, but not all. In the chaotic conditions of 1945–1946, it was enough to be seen wearing some discarded Nazi clothing, to be heard talking about Hitler, or simply to be in the wrong place at the wrong time, in order to disappear behind barbed wire. The civilian population did not have enough to eat. The prison population starved. When the camp was closed in 1948, the survivors were made to swear that they would never talk about it. And they kept their word, because they knew that anyone who mentioned Stalinist crimes could be accused of Nazi sympathies and sent back to the Gulag. So they held their tongues—in some cases for forty years, until the *Wende* and the election convinced them that Stalinism had ended in East Germany.

Now many "de-Nazified" East Germans are talking. For Fünfeichen was just the beginning of a nationwide attempt to track down and dig up the remains of the Stalinist era. Almost every week the East German newspapers carry pictures of men deep in dirt, uncovering skeletons. No one knows how many will be found, but there were eleven Soviet camps. They contained 130,000–200,000 Germans, of whom 50,000–90,000 died. So there must be thousands of corpses hidden all across the country, many of them in the most terrible places of all: Sachsenhausen, Bautzen, and Buchenwald, where the Nazis murdered Jews.

In some cases, therefore, the Stalinist terror was superimposed on the Nazi terror. Their victims were buried in the same ground. And their past is being dug up in the same manner, like a dirty secret, hidden in the foulest corners of the twentieth century.

Whatever the body count may be, it will not prove that Nazism and Stalinism were two varieties of the same phenomenon. The new East German government made no such suggestion. But it felt compelled to confront all of the crimes that have weighed on German history since 1933. So it apologized to the Poles and the Soviets for the suffering inflicted on them by Germans during World War II, and it asked Czechoslovakia to forgive it for the East German participation in the suppression of the Prague Spring in 1968.

This general confession did not have the effect of relativizing the horror of the Holocaust. On the contrary, the government presented its declaration of guilt toward the Jews as the starting point of all its policies: "This guilt must never be forgotten. From it we intend to derive our responsibility toward the future."

De Mazière announced the policies themselves a week later, when the parliament reconvened on April 19. His speech belonged to another self-constituting ritual of the parliament: as prime minister, he outlined his government's position on a wide range of issues, the opposition replied, and the house voted its support. The session included plenty of debate about substantial political issues. De Maizière committed the government to a 1:1 exchange rate, recognition of the Oder–Neisse border, an environmental clean-up, increased wages, adequate pensions, improved health care, and measures to relieve unemployment. But once again, he embedded his political pronouncements in a series of moral reflections on the burden of the German past:

> Our history is not merely the last five years. As a free government and a free parliament, we bow down before the victims of fascism. We think of the victims of the concentration camps and of the war. We also think of the victims of Stalinism, of the victims of June 17, 1953 [the workers' uprising suppressed by the Communists] and the victims of the Wall. The face of our people has been etched by the war and the postwar order, by the involvement of endless numbers in guilt and sin and ever more historical guilt.
>
> The leaders of the resistance [to the Communist regime] remind us of our responsibility for our history. It is not the PDS [formerly the Communist Party] alone that is responsible for the past of the GDR. My party is also responsible.

> We are all responsible. There is a great deal of history to be worked over in Germany. . . . Germany is our inheritance of historical debts and historical guilt.

With its government installed and its first vote of confidence carried, the GDR entered a new political era. But it carried a heavy burden with it—something that sounded like the historical equivalent of original sin. The new politics, as de Maizière described it, was founded not merely on the collapse of the old regime, but on the fall of man. Its rhetoric seemed to come from the nineteenth century, or from the austere, North German variety of Protestantism that goes back to Martin Luther.

How ordinary people will respond to the voices coming out of the Volkskammer remains to be seen. Perhaps they want nothing more than total immersion in the consumer society of the West. But there will probably be a great deal of mutual misunderstanding before the two political cultures merge, and some hard knocks before the East Germans lay down the breastplate of righteousness and take up the deutsche mark.

LAUCHA REVISITED

May 11, 1990

E lection day in Laucha—the day of *the* election, the municipal balloting on May 6, which will determine whether Herr Lauterbach remains in command of the *Rathaus*. For the last four months Frau Müller and the other members of New Forum had been preparing for the event. But when it finally arrived, the mood had changed in the village.

The change was apparent everywhere when I returned to Laucha in order to follow the course of the election. An entrepreneur from West Germany was selling copies of *Bild am Sonntag*, a tabloid from Hamburg, from a stand in the main square. Judging from the line in front of the stand, business was good. But the newspaper readers seemed to be more interested in the soft-porn photographs than in the political news. And when asked about politics, they sounded dejected. "We have our noses full," said one. "What difference will it make?" remarked another. "Everything used to be decided in Berlin. Now it is coming from Bonn." The only optimist in the crowd was an old woman who said she hoped for the return of the good old days. It turned out, however, that she was referring to the years 1946–1948, when the garden by the old town wall was kept in order and the rest of the GDR was sinking into chaos.

A sense of helplessness and anxiety settled over the village after the national elections of March 18. Like most voters in small municipalities, especially in the south, the people of Laucha had backed the Christian Democrats (CDU), the party that raised the greatest hopes for prosperity through rapid unification with West Germany. Almost all of them voted on March 18 (2,245 of the 2,351 eligible voters—96 percent), and the results deviated significantly from the national pattern:

Party	Number of Votes	Percentage	National Percentage
CDU	1164	51.9	40.9
SPD	373	16.6	21.8
Alliance of Free Democrats (Liberals)	304	13.5	5.2
PDS	180	8.0	16.3
Alliance '90 (New Forum)	58	2.5	2.9
DSU	48	2.1	6.3

Not only did the CDU do far better in Laucha than in East Germany as a whole, but the PDS (the former Communist Party) did far worse. The right-wing Democratic Social

Union (DSU) also did worse, although it was generally
strong in the south. And the Liberals (Alliance of Free
Democrats) won an unusually large percentage of the
vote, probably because Laucha had been a Liberal strong-
hold under the Weimar Republic and there was still some
life in its old political tradition.

New Forum failed as badly in Laucha as everywhere
else on March 18, but it had always presented itself as a
loose affiliation of local movements rather than a national
party, or a "party" at all. For Annemarie Müller and the
other members of her group, the crucial test came on May
6. The Müllers could not be candidates themselves, even
had they wanted to, because the General Synod of the
Lutheran Church had instructed pastors who took up
public office to resign from their parishes. But for weeks
before the election, the vicarage in Laucha was full of
people designing posters, writing circulars, and arranging
meetings. Their campaign materials looked amateurish
compared with those of the CDU and the Liberals, who
received handsomely printed, multicolored posters from
their central offices in Berlin, or perhaps even from Bonn.
But villages in East Germany are not easily taken by media
blitzes. Everyone knows everyone in Laucha, and public
opinion is mobilized most effectively by word of mouth.

Tongues were wagging during the last weeks before the
election because the former Communist mayor, Helmut
Lauterbach, announced that he would cut himself off from
the former Communist Party (PDS, earlier SED) and run
as an independent. The PDS had done so badly in March
that it seemed likely to drag him under in May. Moreover,
the municipal election law favored independent candida-
cies, and voters were believed to look upon them favor-
ably; personalities matter more than parties at the level of
local politics—or so everyone thought, although no one
knew what to expect. Acting on the accepted wisdom, the

CDU had chosen two of the best-known men in the village, a postman and an innkeeper, as its top candidates. Then, a few days before the election, word leaked that the CDU had made a deal with Herr Lauterbach. In order to stop New Forum and the Liberals, it would support him for mayor. (The voters elect nineteen town councilors and the councilors elect the mayor; so the system leaves plenty of room for coalitions and cabal.) Frau Müller got out her India ink and penned another poster:

> Do you want the CDU along with its favorite, Mayor Lauterbach (ex SED)? No! Vote for New Forum.

In fact, she explained, the poster wasn't really necessary: to spread the word, she merely had to set the grapevine to work.

New Forum put up twelve candidates of its own. At the head of its list it chose Wilhelm Ebbinghaus, a popular engineer who had just founded a consulting agency that prepares plans for new enterprises in the region. There are plenty of projects in the air but nothing solid on the ground. Still, Herr Ebbinghaus is convinced that new business will pour in from West Germany. He is so convinced, in fact, that just before election day he announced he would not stand as mayor, although he would willingly serve as a town councilor. He decided that his own new business might become so demanding that he could not run it and the town's affairs at the same time. The decision may have been prudent from his point of view, but it left New Forum without a top candidate and it gave Herr Lauterbach more room to re-enter the mayor's office through the back door.

There was a certain amount of drama, therefore, when the citizens of Laucha folded up their *Bild am Sonntag* and began to appear in the voting booths. But it would be

wrong to describe the election as a Homeric battle between the old regime and the new. A tour of the town's
three polling stations turned up nothing but gloom. A
worker in a winery in Frybourg said that everyone was
worried about the economic effects of unification. Many
factory workers lived on tiny farms. They supplemented
their wages by selling tomatoes and lettuce and by slaugh-
tering the occasional pig. But now they would be wiped
out by the cheap produce from the Common Market. The
full-time farmers on the cooperatives would be harder hit,
because there were too many of them and they were too
inefficient to compete with Italy and Spain.

I asked a woman who had just cast her vote what was
the dominant issue in the election. "The deutsche mark,"
she said angrily and walked away. A technician in the local
food-processing plant explained that the currency union
would not open up any opportunity for local entrepreneurs, because no one had much capital. The banks would
not grant loans without 100 percent security. That meant
you would have to put up your house as collateral, but
who owned a house? And who would risk it if they had
one? For his part, he was eager to work for an efficient,
progressive, and high-paying West German enterprise,
but the enterprise would have to come from the West. At
present, 70 of the 230 workers in his plant had been given
notice, and the others knew that it would never turn a
profit until the work force was reduced to 100.

With such remarks ringing in my ears, I found it hard to
think of the election as a contest between candidates. Still,
in deciding who will sit in their *Rathaus*, the people of
Laucha will begin to determine the affairs of their community for the first time in half a century. They will participate in the public business, even if they cannot control the
local economy. Besides, I wanted to know what would
happen to Herr Lauterbach and Herr Ebbinghaus. So

when a letter arrived from Frau Müller a few days after I had returned to Berlin, I tore it open eagerly.

> Hurray, we won! We were completely taken by surprise. New Forum received the largest number of votes in all Laucha. That shows that our head candidate, Wilhelm Ebbinghaus, has the confidence of the people. He received the greatest number of votes by far.

The breakdown of the nineteen seats in the town council was as follows (each voter got to cast three votes, which could be split among the parties or concentrated on a single party or candidate):

Party	Votes	Seats
New Forum (Alliance '90)	1599	6
CDU	1537	5
Alliance of Free Democrats (Liberals)	1280	5
PDS	382	1
Independent (Lauterbach)	303	1
Farmers Union	193	1

New Forum will take over the town council in a coalition with the Liberals. It will turn Herr Lauterbach out of the mayor's office and replace him with Herr Ebbinghaus. Moreover, Herr Ebbinghaus will accept. He received such a heavy endorsement from the voters that he decided to take on the job of mayor and to devote himself full time to municipal affairs. What will become of his consulting business? Another example of a GDR enterprise that will not get off the ground.

PART V

RETROSPECTIVES

TIME AND MONEY

West Germans spend money and save time; East Germans do the opposite. There seems to be a limitless supply of time in the GDR, and people spend it profligately, taking breaks, standing in lines, leaning on shovels, stopping for chats, and watching the world go by. East Germans are perfectly capable of spending money, too, but they don't have much to spend it on. The stores carry a very limited range of goods, enough to satisfy basic needs but not to arouse consumers' appetites. So consumers sock away their wages in savings accounts, waiting for the day when their name will rise to the top of the waiting list for a car or a television or a washing machine. Important items of that sort are extremely rare and therefore extremely expensive. East Germans usually have to wait fifteen years to get a modest Trabi, and it usually costs them 15,000 East marks—more than a year's wages for most people. They do so much saving and waiting, in fact, that time does not seem to be money in the GDR; money is time.

The two cannot be converted into one another according to a fixed ratio, because there is little connection between how much people make and how much they work. Most people earn a fixed salary, usually 800–1,000 East marks a month. They do not get bonuses for overtime or increased output. On the contrary, they take home the same amount in wages no matter how much or how little they work; and they proceed automatically through the stages of a career according to a preordained pattern set by a planning commission. Why work harder or move faster? Most businesses are vastly overstaffed, and most staffs are greatly underemployed. So employees knock off to buy the day's groceries or to have a beer. Many work shifts stop at lunch time or shortly thereafter, rather than at 4:00 or 5:00 as they are supposed to.

The system does not make for efficiency, but it promotes an easy-going sociability that is unknown in the West. If you have an appointment or an interview with a West German, he dispatches with the business rapidly and lets you know as soon as you overstay your time by none too furtive glances at his watch. Should you fail to get the hint, his phone will ring: his secretary, programmed like an alarm clock, calls to say that x or y is waiting. She is the keeper of his calendar, an inexorable, inflexible Cerberus who guards his time as if it were the company's greatest asset. Perhaps it is. So you gather up your affairs and stumble out the door, stammering, "Thank you for your time."

Not so in the GDR. Important personages have secretaries, and the secretaries also tend to be women, but they offer you coffee and pass the time of day with you while you wait—because if you are on time, the boss is late; and if he is on time, he might join you in the coffee break, talking about soccer and the children. Your interview goes on and on. When you have wasted so much of his time that you can hardly bear the guilt, he opens up a new subject of discussion. You walk out with him, after hours. The secretary has already left, or perhaps it is not yet 5:00, but she quit early in order to run an errand.

Ordinary people generally do not have telephones. When they have something to say to a friend, they go the friend's house or meet him in a pub and have a talk. East Germans talk and talk. They used to watch their language when they thought the Stasi might be listening, but mainly they kept their talk to a limited circle of friends and a restricted range of topics. It was small talk, and it took up a large proportion of the day. With the Stasi gone and the elections set for March 18, 1990, the day was filled with political talk. The politicians themselves lacked the rhetorical smoothness of their counterparts in the West, but they had plenty of staying power. Rallies usually began late and went on forever. After the elections, the new deputies in the parliament found it very difficult to restrict themselves to the allotted time for speeches and rebuttals. They were baffled by a problem that could never have arisen only a few months earlier: the contradiction between freedom of speech and the tyranny of time.

The same problem is playing itself out on East German television, now that censorship has ended and commercials have begun. Before the revolution, television programs did not always begin punctually on the hour or the half hour. Afterward, the sponsors enforced a strict schedule; masters of ceremonies visibly tensed as the clock

ticked closer to the end of their programs, and the offer-
ings began to betray a Western-style of time consciousness—contestants in quiz programs racing against the
clock and newscasters slicing their reports into the thin-
nest of "bites."

Trains run pretty much on time in the GDR; but if a
train crosses the road while you are driving in the country,
you often have to wait fifteen minutes or more. An attend-
ant winches down the barrier by hand, at a snail's pace.
You stop, get out, and strike up a conversation with the
other drivers, for a line soon forms and there is plenty of
time to talk. Speed limits are lower than in West Germany,
and the cars go slower. As most of them have only two
pistons, they can't work up much speed. But why barrel
down a superhighway at 100 miles an hour like a Wessi?
What's the rush? The East Germans don't even have an
expression for the "fast lane."

And they still have plenty of horse-drawn carts. On
country roads before November 1989, you were more
likely to see a horse than a Mercedes. When East Germans
wanted to catch a glimpse of a Mercedes, they got on their
bikes and peddled off to one of the *Autobahns* linking West
Berlin with West Germany. They spent hours on bridges
over the *Autobahns* watching the Wessis whiz by. Turn-
pike gawking exists in other countries, but in the GDR it
used to be a major spectator sport. Nearly every bridge
had its cluster of Wessi watchers, people who were fascinated by the foreign variety of speed and who had plenty
of time on their hands.

If you are a Wessi driving in the East, nothing—except
for railroad crossings—is more frustrating than the traffic
lights of the GDR. I timed a half dozen red lights in downtown Leipzig. Each one lasted a full minute—nothing to a
Leipziger, but an eternity to someone from the West. In
West Berlin the red lights last thirty seconds, and people

sometimes tell a joke that used to be popular in New York. Question: What is the definition of an instant? Answer: The time it takes after the light turns green for the West Berliner in the car behind you to blow his horn.

The patience of the East Germans is amazing, unless you compare them with the Russians and the Poles. Unlike the Germans in the West, they stand in line at bus stops and let people out before they climb in. They stand in line everywhere, in stores, theaters, and public toilets. When you enter a restaurant in the GDR, you do not help yourself to a seat. You queue up at the entrance; and if there is no line, you stand there anyway, even if every table in the place is free, until a waiter feels moved to seat you. Waiters, salespeople, everyone in the service industries treat their customers with indifference or contempt. Why should they do otherwise? They work for the state, and the state pays them the same amount of money whether they have customers or not. So the customers stand and take it. I once waited nearly an hour in a taxi queue outside the railroad station in Halle. Some taxis were parked a few meters away, but the drivers wanted to chat among themselves rather than to drive off with passengers, and nobody protested. Waiting and queuing are so fundamental to the social order in the GDR that East Germans often refer to a line as a "waiting collective" *(Wartekollektiv)* or a "socialistic waiting-association" *(sozialistische Wartegemeinschaft)*.

Money, by contrast, is not so fundamental—or wasn't before the monetary union took effect on July 1, 1990. Even physically, East German money is unimpressive. The bills look cheap and feel flimsy in comparison with the bigger, sturdier, and better-printed bills of West Germany. The coins, made of low-grade alloys, don't weigh enough to the Western touch and don't have the right ring to the Western ear. A GDR one-mark piece is unsatisfactory for flipping, if you want to decide who goes first; and a pocketful of change is no good for rattling, if you want to strike the pose of a casual big spender.

Bills and coins do not have much intrinsic value. They are symbolic objects that can be exchanged for other things according to conventions; and their conventional value is determined in large measure by governments, because governments have a monopoly on their production. So a ten-mark note does not merely carry a simple message: "This piece of paper can be swapped in stores for goods priced at ten marks." It says something about the government that issued it. In an attempt to control this larger statement, the government of the GDR covers its bills with pictures of socialist heroes and labor. The ten mark note shows Clara Zetkin, the feminist socialist, on one side and a laboratory on the other. It is meant to be edifying and progressive, but to the Western eye it looks like kitsch. Frau Zetkin has the air of a rumpled grandmother, and the laboratory is full of archaic paraphernalia, something that might have been used by Dr. Caligari or Buck Rogers and that evokes the 1940s rather than the future.

How can you take such money seriously? The East Germans don't. When they talk about "real money," they mean West German marks, the impressive notes with the engravings of portraits by Holbein and Dürer. To get a job done by a skilled worker in East Berlin, you often have to pay in "violins"—that is, twenty West mark notes, which have a violin on the back. Workers in the construction industry, where labor and materials are particularly scarce, commonly get paid in West marks. So do doctors in the university hospital in Leipzig, which lost so much of its staff by emigration to the West that it nearly had to close down. And high Party officials rewarded themselves with millions of West marks, which they stashed away in secret accounts in West Berlin and Switzerland, according to information that came to light after the collapse of the Honecker government in October 1989.

"Real" money buys things that lie beyond the purchasing power of the East mark: stereo systems, transistor radios, washing machines, and all sorts of Western luxuries that are not available in the GDR—or rather, not in normal stores, for special "Intershops" sell Western goods against West marks. The West mark also works wonders where supply lines are clogged. If you have enough of them, from relatives in West Germany or from labor in the black market, you can sometimes buy a Trabi right away instead of waiting fifteen years. The East German government pilfered its own museums in order to have an adequate supply of art objects to sell for West marks to the West. The West German government also used its marks to buy the freedom of political prisoners and to finance all sorts of inroads into the GDR—the *Autobahns* to West Berlin, for example, and the S-Bahn railway system connecting West and East Berlin. Shady characters working out of the Bahnhof Zoo in West Berlin and the Friedrich Strasse station in East Berlin had bought and sold both currencies for years, thereby establishing an unofficial exchange rate. In late 1989 and early 1990, they usually gave five East marks for one West mark, but sometimes a hard bargainer could get them to pay twelve to one and more. It was as if the GDR itself were being put up for sale in dirty men's rooms and squalid cafés.

There was so much trafficking in West marks, in fact, that East Germany developed a dual currency system and West Germany penetrated the GDR economy long before anyone dreamt of a currency union. Once the Wall fell and the East Germans had unlimited access to Western "greeting money" *(Begrüssungsgeld)*—100 DM a head—there was no turning back. A family of four could show up at a West German bank and claim 400 DM, the equivalent of a month's income, simply by presenting their passports. It was an extraordinary sight to see them line up for their cash at the bank branches near Checkpoint Charlie or to watch them wander into the fancier branches in the Grunewald and Dahlem sections of West Berlin.

I followed a group of them into a Grunewald bank a few days after the Wall's collapse. They stood quietly in line before the cashier's window, looking a little bewildered by the unfamiliar surroundings—the thick carpets and plush armchairs, the clicking electronic typewriters and winking computer screens. Ossis (East Germans) stand out everywhere in the West. They wear a peculiar kind of acid-wash blue jeans and imitation leather jackets, and they have different haircuts: short in front and long in back in the case of the men, teased and fluffed rather than blow-dried in the case of the women. But they looked especially out of place in the bank, surrounded by West Berlin customers and bank employees in the current, casual style of Western dress: baggy trousers, blousons, loose cardigan sweaters, and Italian-tailored jackets with heavily padded shoulders. The Ossis seemed to pull together, finding comfort in forming a line against the foreignness around them. When at last the cashier dealt out their money in crisp new bills—a fifty, two twenties, and a ten for each of them—they did not snatch at it. Instead they tried to fold it nonchalantly in their pockets. They walked out the door without a word and then, once outside, gathered together in a group and started talking excitedly.

Back in the bank, you could see annoyance on every Western face. The locals had been delayed a good ten minutes by the alien intrusion. And when they reached the window of the cashier, they collected impressive piles of

100 DM notes, which he dealt out in a loud voice: "800! 900! 1,000! Thank you Frau Müller. *Aufwiedersehen.*" West Germans seem uninhibited about money. They talk about it openly, as if it were not a dirty secret, and carry large sums of it around with them, because they usually pay in cash rather than by check or credit card.

East Germans switched to this system on July 1, 1990, when the West German government finally agreed to convert East Germans' wages and savings into West marks at differential rates of 1:1 and 2:1. Suddenly the old East marks in their bank accounts were transmogrified. Now they, too, could step up to a cashier's window and call for new bills of "real" money, as much as 2,000 DM at a time. In fact, they took out modest amounts and kept most of it in their purses.

When the largest department store in East Berlin, a state-owned monstrosity on the Alexanderplatz called the Zentrum am Alex, opened for business on Monday, July 2, it was crowded but not mobbed. With help from a West Berlin supplier, Kaufhof AG, it had suddenly ceased to be a show window for socialism and had turned into a gigantic cornicopia of Western and Japanese goods: Barbie dolls, Lee's blue jeans, Swiss watches, and Yamaha synthesizers. The East Berliners swarmed over the merchandise, but they did more looking then buying. In the book section, a saleswoman reported that Hollywood romances were selling best. Lee Iacocca's *Iacocca* (entitled in German *An American Career*), James Michener's *Texas,* and sex books also sold well, as did travel guides, atlases, foreign dictionaries, and some (formerly) dissident GDR literature, like Walter Janka's *Difficulties with the Truth.* A saleswoman in the cosmetics section said business was great. At first she had found it difficult to distinguish between the ten-mark and the twenty-mark Western bills, but she loved the merchandise. She sprayed me with a sample of Old Spice, and I thought I was really in the West.

I was, despite the oppressively Stalinist architecture of the setting. Outside on Alexanderplatz, young women in mini-skirts were selling Lucky Strikes from a red Cadillac convertible; West Berliners were peddling the *Orion Sex Catalogue* from a truck, and Poles were doing a lively business with the old shell game. Instead of shells, they used plastic disks, which they shuffled about on cardboard strips laid across public garbage cans. The East Germans gathered and gaped. Occasionally one would open a wallet full of brand new West marks and venture a twenty-mark note on a guess as to which disk had a colored underside. None of them ever won.

The conversion to capitalism seemed to happen overnight on July 1–2, but it had been prepared for years by the penetration of the West mark. In retrospect, the decisive moment came during the two weeks after the opening of the Wall, when nearly everyone in the GDR streamed into West Germany, received a fistful of cash, and spent it on things they had not been able to buy at home. It was an amazing phenomenon: virtually the entire population of one country emptied into another and tried out an alien economic system. The East Germans engaged in a gigantic *dégustation* of Western consumerism, a mass test drive through the free market, and came back convinced. From then on, the push to unification could not be stopped. The politicians simply rode it or tried to rein it in—all except for Helmut Kohl. He made the campaign of the East German Christian Democrats into a capitalist takeover bid. His rhetoric turned into a rhapsody on the West mark: "The deutsche mark is one of the world's strongest, most stable and widely accepted currencies and is the basis of our prosperity and our economic prowess." After the smashing victory of the Christian Democrats in the March elections, the most common comment by East Germans was, "We voted for the deutsche mark."

By then it was clear that the two German currencies functioned as much more than signs of what you could buy in each country. They had become emblems of alternative economic, social, and political systems. They also operated as codes that embodied distinct ways of thinking. Consumers considering the pros and cons of a purchase, use money to make their calculations. If they travel to a foreign country, they must switch from one currency to another and change their mode of calculating. At first they translate back into the old system; then they adopt the new one and with it a new code for the transactions of everyday life. The new money becomes progressively more "real." They cease converting it mentally into the currency of their home country and begin thinking with it, using it as a fundamental standard of measurement. Anyone who has switched from calculating in miles to kilometers and from Fahrenheit to Centigrade knows how such a change can affect one's notions of near and far and hot and cold. Systems of measurement inscribe themselves in the mind and shape general habits of thinking, the overall attitudes known in France as *mentalités collectives* and in Germany as *Weltanschauungen.*

Of course, a great deal more than money goes into a view of the world, but money is more than a means of exchange. So a country cannot adopt the currency of another country—especially one with an antithetical social system—without affecting its citizens' worldview. In the view that prevailed under the old regime of the GDR, East marks seemed unreal, because they had no stable relation to things. Of course, prices in a socialist economy are not supposed to be determined by supply and demand. But in the GDR they also looked irrational if considered from the viewpoint of social engineering. The government fixed them capriciously, so that some articles seemed impossibly expensive and others absurdly cheap. In 1950 it set the price of the most common bread roll in all GDR bakeries at 5 pfennigs (somewhat more than half an American penny), and kept it there for forty years, while it raised the price of a one-pound container of coffee to 35 marks, the equivalent of a day's wages for most working people (about $11.50 at the exchange rage prevailing in 1989). A two-room apartment commonly cost 100 marks ($33.00) or less a month, and a personal computer 25,000 marks ($8,250)—if you could find one. Many goods were simply unavailable, so their prices did not matter. What counted was access to things.

Access to things was mediated by persons, not by money. It worked according to the Leninist principle of "who–whom"—whom do you know who can get something for you. The system combined two elements, an economy of scarcity and a Communist dictatorship, each of which favored influence peddling. As a consequence, people acquired goods by pulling strings rather than by making money, and a privileged class grew up around the Party members who controlled the dispensation of goods. The *Privilegierte* in the GDR inhabited a separate world of Western products and pleasures. They drove about in Volvos, relaxed in saunas, vacationed in Swiss-style chalets, and ate fresh fruit and vegetables all year round. The last thread that bound the apparatchiks to the people finally snapped in December 1989, when East German television transmitted pictures of the Party chiefs' hunting lodges and houses in the Wandlitz colony of East Berlin.

The most revealing episode concerned Günter Schabowski, a key member of the Politburo, who tried to help Egon Krenz patch together a government that would save the system after the fall of Erich Honecker in November.

Schabowski made a great effort to put himself across as a man of the people in a television interview that focused on his private life. When asked what he did after a hard day's work in the Politburo, he said that he came home, threw off his coat, flicked on the television, and opened a can of cold beer. That finished him with the public, because everyone knew that only Western beer came in cans and only a *Privilegierter* would keep it stocked in his refrigerator. Schabowski had lived so long in the separate world of the apparatchiks that he had forgotten how ordinary people drank their beer.

In the end, the East Germans got rid of Schabowski and the East mark, too. When given their first opportunity since 1933 to vote in a free election, they chose something that they called a free market economy. But what was that? Most of them had carried some West marks in their wallets and had spent them on Western goods in Western stores. But they had never adopted a Western rhythm of work or a Western mode of calculating time and money. Having changed their political system, they faced the more daunting but less dramatic task of remaking their basic codes for ordering the world. It was a revolutionary undertaking, even though it did not conform to the recipe for revolution devised by Marx and Lenin.

THE POLISH MARKET

P olish economy" in German slang means disorder and
mess, but in West Berlin it conjures up a place—
"the Polish market," a huge open area along the
Reichpietschufer not far from the Wall. Polish
peddlers have turned the area into a gigantic flea market
and also into an economics lesson in the problems that
arise when East meets West.

Soon after the opening of the Wall, Poles began to set
up shop in the vast vacant lot. Their "shops" consisted of
plastic sheets spread over the mud and covered with
junk—old clothes, crockery, pots and pans, toys, tools,
flashlights, clocks, embroidery, and anything else they

could dredge out of basements and attics. With the collapse of their economy, they were ready to sell anything for deutsche marks, and they found plenty of buyers among West Berlin's bargain hunters, most of them working-class and Turkish. Since the Polish border is only sixty miles from Berlin, the Poles could load their cars with bric-a-brac and dispose of it a few hours later in a booming, capitalist economy, which had suddenly become near instead of near and yet so far.

They did not need visas to enter East Germany; and they had no difficulty in passing from East to West Berlin, because the West Berlin authorities admitted everyone who came through the Wall. Indeed, the "red-green" government of West Berlin (a coalition of Social Democrats and the Green Party) went out of its way to be hospitable to Eastern Europeans. So the police did not trouble the Poles about authorization to peddle their wares or about paying taxes on their sales.

At first, the peddlers went about their business furtively. When a policeman came in sight, they swooped up their goods and ran, like sidewalk vendors in Paris and New York. They often kept everything in a bag; then when a potential customer walked by, the would suddenly unzip it, as if they were flashers exposing a criminal secret. But they soon learned that one could buy and sell with impunity in the capitalist world. They displayed their goods openly and bargained for the best price they could get. Few could speak German, but all of them knew the magic word, "deutsche mark," and they handled the rest with their fingers—an ancient mode of negotiation that was all the more effective in that most of their items cost less than ten marks. Ten marks went a long way in the currency markets of Warsaw. They bought more than a day's wages for a Pole, though a West Berliner could earn them easily in half an hour.

By mid-December, the Polish market had become as crammed as the Casbah. Every blade of grass had been ground into the mud, and every square yard of mud had been occupied by a Pole, who stood elbow to elbow with other Poles in rows that filled the entire area. The customers walked between the rows, looking suspiciously at the goods displayed on the plastic sheets at the sellers' feet. Occasionally a customer would pause before an item, and the fingers would begin to fly as buyer and seller locked in bargaining—a dialogue of the deaf, for most of the customers were Turks who had no more German than the Poles themselves.

What everyone had in common was self-interest, the desire for a bargain on one side and for profit on the other. An air of acquisitiveness hung over everything, unmitigated by the small talk and decorative touches that soften commerce in ordinary shops. Here there were no shops at all. Just goods, laid out in the mud, and buyers and sellers haggling over them. There was no overhead, either, nothing but the gray, north German sky. Nor was there any bookkeeping or tax-collecting. Trade had been reduced to its simplest: pure supply and demand. And the traders represented humanity at its crassest: pure Economic Man, a combination of the creatures imagined by Adam Smith and Thomas Hobbes, with the Hobbesean element uppermost.

This phase of unadulterated capitalism did not last long, however, because the Poles soon emptied their attics and had to seek another source of supply. They found it in the border area between the capitalist and socialist economies, where they could play one system off against another. Poland itself had already switched to a market economy, and priced had skyrocketed. But the authorities in the GDR continued to set prices according to socialist principles—that is, in line with an economic plan rather than in response to demand. As a result, prices for East German goods had little relation to their market value. Certain items, such as common varieties of food and clothing, cost a fraction of their price in the West, while others, such as washing machines and stereos, cost three or four times as much, if they could be found at all. The Poles bought the cheap articles in East Germany and then sold them in West Berlin, where they found plenty of down-market consumers who were happy to purchase T-shirts, shoes, and cigarettes at half price without a value-added tax. Sometimes the Polish entrepreneurs managed to get their hands on vodka from their home country, Russian caviar, or shawls woven in Romania and Bulgaria. These attracted a middle-class element to the Polish market. And once they had accumulated a few West marks, the Poles crossed back over to the socialist world and bought still more, this time with "real" money, which had tremendous purchasing power and could be exchanged at a tremendous profit on black markets everywhere in the East. Anyone willing to spend enough hours shuttling across the border and standing in the mud could transform a few Polish zlotys into a small pile of deutsche marks, and the pile would grow with every expedition between one economy and another.

By January, a new generation of merchandise had appeared on the plastic sheets. Gone were the knick-knacks from grandmother's attic. In their place were shiny new items straight out of the people's emporiums of the GDR, along with luxury goods creamed off economies farther East. On a tour of the market on January 8, I found a great many East German labels on things like combs, cutlery, and clothing. In a typical scene a Turkish woman dressed in baggy pants with her head in a shawl plucked a child's pink nightshirt from the plastic sheet in front of a Pole. She unfolded it, frowning skeptically, then shot an inquiring look at the Pole. He held up ten fingers. She deepened her frown and held up five fingers. They continued back and forth for several minutes, until she got him down to eight fingers and he got her up to six. But then neither would budge; so the Pole took the nightshirt back, folded it elaborately, and returned it to the plastic. Meanwhile, the Turkish woman pretended to walk away. But at last she wheeled around, holding seven fingers in the air. That settled it: the Pole pocketed 7 DM, and the Turk stuffed the nightshirt into her shopping bag, both of them looking as though they had made a tremendous sacrifice.

Of course, the real sacrifices were being made by the East German people, and they resented it. GDR newspapers and television carried stories about the pillaging of the home economy. According to one, East German stores had sold three times as many pairs of children's shoes in 1989 as there were children in East Germany. A wave of hostility to foreigners, and especially Poles, swept through the country. The government finally decreed that foreigners could not buy certain staple goods unless they produced a residence permit, and it began to inspect people leaving the GDR more carefully than it vetted those who entered.

Things also soured on the West Berlin side of the border. On March 10, the police reported that at least 10,000 persons had crowded into the market and that 2,000 cars with Polish license plates were parked in the street surrounding it. Poles also arrived by bus and by train. When they did not dispose of their goods, they camped out—in cars, or cellars, or doorways—and tried again the next day. As the area lacked public toilets, they urinated and defecated wherever they could, sometimes in the entrances of apartment buildings. The residents protested, and the authorities began to worry about a political revolt.

By this time, the Polish market had ceased to be strictly

Polish. The most impressive peddlers came from Romania, Bulgaria, the Soviet Union, and other remote areas in the devastated economies of Eastern Europe. Peasant women with their hair in babushkas and their mouths full of flashing gold teeth stationed themselves behind displays of hand-embroidered tablecloths and hand-painted pottery, much of it exquisitely beautiful. Instead of bartering, they stood their ground and waited things out, and in the end they usually got their price: 50 DM for a tablecloth from deepest Moldavia, 150 DM for a Byelorussian lacquered box. You could pick up Communist gee-gaws—watches with "perestroika" or Soviet and American flags painted on their faces, and the usual run of Russian wooden dolls—for less than two dozen marks. Or you could simply walk around and wonder at the endless variety of the human species and its products. *Vanitas vanitatum:* all is vanity, or everything seems to be, when it is spread out for sale on plastic sheets in the mud. But the Polish market did not look like Vanity Fair. Instead of Thackeray and Ecclesiastes, it called up thoughts of Dostoycvsky and *The Grapes of Wrath*.

For the Polish market was not merely an outlet for everything produced in Eastern Europe; it became a magnet for the dispossessed. Every day a train known to the East Germans as the "Orient Express" arrived in East Berlin from Bucharest and dumped hundreds of Romanians in the city. They swarmed into the West, begging, stealing, and camping out in parks and subways. In wealthy sections like Dahlem, housewives warned one another to keep their doors locked and their children within sight. Latent hostilities to gypsies and Slavs rose to the surface, stirring memories of the Hitler years. *Auslanderfeindlichkeit* (hostility to foreigners) became an issue in West as well as East Berlin.

But East Germans also found themselves treated as foreigners when they crossed into the capitalist half of the city. Gone were the magic moments of November, when the "Ossis" were embraced as brothers. Their Trabis, which had once looked so endearing, now simply smelled bad, sounded worse, and tied up traffic. Their children, who had seemed so well behaved, now got underfoot. And their hunger for consumer goods, which once was welcomed as a sign of the defeat of socialism, now threatened the consumption of the Westerners. "Where is the cream?" asked an old woman, contemplating the empty shelves in her neighborhood grocery store one day in Dahlem. "In Prenzlauer Berg," came the reply from the checkout counter—an allusion to the customers from the working-class districts of East Berlin who were cleaning out the supplies in the West. According to another version of the story, the answer was, "In Warsaw."

The supreme symbol of the consumer confrontation between East and West was the banana. Bananas were rarely available in socialist countries, not so much because of their cost as because of the inefficiency of the distribution systems: by the time the fruit had been stocked and distributed from central warehouses, it had usually rotted. So one of the first items bought by East Germans in West Berlin was a banana, and one of the most crowded corners of the Polish market was a banana stand, where the Eastern Europeans gave in to the temptation to taste the wonders of capitalism and spent their deutsche marks as soon as they had earned them. But banana consumerism had its negative side. West Germans sometimes derided the GDR as a "banana republic," and left-wing critics within the GDR itself harped on bananas as the symbol of a sell-out to capitalism. During the campaign for the March elections, one poster displayed a banana in place of the hammer and compass in the center of the GDR flag. Another showed a child clutching a pickle, grinning idiotically and saying, "My first banana." The theme went all the way back to the ninth of November. Soon after the Wall had opened, a West Berliner stationed himself at one of the entry points with a huge pile of bananas and handed one to each East Berliner who came through. Before long, the crush had become so great that he started to toss them out to people. But then he was stopped short by a voice from the crowd, which cried, "We are not apes."

The tendency to see outsiders as something less than human is especially dangerous in Berlin. Since 1945 West Berlin has survived as a capitalist island in an alien ocean of socialism, and since November 1989, it has been flooded with aliens who are refugees from socialism. They streamed through the Wall and into the Polish market, where they tried out capitalism in their own way, on little plastic sheets. By April it seemed as though all of Eastern Europe was standing in the mud and selling its wares, and the Berliners had exhausted their capacity to tolerate disorder. The police closed the market on April 28. The peddlers scattered, regrouped from time to time and place to place, and finally disappeared.

With the establishment of the economic and currency union on July 1, the Eastern Europeans lost their opportunity to profit from the disparities between incompatible economic systems. All that remained were disparities in wealth and ethnic background. The Polish market had given them a chance to experiment with capitalism on a small scale. Now they had to confront an alien economy along the whole Western front. Would it be capitalism red in tooth and claw or capitalism with a human face? No one could say, but the experience of "Polish economy" in the Polish market left little room for optimism.

BORDER CROSSINGS

Anyone who has ever done it knows the feeling—the
slight tightening in the pit of the stomach, the
hint of perspiration on the brow, the compulsion
to avoid any suggestion of irregularity or even
levity—for it is *Ernst,* serious business, the crossing of the
border into the GDR. Or rather it was until the border
disappeared. Of course, the border did not vanish overnight. It gradually crumbled, and the stages of its crumbling illustrate the way a regime falls apart. I distinguished
four.

Stage one: September 1989. When I arrived in Berlin,
the border was intact. Despite the disappearance four

years earlier of the mines and the rifles that fired automatically at anyone who tried to dash across no man's land, the Berlin Wall looked forbidding. It showed its ugliest face—the guard towers, the dog patrols, the scorched earth between the outer and the inner walls—when you crossed over it to enter East Berlin at the Friedrichstrasse station of the S-Bahn (Berlin's elevated municipal railway). Friedrichstrasse was the end of the line, the last stop in the West. You got out, clutching your passport, climbed down into an underground cavern, and waited in line for clearance by the border police, who manned the barrier where the East began.

Clearance often took half an hour or more. You had to pass several observation posts and surrender your passport to a succession of guards. They looked at it, looked at you, looked at the mirror placed in back of you, consulted a computer, took some mysterious notes, and eventually waved you on, always expressionless, always without exchanging any talk. If you had a suitcase, you had to turn it over for inspection. If you carried any Western books or newspapers, you had to leave them behind. You also had to exchange 15 DM at the official rate of one to one, whether or not you could find anything on which to spend the East marks. And when at last you thought you had reached the end of the inspecting and registering, you might be pulled out of the line for further interrogation. One friend of mine always had to undergo an interrogation because the police suspected he had friends among the GDR dissidents. Another refused to attempt a crossing because he thought the police might arrest him for spying—not that he worked for the CIA: he simply feared that the East Germans wanted a hostage in order to arrange a trade for one of their spies who had been captured in the West. The underground border station at Friedrichstrasse gave rise to such fantasies. In Kafkaesque fashion, you felt you must be guilty, although you didn't know your crime.

Travel by car was even worse. You could not drive around freely in the GDR; and if, after many weeks of negotiations, you received a visa to visit a specific town, you had to check in with the police and leave your passport at the hotel, which always charged outrageous prices for anyone with Western currency. Before letting you back in West Berlin, the border police made you get out of the car, searched through all your belongings, looked through the trunk, pounded the seats in order to verify that no refugee was hidden in the upholstery (the Checkpoint Charlie Museum displays a Volkswagen in which a woman had been hidden under the lining of the front seat), and ran a special mirror under the chassis to make sure no one had been strapped beneath it.

Stage two: December 1989. After the opening of the Wall on November 9, the border remained intact but permeable, and the police suddenly became human. They had also been disarmed. Having carried machineguns in the 1960s, rifles in the 1970s, and hip pistols until recently, they now had no weapons at all. Because I had registered as a resident of Berlin, I could cross the border simply by showing my identity card *(Senatsbescheinigung)*. I no longer had to exchange the 15 DM, but I still had to submit bags and packages for inspection.

One evening, a border guard reached into my shopping bag and pulled out the *Züddeutsche Zeitung*, a solid, serious daily published in Munich. He held it at arm's length, making a face. "Why don't you try something more adventurous?" he asked. "Like *Neues Deutschland?*" I replied, referring to the organ of the Communist Party. "Not at all," he shot back with a laugh. "Have a look at *Junge Welt* and *Morgen.*" He was recommending the new style of journalism in the GDR, which combined hard news with muckraking, much of it at the expense of the Party.

A few weeks earlier while traveling in West Germany, I drove to a different kind of border—the electrified, barbed wire "wall" that divided the two Germanys in the middle of the countryside of Lower Saxony. The barbed wire looked convincing enough as a barricade, but it seemed oddly out of place. It went against the grain of the landscape, slicing across hills that blended into one another as if the Cold War did not exist. At one point outside the little town of Hornburg in West Germany, a path led directly to a village in the GDR, not much more than a stone's throw away. The border police guarding the crossing from the East had strolled over to have a smoke and a chat with their opposite numbers in the West. None of them checked the identity cards of the peasants passing back and forth on foot. When I asked them why, they explained that everyone knew everyone in this part of the world, at least among the older generation. Villagers born after 1961 had never had any contact with their fellow Saxons on the other side of the border. But they made up for lost time after November 9. By now the East Germans had become regular customers in the Hornburg supermarket. I could see a long column of them winding their way across the brow of a hill. They were loaded down with shopping bags and looked like army ants returning with the day's booty from the consumer society that once seemed to lie on the other side of the world.

Stage three: March 1990. After the East German elections of March 18 made it clear that the two Germanys would unite, the border seemed to be more artificial than ever. At Friedrichstrasse, the guards waved you by with barely a glance at your papers, and the police at the border crossings for cars became downright friendly. Instead of demanding your passport, some of them politely requested you to fill out a form. It was a questionnaire designed to discover the preferences of foreigners so that the GDR could develop its tourist industry. Not only did it ask whether you spent most of your money on food, souvenirs, amusements, or gasoline; it also inquired whether you changed money illegally and, if so, how much. The police promised to respect your anonymity: they did not want to crack down on the black market, they explained, but rather to do consumer research.

By now, boat tours circulated through Berlin's canals as if the city had never been divided. Police chased criminals across no man's land as if it belonged to them. When emergency calls came from the other side of the border, rescue squads and firemen did not hesitate to dash into what had once been impenetrable, alien territory. Large parts of the Wall had been replaced by a consumer-friendly fence, and the booming trade in wall souvenirs had devastated what was left of the original structure. Even the guard houses no longer looked menacing. An East German entrepreneur had converted one of them in the outskirts of the city into a fast-food stand. Sunday strollers ate sausages beneath a Coca-Cola sign where machinegunners once kept watch over no man's land.

Stage four: July 1990. After the currency and economic union went into effect, the last segments of the border disappeared from Berlin. No longer did the police wave you past the checkpoint at Friedrichstrasse; they themselves were gone, and their apparatus with them. When the S-Bahn rolled into the station, it arrived on the regular, East Berlin track, discharged its passengers, and continued on toward Alexanderplatz. Nothing was left from the Great Divide of the Cold War at places like Checkpoint Charlie, where Soviet and American tanks had once squared off, and the Glienecke Bridge, where spies were exchanged. People walked back and forth at those places, as if to prove the border's nonexistence by pacing it off

with their feet. Bicyclists pedaled up and down no man's
land. And the East–West traffic resumed along streets and
trolley tracks that had lain unused under the Wall for
twenty-nine years.

Berlin was at last united: one city! It felt odd to be able
to walk or ride in any direction—as far as you liked, to
Alexanderplatz or to the Polish border at Frankfurt-an-
der-Oder—without coming up against a political barrier.
Of course, cities are not simply political units. They are
organic wholes, so it would take some time for the social
tissue of the two Berlins to grow together. But unification
was occurring nonetheless, in all sorts of unexpected and
invisible ways.

One was microbiological. Rabies had disappeared from
West Berlin a decade or so after it was sealed off from East
Berlin and the surrounding areas of East Germany. Foxes
carrying the disease could not get past the Wall and the
dogs patrolling it. But by mid-March three rabid foxes had
been found dead in West Berlin. At that time there were
already thirty-five openings in the Wall, and the West Berlin veterinarians decided that the only way to defend their
half of the city was to innoculate all dogs in both halves
with a special serum to be provided by Bonn.

There was also a moral dimension to unification. The
GDR had always refused to pay reparations to Israel because it claimed that it had no share in the responsibility
for the Holocaust. As soon as the new parliament convened after the March elections, it reversed that policy
and agreed to pay the reparations. By acknowledging East
Germany's part in the common German past, it opted for
unification through the assumption of a common guilt.

On a more mundane level, the two Berlins prepared to
unify by linking their underground drainage and sewage
systems, sharing their sources of drinking water, and coor-
dinating their network of canals. It was still nearly impos-

sible to telephone from one part of the city to the other at the end of July. In fact, I had to take the subway to East Berlin in order to make a phone call to Leipzig. But the two federal governments announced a plan to integrate their phone and postal systems. Bonn was to contribute 5 billion DM toward the creation of a super-modern, pan-German telecommunications network, while doubling the number of telephones in the East.

Despite close cooperation between the major parties, East and West Berlin continued to be separate political units; and they had not merged many of their social services by August 1990. But they had removed the last obstacles to the free circulation of people, and the circulation of goods had increased to a dizzying pace, thanks to the most important measure since the opening of the Wall: the extinction of the East mark. Of course, economic union seemed certain to have negative effects on East Germany, but no one could calculate their cost. Unemployment? Inflation? Alienation? There were plenty of prophecies of doom, especially after the West German soccer team won the World Cup on July 8, and a group of nationalist skinheads celebrated by smashing store windows and bashing foreigners in Alexanderplatz.

Yet British soccer fans often behaved far worse, and for my part I saw neo-Nazism more as a specter haunting the Western imagination than as a reality threatening East Germany. When asked about the East Germans' problems in adjusting to the new economic order, I preferred to cite a different case of deviance. An hour and a half before the deadline for turning in East marks for West marks in the GDR, a man holding a pistollike instrument under his jacket entered a bank in the town of Herzfelde and ordered the cashier to fill his sack with money. She stuffed it with the day's take of East mark notes, which were waiting to be carried off to the incinerator. The robber grabbed the sack and ran. Presumably he did not discover his mistake until he stopped to count the haul. I imagined him sitting before a pile of worthless marks and cursing the West German capitalists.

Such incidents aside, the union of the two countries seemed remarkably successful by the time I left Berlin in early August. I could scarcely believe that so much had happened within one year. Physically, the city had hardly changed, yet it looked entirely different. A Gestalt switch had taken place in the collective imagination, in the mental geography that had imposed some order on the world since 1945; 1945–1990 had been a good run for a worldview, but it was finished now. The basic division of East and West no longer made sense. It had come to an end right here in Berlin, where the sharpest line had been drawn and the border, now nearly imperceptible, once had been a question of life and death.

THE REVOLUTION
IN THE MUSEUM

Whenever they take up history, museums turn into mausoleums. They mummify the past, draining the life out of it and displaying it in cases, as if it had taken place among extinct, exotic species, pterodactyls and brontosauri with medals and magna chartas. No one ever left a museum thinking the past could happen to us. It happened to them, our remote ancestors, and we keep it at a safe distance, under glass.

The Museum for German History in East Berlin is a perfect example of the genre. It contains dozens of dummies in glass cases wearing antique costumes. Children on school outings file by, chewing gum and looking blank.

How could these strange figures in chain mail and wigs have anything to do with them? Last year the directors of the museum attempted to deal with this problem by organizing an exhibition on daily life in the GDR. Unfortunately, however, they also had to celebrate the fortieth anniversary of government by the Communist Party (SED). So the exhibition, entitled "The GDR, a Socialistic Fatherland," turned into a collection of Communist kitsch: old programs from Party congresses, banners from May Day parades, medals from heroes of socialist labor, uniforms of border guards, copies of *Neues Deutschland* announcing fraternal visits from Moscow, technological bric-a-brac demonstrating the triumph of socialist science, and photographs showing all sorts of stirring scenes—peasants carrying the harvest home to the collective farm, construction workers striding beams of new apartment buildings, and bashful girls presenting roses to a grandfatherly Erich Honecker.

But when the exhibition opened in the fall, a revolution exploded in the streets of the GDR. On November 4, at the high point of the agitation against the government, nearly a million people took part in a rally in East Berlin. They listened to speeches by political activists, and they spoke out themselves, not merely by shouting their approval but also by carrying placards, hundreds of them, which stuck out above the crowd as far as the eye could see. In workshops and apartments throughout the country, ordinary people had lettered, sketched, stitched, and cobbled together a whole program for the transformation of society. They paraded it through the streets of East Berlin on November 4, calling for the end of the Communist dictatorship and the creation of a truly democratic republic in East Germany.

No one had organized this great outpouring of words. It happened spontaneously, and so it was endlessly varied and inventive. The signs were scrawled on pieces of cardboard, mounted on broom handles, patched together from bits of cloth, painted on sheets, written across the backs of old coats and umbrellas and kites. Their lettering was often clumsy, their wording maladroit. They made all kinds of demands, not merely for a change of government but for the deprofessionalization of sports, the end of Saturday classes in schools, and the creation of bicycle paths. Nothing could be further from the regimentation of the Nuremberg rallies. But when the signs and banners all came together in Alexanderplatz, they seemed to say collectively, "We have recovered our speech, we the people of East Germany, who were forced to hold our tongues for forty years."

At the end of the rally, as he looked out over the sea of faces and the signs raised above them, one of the speakers said, "The mass of the placards carried here is really overwhelming. I think it would be good if we could save them and make them available as a new kind of art exhibition." The demonstration had turned into an historic event, the placards into documents. They were deposited at the speakers' stand and carried off for safekeeping to the Museum for German History.

Five months later, on April 12, the museum put the signs and banners on exhibit. Instead of displaying them under glass in a space of their own, the curators hung them from the ceiling and draped them over the objects in the exhibition on "The GDR, a Socialistic Fatherland." The result is staggering: one layer of time imposed on another and seen through a third, the present. By examining the slogans of November 4 juxtaposed against the propaganda of 1949–1989, the visitor can watch the revolution bursting out from the old regime; and at the same time, he can see it congeal as a piece of the past, history only a few months old.

So much has happened since November 4 that the dra-

matic events of last autumn already seem far away. After
the gigantic rally in Alexanderplatz, the Wall was opened;
the East Germans acquired the right to travel freely and
poured into West Germany; the last attempt to perpetuate
the rule of the Communist Party under Egon Krenz ended
in failure; a caretaker government under Hans Modrow
took over the administration; free elections were held, and
a coalition government dominated by the center-right
began to negotiate terms for the admission of the GDR
into the Federal Republic of Germany. Now that attention
has centered on the bread-and-butter questions surrounding unification, the ideals expressed last autumn seem to
belong to a distant past.

You take a step back into the past as soon as you enter
the exhibition. First you confront a sign: "Attention! You
are leaving the territory of the Federal Republic of Germany." You walk through a door and come smack up
against a huge section of the Wall that once divided East
and West Berlin. After rounding the Wall, you step into a
passageway formed by a wire fence with more warning
signs: "Border zone. Passage not allowed." Although you
are only crossing through a courtyard, the props, which
are all genuine, suggest the experience of venturing across
the no man's land between the two Berlins; and some ancient cannon from the permanent collection, which point
at you from the sides of the courtyard, heighten the effect.

Not that you feel afraid. You know that you are surrounded by relics from a border that once was deadly but
now has virtually disappeared. So one of the first placards
that strike your eye, "No more fear," has an odd look to it.
How could you be afraid of the figures evoked in the old
exhibition, mannequins dressed as border guards defending "Forty Years of Socialism"? Draped over a mannequin
in a soldier's costume is a banner saying, "No force," and
on another a placard with the words, "Community service

in place of the draft." But on November 4, fear was uppermost in many minds, and so it appears on many placards: "Freedom of opinion without fear," "Let us be free of fear," "For forty years: fear as a method."

The method, as the East Germans understand it and the signs express it, was simple: unlimited use of the secret police (Staatssicherheitsdienst, or State Security Service, Stasi for short). "More security from the security," said one placard. "Security, yes. Stasi, no," said another. The theme continued through endless variations, several of them written across puppets and cardboard cutouts dressed as spies: "All citizens in the Stasi," "State security? But who is the state?" "When Adam delved and Eve span, where was then the Stasi-man?" (a modern version of a revolutionary slogan that goes back to the sixteenth century). In November 1989, most East Germans suspected they were being spied on by Stasi agents in their apartment buildings, offices, or factories. They did not discover the full extent of the espionage until January, when a report by the new government revealed that at least 2 percent of the adult population worked for the Stasi and that the Stasi files contained dossiers on 10 million persons. Since then, however, the Stasi state-within-the-state has been dismantled. Its leaders are in jail, its rank and file unemployed. So the posters seem to come from another world.

Perhaps that is why the East Germans enjoy the exhibition so much. They stream through it, looking hard and laughing harder. Here, held up for ridicule, are all the orthodoxies of a regime that seemed all-powerful only a few months ago and that now is a thing of the past. The ridicule itself can be inspected, because the words that once flowed through the streets are now fixed on walls and suspended from ceilings. The crowds walk round them, touch them, photograph them, and expound them to one

another. Children stop in front of a child's finger-painting
of a railroad with the word "Travel" written across the top
in an adult hand. Their parents explain that people were
not free to travel outside the GDR before November 9.
Teen-agers get a laugh from signs that say: "I want to visit
my girl friend in Holland," and "I want to visit my friend
in West Berlin." A woman takes a photograph of her husband standing with his arm around the shoulder of a heroic, socialist-realist bust of Karl Marx from the old
exhibit. Next to it an equally bombastic bust of Lenin
seems to be whispering something into Marx's ear, and
above them a sign from the November demonstration
says, "Socialism: who destroyed its meaning?"

Another section from the old exhibition illustrates the
prosperity created by forty years of socialism. It shows
photographs of happy couples entering new apartment
buildings, and it contains a reconstructed living room
from one of the apartments: heavy, stuffed furniture gathered around a television set; on the wall a photograph of
Honecker; and over the photograph one of the placards
saying, "Workers! Your houses in Wandlitz are in danger!" Wandlitz, the closed off, luxury colony built for Honecker and the other leaders of the Party, provoked some
of the angriest protests last fall. The signs convey that
anger and the general resentment of the privileges of the
Party elite:

> Wandlitz, show your face. (Wandlitz zeigt dein Antlitz.)
> Stop privileges. (designed in the shape of a stop sign)
> Hey you up there, give up your privileges. Give them to
> the pensioners. Give them to the handicapped. And give
> them up for green trees.
> Reforms. No privileged class.

The resentment of privilege belongs to a democratic
impulse, which goes back at least as far as the French

Revolution; so there are some ancient motifs mixed in among the modern. One sign appears in the form of a phrygian bonnet; another simply says, "1789–1989." And a third plays with an anachronism: "Stalinists off the throne. To the people the crown" ("Stalinisten vom Throne, dem Volk die Krone").

Against this chorus of revolutionary themes from the distant past, other placards comment on current events— or rather, events that were current last November. When asked why there was no perestroika in the GDR, Kurt Hager, the chief ideologist of the regime, had replied that he saw no need to change the wallpaper in his house just because his neighbor had done so. The protestors therefore covered their signs with wallpaper. One huge placard consists of nothing but chunks of wallpaper and the words, "This placard is uncensored." Another says simply, "Hagerquark" (Hager rubbish). Strips of wallpaper pasted end to end on the floor provide a path through the exhibition.

Along the way, the posters pillory all of the leading figures in the last Communist government, above all Egon Krenz, who was trying to pass himself off as a reformer in November after having congratulated the Chinese on the Tiananmen massacre in June. Krenz was known for his toothy smile, which East Germans commonly took as the essence of hypocrisy. So in one poster he appears, smiling wickedly, as the wolf impersonating grandmother in Little Red Riding Hood. The caption simply reads, "Grandmother, why do you have such big teeth?"

Today, however, Egon Krenz is nobody. He does not exist anywhere in the current political spectrum and is not even important enough to be in jail. The East Germans remember him only as a passing phenomenon, the Party chief who, for a few weeks at the end of last year, tried and failed to hold the old regime together. Most of the other references in the placards seem equally out of date. They include fierce demands for freedom to travel, the end of censorship, the creation of new political parties, free elections—all of them burning questions on November 4 and now well-established rights that have become part of everyday life in the GDR.

Nowhere among the cacaphony of protest can one hear a hint of the demand that swept everything before it in the elections of March 18: the push for unification with West Germany. Instead of advocating a Western type of government, the placards call for socialism. They take the professed principles of the GDR for granted and turn them against the Communist regime:

OUR GOAL: POLITBUROCRATIC
[with "politburo" crossed out and "demo" inserted over it]
SOCIALISM.

[To the Politburo:]
COMRADES, DON'T SAVE YOUR JOBS; SAVE
SOCIALISM

THE SED [Communist Party] DID NOT
DISCOVER SOCIALISM; IT MISUSED IT.

TURN LEFT TO GET TO THE RULE OF LAW.
[Links Um Zum Rechtstaat.]

43 YEARS OF THE LEADING ROLE OF THE SED—NO!
THE INVASION OF PRAGUE.
28 YEARS ENCLOSED BEHIND THE WALL.
HURRAHS FOR THE PEKING MASSACRE.
ABUSE OF POWER.
FEAR.
PRIVILEGES FOR BUREAUCRATS.
NO SECURE RIGHTS.
MISEDUCATION INSTEAD OF PUBLIC EDUCATION.
WE WANT A NEW COMMUNIST PARTY!

The signs and banners express a revolutionary impulse that arose from within the political tradition of the GDR and that now seems to have evaporated. They belong to a moment, the feverish seven days from November 4 to 10, when the protest movement acquired such force that the regime collapsed before it. That moment has gone, like the system it destroyed. And yet you can see it as a replay on a television set standing amid a pile of Communist paraphernalia in the middle of the exhibition.

There on the videotape are the very placards that surround you in the room. There is Christa Wolf, the GDR's most celebrated author, before the crowd in Alexanderplatz. She can turn a phrase. But instead of developing her own eloquence, she weaves together phrases from the signs: "Freeloaders resign!" ("Trittbrettfahrer zurücktreten"); "A suggestion for the first of May: the government should parade past the people" ("Ein Vorschlag für den 1. Mai: Die Führung zieht am Volk vorbei"). The crowd roars, hundreds of thousands, as far as you can see. "None of that is from me," says Christa Wolf. "That is the literary property of the people. Amazing transformation. The sovereign people of the GDR go into the streets in order to recognize themselves as the people. And this, for me, is the most important sentence of these last weeks— the call repeated a thousand times: 'We are the people!' "

That call went round the world. It bounced off satellites and into houses everywhere. But here, in the history museum, it sounds out of place, or rather, out of time. A thin slice of the recent past spread out over a thicker cut of the last forty years makes the present seem out of joint. Perhaps revolutions always work that way. They sever the connections between yesterday and today. So yesterday's revolution in today's museum does not provide a foundation for a new regime. Instead, it undercuts one's sense of standing on solid ground.

At the same time, the exhibition is a tribute to the endless inventiveness of ordinary people in extraordinary situations. The fourth of November channeled the graffiti impulse into a spontaneous and collective explosion of pop art. It rocked a regime, and it still moves the observer, even though it belongs to a past that can never be recovered, no matter how much of it is gathered up in galleries and replayed on videocassettes. Here in the museum, it seems to say in spite of itself: The revolution is over.

INDEX

Party of Democratic Socialism, *see*
  Communist Party (PDS)
Pasternak, Boris, 197
PDS, *see* Communist Party (PDS)
Peaceful Revolution, 36
peddlers, 297–98, 301, 303
PEN organization, 200
perestroika, 66, 68, 100, 176
  East German censorship of, 191–2
Piche, Lothar, 256–57, 260
"planification," 90
Plaste und Elaste, 168
Poland, 68, 108, 119, 123, 158, 180,
  225, 271
  East Germany's apology to, 272
  market economy and, 298
"Polish economy," 296, 303
Polish market, 177, 296–303
  black market and, 299
  hostility to foreigners and, 300–3
  immigrant peddlers and, 301
Politburo, 11, 22, 85, 88, 90, 93,
  107, 187, 193, 214
  resignation of, 89
pollution, 159–60, 171–72
Potsdam, 133
Potsdamer Platz, 117–18, 155
Prague, 67–69, 70–73, 89
Prague Spring (1968), 272
Prenzlauer Berg district, 139, 141,
  145, 147
  described, 144
  Local 650 of, 253
prices, 121, 293–94, 298–99
privilege, 173, 174
Prokop (Wegener's friend), 54, 55
Protestant Synod, 264
Publishing and Book Trade
  Administration, 187, 191, 195,
  200, 202
  divisions of, 193
pubs, 138–47
  ambience of, 139
  for Communists, 143
  described, 139

etiquette of, 140
immigrant workers and, 140–41
for Nazis, 143
Westernization of, 145

Quadriga statue, 115, 118

rabies, 309
"radicalization," 222
Ragwitz, Ursula, 196–98
Reagan, Ronald, 40
"red-green" government, 297
Reformation, 95
refugees, 141
  citizenship and, 72
  trains of, 67, 69–70
  in West Germany's Prague
    embassy, 68–69, 70–73
Reich, Jens, 235, 237
Reichstag Building, 81, 86, 118
Reisekader, 19
Republican Party, West German, 228
reunification, *see* unification
revolution *(Vormärz),* 89
revolution of 1848, 89
"revolution tourism," 109–10
Richter, Ingo, 241
"Robert in Wonderland" (Berger), 35
rock concert, 118–19
Romania, 109, 119, 158, 301
Round Corner, 130, 131, 133, 135,
  137
Round Table, 23, 24, 126
  of Bitterfeld, 163
  coalition government and, 226
  of East Berlin, 215, 244
  of Halle, 170
  of Laucha, 215–16
  Modrow and, 125
  Monday demonstrations and, 130
  Social Democrats and, 227
  Stasi headquarters riot and, 121,
    124–25

Sachsenhausen, 272
Sauer, Manfred, 125
Sauer, Stefan, 101
Sauer report, 125
S-Bahn railway system, 289, 305, 308
Schabowski, Günter:
  ambiguous announcement of,
    11–12, 22, 85, 107
  as *Privilegierter*, 294–95
Schalck-Golodkowski, Alexander,
    88, 92
Schalck System, 88
Schirmer, Herbert, 202
Schleiermacher, Friedrich, 172
Schmidt, Helmut, 250
Schnur, Wolfgang, 258–59
Schöneberg Town Hall, 108
Schopenhauer, Arthur, 179
Schwerin, 235, 239
Secretariat for Ideology, 193
Section for Marxism-Leninism, 100
Sector for GDR Literature, 188
SED, *see* Communist Party (SED)
slogans, 79–81, 317–20
Smith, Adam, 298
Social Democrats, East German, 15,
    25, 143, 225, 228, 229–30, 231,
    234, 239–43, 245, 246, 252,
    253, 257, 259, 261
  coalition government and, 265–67
  election results of, 248
  Laucha election results of, 276
  Round Table and, 227
Social Democrats, West German,
    225, 229–30, 241, 253
  coalition government and, 266–67
  Green Party coalition with, 297
  Lafontaine and, 227
socialism, 79, 87, 89–90, 97, 153
  capitalism compared to, 178
  Church and, 208
  concrete, 172–73
  jokes about, 177
  placards calling for, 319
  Stalinism and, 192

"socialistic waiting-association," 287
Socialist Unity Party, *see*
  Communist Party (SED)
Solidarity, 234, 236
Soviet Union, 13, 25, 40, 70, 91,
    119, 180, 301
  East German censorship and, 190,
    192, 198
  East German politics and, 226
  East Germany's apology to, 272
  Katyn massacre admitted by, 271
Spain, 279
Spanish Civil War, 183
SPD, *see* Social Democrats, East
  German; Social Democrats,
  West German
Speer, Albert, 110
Spiegel, Der, 258
spies, 135–36
Springer media conglomerate, 186
Sputnik, 100
Stalin, Joseph, 117, 123, 233
Stalinism, 14, 24, 68, 104, 107, 237,
    240, 273
  in East Germany, 175
  election of March 18 and, 272
  Nazism and, 271, 272
  socialism and, 192
"Stalinismus," 134
Stasi (State Security Service), 14,
    23, 24, 142, 171, 202, 210, 211,
    212, 215, 285, 316
  blackmail technique of, 151–52
  Böhme and, 258, 259
  citizens' committees and, 93
  demonstrations put down by, 70
  disbanding of, 97
  East German consciousness of,
    132–33
  East German obsession with, 122
  elections and, 206
  as Gestapo continuation, 271
  goal of, 125
  Halle headquarters of, 171
  jokes about, 133